THE DAY OF
GOOD
NEWS

The Day of GOOD NEWS

Essentials in Personal Evangelism

Bob Gabelman

Xulon Press

Xulon Press
2301 Lucien Way #415
Maitland, FL 32751
407.339.4217
www.xulonpress.com

Due to the changing nature of the Internet, if there are any web addresses, links, or URLs included in this manuscript, these may have been altered and may no longer be accessible. The views and opinions shared in this book belong solely to the author and do not necessarily reflect those of the publisher. The publisher therefore disclaims responsibility for the views or opinions expressed within the work.

Unless otherwise indicated, Scripture quotations taken from the New American Standard Bible (NASB). Copyright © 1960, 1962, 1963, 1968, 1971, 1972, 1973, 1975, 1977, 1995 by The Lockman Foundation. Used by permission. All rights reserved.

Paperback ISBN-13: 978-1-66284-752-3
Hard Cover ISBN-13: 978-1-66286-741-5
Ebook ISBN-13: 978-1-66284-753-0

Dedication

To KATHLEEN, MY bride of 40 years. You have stood by my side during my entire Christian life, often encouraging me in the God-given gift to win the lost to Christ. I could not have done what I have done without your faithful support and counsel. I love you. To my five children, Jared, Shiloh, Nathan, Angela, and Hannah, you have shared your father through many years with the unreached souls of this world. Each of you have become men and women whom I am incredibly proud of. I love you!

Acknowledgments

To my Heavenly Father, who so loved the world that sent His only begotten Son to redeem mankind through His selfless life, death, and resurrection. To Jesus Christ, who saved me from my sin and lost condition and sent us the Holy Spirit. To the Holy Spirit, who is my faithful friend and guide on this journey. Thank you for your patience with me. To my faithful bride, Kathleen. You have walked by my side these 40 years. To my children, who watched their father step out into the blazing heat or freezing cold week after week to seek and to save the lost. To all my pastors and spiritual leaders over the past 43 years, who have equipped me for this work. You have faithfully discipled me and formed in me the character of our Lord Jesus Christ. To Cheri, who gave countless hours to edit and refine this book. I did not know how much help I needed till I started seeing your edits and refinements.

FOREWORD

My name is Pastor Bob Groeneman. During the 24 years my wife Tammie and I were youth pastors in Northern Colorado, we had many wonderful people come alongside to help in the ministry. None were more faithful than Bob and Kathleen Gabelman. During the ten years of ministering together in Colorado, Bob had one great passion: soul-winning.

You see, Bob had such a heart for people that he spent hours every Friday night walking the streets of nearby cities to seek and save the lost. No matter how cold it got on those Colorado nights, year after year, Bob regularly went out to share Jesus with whomever God led him to: students, businessmen, gang members, satanists, drug addicts, runaways, and the homeless.

Bob was relentless!

Bob would challenge and amaze all of us other youth leaders with the supernatural stories of miracles he saw while sharing the gospel, praying for people, and simply obeying Jesus.

Bob was inspiring!

I am thrilled that you are about to hear these same miracle stories that awed us over the years.

Bob was an extremely faithful ministry leader, helping us lead 20 winter and summer camps, 5 mission trips, and our many mall outreaches. Evangelism outreach is where Bob would really shine as he trained our students to effectively share their faith. When Bob became a full-time missionary, he began to put the wisdom he gathered on the streets into evangelism classes for their ministry school in Mexico. I was excited to hear that Bob was writing down the most anointed of these messages for all of us to read, and I was extremely honored to be asked to write the foreword to this amazing book.

Bob is probably the most honest and constant friend I have ever had. We have laughed about the same things and worked for the same wonderful Savior. We have seen Jesus glorify himself over and over again. All of it with so much joy!

In the pages of this book, you are about to meet and learn from my faithful friend Bob Gabelman. I guarantee he will challenge and inspire you, just like he has me.

Pastor Bob Groeneman
Pismo Beach, California

PREFACE

I STARTED WRITING this book in 2010. I laid out the chapters and wrote the first chapter at that time. Then I laid the project down. During the months and years that followed, numerous people whom I had never met approached me, telling me I had a message to share and I needed to get to it. My feeling was, "Does Christianity really need another book?" I never really answered my own question.

Kathleen, my dear wife, kept encouraging me, the way only a wife can, to write the book. Over the years she had heard the many stories in this book and wanted me to write them down for our children and grandchildren's posterity. Still, I dragged my feet on the subject.

Then, March of 2020 came upon the world. The world took a pause as a result of COVID-19. With lockdowns and shelter in place orders I found myself with a whole bunch of downtime. To add to the situation, my sciatic nerve in my back went haywire, and I found myself unable to stand or walk without pain for six months.

Then, one morning as I sat in my backyard, watching the birds and butterflies, I contemplated what I was to be doing during this international pause. It was during my personal devotion time that I heard that still small voice of the Holy Spirit say, "What about that book?" Around the same time, I heard another familiar voice, the voice of Kathleen, say, "What about that book?" Soon after, my old friend Pastor Bob, whom you will meet in the book, said to me, "You should write it; if it blesses even a few people, it will be worth it."

So I was hooked. I determined to write the book. First, I had to find what I had started 10 years earlier on my computer. That computer was long gone, though, and I could not find what I had begun.

I then set out to reconstruct what had been in my heart 10 years ago. I laid out the chapters and wrote the first chapter again. One day, I found an old external hard drive and plugged it in to see what was on it. Guess what. I found the beginnings of *The Day of Good News* from 2010. In comparing the first draft with what I had again started, I found that all but one chapter differed from the original. Comparing the first chapter was amazing. They were identical.

Over the next six months into August 2020, I wrote for about four hours each day. Four times during that period my computer crashed and only when working on the manuscript. It had never crashed before and has not crashed since. The third time it crashed, it took 10 days to restore it. Fortunately, I had been saving my work each day on multiple flash drives.

By August 2020 I had finished the rough draft of the book, and it was rough. Another significant event took place at that time. My back was healed, totally and completely. At that time, I approached some people I knew to see if they would be interested in publishing it. Sadly, that did not work out.

At Christmas, quite unexpectedly, a longtime faithful supporter of ours since we have been working on the mission fields approached me and offered to edit the book. She also directed me to a publisher, who has shown interest in the book.

What you have in your hands is my story. I started sharing the Gospel in early 1979. I have shared the Gospel message at least 20,000 times. About 1997, I was out on the streets witnessing on a Friday night. As I walked along, I heard the voice of the Holy Spirit say, "Bob, it's time to reproduce yourself."

After 18 years witnessing on the streets, I had learned essential evangelism techniques. It was then that I began to write a training manual called "The Essentials of Effective Evangelism," which is the basis of this book.

To this point, I have taught this subject upwards of 60 times, to thousands of God's people in the United States, throughout Mexico, El Salvador, Cuba, and China. In China, we taught in underground churches and Bible schools, with the threat of arrest if caught. In Cuba, I was arrested after teaching this material to a gathering of 120 pastors. After four-and-a-half hours of interrogation over two days, and under a threat of prison, I was deported. My crime was teaching in an illegal church to illegal pastors.

What you have in your hands is illegal in some places on the earth. But the kingdom of Heaven rejoices at the sound of the proclamation of the Good News of salvation through Jesus's life, death on the cross, and resurrection from the grave.

I hope you will be blessed, encouraged, equipped, and motivated to share the most powerful message this world has ever known.

Working together in the harvest,
Bob Gabelman

TABLE OF CONTENTS

1

This Day Is a Day of Good News

"This generation of Christians is responsible for this genera-tion of souls on earth."[1]—Keith Green

"Then they said to one another, 'We are not doing right. This day is a day of good news, but we are keeping silent; if we wait until morning light, punishment will overtake us. Now therefore come, let us go and tell the king's household.'"
—2 Kings 7:9

THE SITUATION IN the city of Samaria was desperate. The king of Aram had surrounded the city, allowing none to enter or leave. Food was scarce and hope had departed. The people were starving and dying without hope. Elisha, the prophet of God, had promised the king that things were about to change. Outside the walls, at the city's gate, sat four lepers. They could not enter the city because of their unclean con-dition, nor could they leave its gates. They discussed among themselves their state and their options. "Why do we sit here until we die? If we go into the city we will die. If we sit here any longer, we will die. If we go over to the enemy's camp, perhaps we will die, or perhaps they will let us live" (2 Kings 7:3,4).

So they went, and what they found was unexpected. The camp was abandoned. The tents and all the provisions were there, the fires and the food upon the fires were there, but the army had fled. When the four lepers entered the first tent, they ate and drank and took everything of value and hid it. Then they entered a second tent and did the same. Upon returning and entering a third tent, they paused and considered what they had found. Then they said to each other, "We are not doing right. This is a day of good news, but we are keeping silent." Back in Samaria their families and friends were dying without hope. So they returned and announced the good news of what they had found. And the people of the city rushed out to lay hold of the abundance of provisions left by the Aramean army.

Today is the day of Good News. In our hometowns and in our cities, people are living and dying without the hope that the Gospel offers. Our families and friends, our co-workers and classmates are all heading into eternity without the hope that Jesus offers in the Gospel. We are like those four lepers. We have found the Source of hope and abundance, not just in eternity but here and now in our daily lives. That Source is Jesus. He is everything to us. And many of our friends and families would rush to Him if we didn't remain silent about Jesus.

Since 1979 I have been able to share the Good News of salvation nearly 20,000 times. This is only by God's grace working in me. His grace, His divine influence, has moved me to touch His heart for this world. In this book I would like to share with you some simple essentials I have found in effectively sharing the Good News of salvation with the people God has placed in my realm of influence. We all live within a realm of influence. That is the world around us where we have contact with people every day. In that realm are our families, our friends, our neighbors, our co-workers, our classmates, the people we see every day in the markets and stores, in the parks, and on the streets.

I walked along the street one night in Denver, Colorado, and met a man named Saka. Saka was from the Democratic Republic of the Congo. He had only been in a church service one time in his life in his native country. As we walked along, I shared with him the Good News of Jesus's sacrifice for our sins. I stopped on the street and turned to Saka and asked him, "What do you think of this message?" He looked at me, and his eyes grew big. With much animation he cried out, "Dat's Goood News! Dat's Goood News!" I responded, "That's what God calls it, Good News!"

The Gospel is "Good News," and our message to our world must be good news. Sometimes I hear people's message, and it does not sound like Good News. I remember a time I was in the central park of Mexico City, Parque Alameda. We had a group from the United States sharing the Gospel through dramas. As I walked through the park, a man with a portable speaker was shouting at people that they were going to hell. As I walked by, I heard him say, "And you, in the orange hat, you're going to hell." I was the man in the orange hat, and I thought to myself, "That message doesn't sound like good news."

Imagine the scene in the movie *Titanic* where all the people are drowning in the icy waters when a lifeboat arrives to help them. Now imagine a man standing on the edge of the lifeboat shouting at the drowning people, "You're going to drown, and you, you're going to drown, and you, over there, you're going to drown. You wretched swimmers, you're all going to drown!" Now that's not good news. Good News would sound like this, "You don't have to drown. Get in the boat. Let me help you get in the boat." Our message to our world should sound like the latter and not the former.

I was in the city of San Vincente in El Salvador a number of years ago. We were taking a group of young people into a national secondary school (high school) in the city, to present a program based on good values and good choices. Again, we use dramas to present our message. This school had over 700 students in the morning session and 700 more in the afternoon session. In El Salvador we can share the Gospel message, pray with the students, and distribute Bibles during these events. As we walked down a street to the entrance of the school, a man called out to me, asking what we were doing. I stepped onto the porch of his home and began to speak with him. He was missing an arm and had knife scars all over his body. Asking what had happened to him, he replied that he had been in a knife fight, but he had "taken care" of the men who had done this to him. This resulted in several years in prison. In the midst of our conversation he said, "I used to be a Christian."

I asked, "What happened?"

He responded, "Well, I kind of fell out of the boat."

I extended my hand to him and replied, "Let me help you back into the boat." With tears in his eyes, he took hold of my hand as I led him in a prayer to rededicate his life to Christ. It was Good News to him.

Our message is Good News! When Jesus announced His ministry in His home synagogue in Nazareth, He took the scroll of Isaiah and began to read what we know today as Isaiah 61:

> *16 And He came to Nazareth, where He had been brought up. And, as His custom was, He went into the synagogue on the Sabbath day and stood up to read. 17 And the book of the prophet Isaiah was handed to Him. And unrolling the book, He found the place where it was written, 18 "The Spirit of the Lord is on Me; because of this He has anointed Me to proclaim the Gospel to the poor. He has sent me to heal the brokenhearted, to proclaim deliverance to the captives, and new sight to the blind, to set at liberty those having been crushed, 19 to proclaim the acceptable year of the Lord." 20 And rolling up the book, returning it to the attendant, He sat down. And the eyes of all in the synagogue were fastened on Him. 21 And He began to say to them, today this Scripture is fulfilled in your ears. 22 And all bore witness to Him and wondered at the gracious words which came out of His mouth. And they said, Is this not Joseph's son? —Luke 4:16–22 (MKJV)*

Here, Jesus announces at the beginning of His ministry what His ministry would look like. He came to restore lost man in all aspects of life: body, soul, and spirit. He would proclaim Good News, heal broken hearts (soul), restore sight to the blind (body), and deliver the captives and those crushed by sin. Jesus did something unique as he read these verses. He stopped in mid-sentence. This was a breach of scripture etiquette. Among the Jews, a teacher should never stop his reading in mid-sentence. Notice when He sat down the people in attendance "fastened their eyes upon Him." Why? Because they expected Him to complete the reading. Jesus was making it noticeably clear what He had come to do. Look at Jesus's message in the Gospel of Mark:

> *14 And after John was delivered up, Jesus came into Galilee, proclaiming the gospel of the kingdom of God, 15 and saying, the time is fulfilled, and the kingdom of God draws near. Repent, and believe the gospel. —Mark 1:14,15 (MKJV)*

The time has come, the kingdom of God is at hand, repent and believe this Good News.

Jesus came to proclaim Good News!

Now let us look at the remainder of the scripture from the reading in Isaiah 61:

> *2 to preach the acceptable year of Jehovah and the day of vengeance of our God; to comfort all who mourn; 3 to appoint to those who mourn in Zion, to give to them beauty for ashes, the oil of joy for mourning, the mantle of praise for the spirit of heaviness; so that they might be called trees of righteousness, the planting of Jehovah, that He might be glorified. —Isaiah 61:2,3 (MKJV)*

Here we see that Jesus stopped short of the portion "to preach ...the day of vengeance of our God." Why did He stop short? We believe that the remainder of verses 2 and 3 are precious Gospel promises: comforting those who mourn, beauty for ashes, oil of joy, and garment of praise. We love these promises, and indeed we should. But Jesus stopped short in His reading. He ended with, "...proclaim the acceptable (or favorable) year of the Lord." Jesus was clearly proclaiming, "The time has come, the kingdom of God is at hand, now believe this Good News!"

Jesus was announcing the season of God's favor toward man. Yes, there is a day of vengeance. But that day is not today. Today is the day of Good News.

I have found that most people in our world have never really heard the Good News of the Gospel. They may think they have heard the message of Christianity, but they have not. Often when I share the simple Gospel message they respond, "I've never heard that before." I have heard this response thousands upon thousands of times.

I met a group of young people one night and asked them if I could share the message of salvation with them. One young man, who was rather large and threatening, responded, "I'm an atheist, and I don't want to hear it."

"Okay," I said, "I respect that." And I turned to the rest of the group and asked if I could share the message with them. They said I could. I shared a simple Gospel message, which only takes about two minutes.

When I finished, I looked at the young "atheist," whose face had a look of amazement, He said, "If there is ever anything I can believe, I can believe that!" The message was Good News to him. Often the message people are hearing is not Good News.

Jesus's message was Good News, and our message must be Good News as well. People really are waiting to hear Good News.

This is the day of Good News!

About 25 years ago I did a demographic study of the earth, and I discovered that 33 percent of the earth's population are Christian believers. That includes 17.3 percent Catholic, 15.7 percent Protestant, Orthodox, Evangelicals, Pentecostals, and so on and so forth. Another

33 percent of the population are people groups that are still considered unreached. That is, no missionary has entered their culture with the Gospel message, no portion of Holy Scripture has been translated into the language of their heart, and/or less than 2 percent of the indigenous group are believers in Christ. The final 33 percent of the world population live within the reach of the established Christian Church within their culture but have yet to be evangelized or have rejected the Gospel message and the claims of Christ.

The world population at the time of this writing is 7.8 billion. That translates to about 2,364,000,000 believers and 5,436,000,000 unbelievers. In other words, over 5.4 billion people are heading into eternity without hope, destined for a hell that God did not create for man. God created hell for the devil and his demons, but He created heaven for man and man for heaven.

Every year nearly 56 million people die. Of those, 18.5 million are destined for the kingdom of Heaven, while 37.5 million are lost for eternity. Every day 151,600 people will die on the earth, with 50,028 souls stepping into their eternal hope, and 101,572 souls that are lost forever. Every hour of every day 6,316 people will die, 2,084 souls will have everlasting life, and 4,232 will be lost. Every minute of every hour of every day, 105 people will die on this earth. Thirty-five are saved, and 70 are not. Every three seconds, six people will die. Two are saved, and four are lost for eternity. This means that a soul enters hell every second. Every second, every second, every second, every second...

How many destinies could be changed if someone had said this to them during their lifetime? "The time has come, the kingdom of Heaven is at hand, repent and believe this Good News"? Would they have responded to the story of the Gospel like Saka, who said, "Dat's Goooood News! Dat's Goooood News!"? Today is the day of good news, and we are still living in what Jesus called "the year of the Lord's favor."

Perhaps you have been given this book by a Christian believer. Perhaps as you sit here, you know you are not right with God. If you were to die tonight, where would you spend eternity: heaven or hell?

Before we continue further, I would like to share the message of Good News. Are you ready? Let us have a look.

Do you know God created you to have a relationship with Him? He wants to be a Father to you. But there is a problem. Sin. God is holy, righteous, and perfect. Our sins separate us from God. What is sin? It is wrong thoughts, wrong actions, and wrong attitudes. These thoughts, actions, and attitudes have separated us from God. Some people believe if they could just do better, God would accept them. But we can never do enough good to satisfy God's requirements for holiness.

Our Father in Heaven is not satisfied that we are separated from Him. So God became a man in the form of Jesus Christ, the Son of God and God the Son. Jesus lived among us, showing us the way to the Father. He announced, "I am the Way, the Truth, and the Life. No one comes to the Father but through me" (John 14:6). Jesus's holy and perfect life led to His death, a crucifixion on the cross on Calvary's hill.

On the cross a transaction took place. Your sins—all your sins, past, present, and future—came upon Jesus, a holy, righteous, and perfect man. And His righteousness became yours. As He hung on the cross, he cried out: "Father! Why have you forsaken Me?" (Matthew 27:46). At that moment, for the first time in eternity, the Father and Son were separated. Jesus took our sins so we could partake of His righteousness. After His death He was laid in a tomb.

But the story did not end there. After three days in the tomb, He rose from the dead. Over 500 people saw Him alive after his death during the 40 days he continued on earth, preparing His followers to take up the task of world evangelism. Many of those who witnessed Him during this time went on to be martyred for their testimonies. They could have easily recanted their stories and been spared from death, but they did not. They were convinced of what they had seen, heard, and touched.

The Bible says that everyone, *everyone*, who calls upon the name of Jesus shall be saved. It also says that if you confess with your mouth that Jesus is Lord and believe in your heart that the Father raised Jesus from the dead, you too shall be saved (Romans 10:9).

I must ask you this: Would you like to make Jesus your Savior and Lord here and now? Do you believe in your heart—this is a deeper belief than believing intellectually—do you believe in your heart that Jesus is the Son of God? Do you believe in your heart that Jesus died for you personally? Do you believe in your heart that He rose from the dead? If you do, make this confession with your mouth.

Say with me: "Father in Heaven, you are holy and good to me. Let your kingdom come, and let your will be done in my life as it is in heaven. Father, I confess I am a sinner. I know I need a Savior. I believe that you sent your Son Jesus to make a way for me to get right with you. I ask you to forgive me of all my sin: yesterday, today, and tomorrow. Jesus, I invite you into my life right now to be my Savior and my Lord. Come and fill my heart with your presence. Send your Holy Spirit and fill me, baptize me, and lead me in the way I should go. Thank you, Jesus, for saving me today. Amen."

Maybe you have made this decision for the first time in your life. The Word of God, the Bible, assures you that you are now saved. Start out by telling others of this decision. If you know some Christians, let them know what you have done. Then, start to read the Bible. I would encourage you to start in the Gospels, the beginning part of the New Testament, with the Gospels of Matthew, Mark, Luke, and John. These Gospels will introduce you to Jesus, His mission, His purpose, the life He lived here on the earth, and His kingdom. Also, pray. Prayer is simply talking to God; it can be like a conversation. Talk to Him, and then listen in your heart, in your spirit, because He wants to talk to you personally as well. When you prayed just now, His Spirit, the Holy Spirit, entered your life and ignited your spirit to new life. That is what it means to be born again. I am thrilled with you and your choice to enter this new life!

In the next chapters I would like to share my story with you, the day of my good news, and the journey I began on January 20, 1979.

"Not called!" did you say? "Not heard the call," I think you should say. Put your ear down to the Bible and hear Him bid you go and pull sinners out of the fire of sin. Put your ear down to the burdened, agonized heart of humanity, and listen to its pitiful wail for help. Go stand by the gates of hell and hear the damned entreat you to go to their father's house and bid their brothers and sisters, and servants and masters not to come there. And then look Christ in the face, whose mercy you have professed to obey, and tell Him whether you will join heart and soul and body and circumstances in the march to publish His mercy to the world.[2] —William Booth

2

My Day of Good News: My Personal Testimony

"The gospel is only good news if it gets there in time."[3]
—Carl F. H. Henry

JANUARY 20, 1979, was a Saturday. I was living in Jacksonville, Florida, in my fifth year of active-duty service in the Navy. As a 22-year-old stationed on an aircraft carrier homeported in the area, I kept a home in the city. I spent that day making deals to buy and sell drugs. Yes, I was serving in the military, but I was a heavy drug user at the time and had been for the past seven years. If you could smoke it, I smoked it. If you could pop it, I popped it. If you could snort it, I snorted it. If you could shoot it, I shot it. Now, I was not a total derelict. My responsibility in the Navy was maintenance and repair of the intelligence system computers, peripheral data equipment, and the shipboard intelligence closed circuit television system.

That evening, after a full day of wheeling and dealing, I came into my home and went to my room. As I sat on the bed, my eye caught a pocket-sized King James Gideon New Testament with Psalms and Proverbs sitting on my dresser. I can say that I was not in any particular way pursuing God at that time, although there were a number of current circumstances in my life that were making me more receptive to the claims of Christ. That day it captured my attention. During basic training we were all issued one of these New Testaments. Since then, I had picked up and read it a couple of times, and a strange sense of awe came over me. I could not explain it then, but I would feel something shift in the atmosphere. But most of the time I just found it hard to comprehend what I was reading.

On this night, the words came alive. I cannot tell you what I was reading at the time, but those words were living. Something began to build inside of me, a divinely understood sense of anticipation, of expectation. I had a realization that I was a sinner, and I was lost. Not only were my actions sinful, but my very nature was to be a sinner. I sinned because I was a sinner. I was born this way, and even changing my actions and behavior would not change that. I became aware that even the best things I ever did were mostly done out of selfish ambition. Also, my current lifestyle really placed me in a tough situation if I should die.

As I continued to read that New Testament, with the fresh awareness that I was headed for a serious bad end, I read that Jesus came from heaven to earth to save me from my current destiny. In the back cover of the book was a plan of salvation with scriptures to highlight each point of the plan. The heavens were opening, and I could begin to see there was hope for me. Finally, at the end of the plan, there was a prayer: a sinner's prayer. I read it and ...nothing happened. I still had this sense of hopelessness. So I turned my face toward heaven and cried out from the depths of my soul, "God, I don't know if you are real, but if you are, will you show me?" I was being sincere. I did not know if God was real, but if He was, I wanted to know!

With that, something began to change in the room. The Holy Presence of a Holy God began to fill the room. I didn't know what to do. It seemed like the room was filling with smoke, like on Thanksgiving when Momma was burning the turkey, and the house would be smoky from about three feet above the floor to the ceiling. I tried to get under the smoke and lay flat on the floor. That Holy Presence began to fill me.

I had enough background to know about being born again, and I knew this was happening to me. For some time, I lay there, unable to move. I felt a cleansing in my heart, soul, mind, attitudes, feelings, and so on. I truly felt forgiven. God the Holy Spirit had entered my heart and ignited my spirit into new life. I became a new person, never to be the same.

Looking back, I can see how Jesus carefully planned my steps to bring me to this point of new birth. I was born and raised in a somewhat devout Catholic family of six children in Akron, Ohio. Our family life was centered on our parish church, and all of us children attended the associated Catholic school.

Most of my family memories were good and wholesome. I made my First Communion in second grade in conjunction with my first confession just before my First Communion. We never missed a Sunday Mass, always attending as a family. We could take up an entire pew, and surely it was a great task to get us all ready and loaded in the family station wagon to arrive on time. Yes, there were those Sundays when my parents' frustration would boil over into arguments during the ride. But like all churchgoing families, when we entered the "Miracle Mile," all would be well. You know the Miracle Mile, that point when you enter the church parking lot, and everything becomes beautiful and wonderful. All is well with the world, and you greet everyone with a cheery "Hello" as you enter the doors of the church.

I became an altar boy in third grade. We first learned the liturgy of the Mass in Latin, before it was changed to English. In those days, I thought God's phone number must be a Latin phrase from the liturgy that always stuck with me: "*Dominus vobiscum, Et cum spiritu tuo.*" This translates to: (Priest) "The Lord be with you." (Response) "And with your spirit." It sounded to me like we were saying, "Et-2 spirit 2-2-0" and therefore must be God's phone number. At that time phone numbers sounded like that.

The first Mass I served as an altar boy was at six o'clock on a Monday morning, with only a handful of people in attendance. My older brother served with me, and Mom and Dad sat in the front row. Over the years I found myself serving the six o'clock morning Mass often.

We were assigned to serve in weeklong intervals. One morning I asked Sister Lawrence, who made the altar boy schedules, why I was assigned the 6:00 a.m. Mass so often. She said, "Because I know you will show up." Ah, the reward for dependability! Many occasions I served that mass alone because the other altar boy did not show up.

During a two-and-a-half-year period when we lived in a house exactly two miles from church, serving the 6:00 a.m. Mass meant waking up at 4:30 a.m. My mother always prepared a warm breakfast for me before I set off into the northern Ohio cold. I think she felt honored and blessed to send me off on such a noble mission. Then I walked the two miles, in my memory always in the snow, to arrive the required 15 minutes before Mass started. I can still hear the sound of my feet crunching the blanket of snow, which seemed to be fresh every morning.

Another memory from those mornings is the smell of the Firestone Rubber factory I walked by each morning. At that time all the major rubber companies were in full operation, so the smell of rubber continually filled the air in Akron. I did not realize what fresh air smelled like until I left for the Navy at 17.

Maybe once a week, especially during the Lenten season, my family would gather in the living room of our home, kneeling down to say the rosary together. Now as I write this, I can see a number of readers—especially Protestant, Evangelical, Pentecostal, Charismatic readers—rolling your eyes. But there was a sincere devotion in my family to our Catholic beliefs. My Dad would usually lead the prayers, although I always felt my Mom was the inspiration behind it. Now, he could say a Hail Mary in a single syllable without taking a breath. I really felt I was hearing those unknown tongues I had heard about in the New Testament.

Being an altar boy, and serving so many weeks of six o'clock Mass from third grade to the beginning of ninth grade, I did become familiar with the Gospels and the Epistles. We seldom ventured beyond those borders into the Old Testament, except for the Psalms. It seemed that every other Saturday afternoon, my mom would pack me off to church to have the priest hear my confession. I do not recall my brothers and sisters being sent off as frequently as I was, and it could be she knew more about me than I thought she did.

In seventh grade my teacher was Sister Katherine. She had something unique about her that I could never quite put my finger on until the night I was born again. I really liked being around her because she was different, with a genuinely sweet, calming presence about her. The night I encountered the glorious presence of Jesus, I understood that it was His presence in her.

Sister Katherine occasionally invited me into the church at lunchtime, putting me up on the altar behind the pulpit and having me read the Gospels and Epistles out loud over the microphone. She helped me in my public speaking, stopping me often to coach me on my diction and enunciation. I never figured out why she did that. Plenty of students were much better than I was, and she was not doing the same with them. Now, when I consider it, I think maybe a prophetic gifting revealed God's plan for my life to her.

During my seventh, eighth, and ninth grade years, 1968–1970, the Jesus Movement was underway. I remember well the Jesus Movement taking place. Akron has a small university and at that time had a couple of popular Christian coffeehouses. A noticeable number of Jesus Freaks were turning up around the city. I was an observer of the movement, interested, but not aligned with it.

A regional band, Glass Harp, put out several albums and played at my all-boys Catholic high school one Friday night after a football game. This three-piece band had a guitar phenom named Phil Keaggy, who was writing profoundly Christian material under a secular guise. The other members of the band, also talented musicians in their own right, wrote songs that were not quite in the same vein as Phil's music. Phil Keaggy left the band at the pinnacle of its influence and began a solo Christian artist career. His music really touched me, and I saw him play in several Christian concerts as a high schooler. Over the years he has released over 50 contemporary Christian albums. But still I remained a nonparticipant observer of the movement.

The middle years of high school were packed with activity. Besides cross-country in the fall and track in the spring, I worked hard to maintain a high grade point average. I also participated in youth meetings in the church. During this period, I developed what would be a twenty-five-year passion for long-distance running. I ran an average of fifteen miles a day in the summer, and I had mapped out three 15-mile courses in different directions from our home. I loved to run, more than compete, but I became extremely competitive, winning many distance races. The portable Sony Walkman hadn't been invented, so I ran each day in solitude. This really developed a portion of my character; I still love solitude today. I love the quiet places, and I love to be alone with myself and contemplate, just to think.

In the winter of my junior year, a great change took place in my life, and not a good one. I took LSD for the first time. By summer I was taking all sorts of drugs several times a week. I also began to drink a lot of alcohol.

This period in my life would last seven years. By the summer before my senior year, I was living on the streets. In five months, I had fallen from a tremendous athlete and student who was being offered college scholarships to a street urchin with no aspirations beyond taking drugs and sneaking into concerts. My senior year of high school is almost a blur, not really worthy of expounding upon.

I dislike taking trips down memory lane. The good old days really were not all that good after all. By the spring of my senior year, I was a mess. I had been arrested three times in the month of April, in three different counties. The Juvenile Court Judge, weary of seeing me, gave this advice: "If I see you again, the consequences are going to be severe, and I will no longer treat you as a juvenile. I suggest you enter the military." Less than two months later, at the age of seventeen, I enlisted in the Navy. A new chapter had begun in my life.

I preached on the righteousness of the law and the righteousness of faith. While I was speaking, several dropped down as dead and among the rest such a cry was heard of sinners groaning for the righteousness of faith that it almost drowned my voice. But many of these soon lifted up their heads with joy and broke out into thanksgiving, being assured they now had the desire of their soul – the forgiveness of their sins.[4] —John Wesley

3

DISCIPLED: MY FIRST STEPS IN CHRIST

"I care not where I go, or how I live, or what I endure so that I may save souls. When I sleep, I dream of them; when I awake, they are first in my thoughts."[5] —*David Brainerd*

I WAS BORN again on a Saturday night. The following morning, Sunday, I had to report to my ship for fire watch, which I did every six days. I had volunteered for this responsibility, thereby violating the unofficial NAVY acronym, Never Again Volunteer Yourself. I wanted to know how to fight my way out of a fire at sea rather than jump overboard to save my skin.

Arriving at the ship that Sunday morning, I was still exhilarated by my encounter with the glorious presence of Jesus the night before. I decided to attend the Catholic Mass in the ship's chapel. It had been about seven years since I had been to Catholic service, but something was different for me that morning. Everything had become new in my life. For the first time in my life, the liturgy of the Catholic Mass came alive. I had been through the Catholic liturgy more than 1,500 times, but on that day it was different. I realized that every aspect of the liturgy would lead you to Jesus. Every response in the liturgy was coming from my spirit.

For all those years Mass had never once engaged my heart, only my head. Now my perspective of liturgical forms of worship has changed. Even today when I participate in the Catholic Mass, the same sense of life comes to me through the liturgy. When I witness to Catholics on the streets, especially in Latin America, I always tell them, "I am not here to convert you to a Protestant. I want you to be the best Catholic in your church. Someone that other people will ask, 'What is different about you?'" I feel my purpose in ministry on the streets is to lead people into a head-on collision with the presence of Jesus. It is the Holy Spirit's purpose to guide them afterward. We will explore this more in the following chapters.

Things really began to move fast in my spiritual growth. Now, remember I was not saved in a church setting. I was saved in my room, by reading the Bible. So there was no one following up with me from a local church on Monday morning. The Holy Spirit really became my guide and comforter. He had moved alongside me and began to direct my way. I quickly developed an insatiable hunger for the Word of God. I feasted throughout the day on that little Gideon King James New Testament with Psalms and Proverbs. Without a doubt, the Word of God is what brought healing to my mind and body after so many years of alcohol and drug abuse.

I had several Christian friends in the Navy. My best friends throughout my seven years of military service were a couple named John and Gloria from El Paso, Texas. John and I had known each other in boot camp. Amazingly, we were always transferred together to our next military assignments. We were roommates for about six months in a barracks in northern California for our first computer systems training. Later we were transferred to Key West, Florida, for our intelligence systems training. We were then transferred on to the same ship for three and a half years of sea duty. Finally, we were both transferred back to Key West for our final assignments before being discharged. In 1975, our first time in Key West, I visited them in their apartment one Saturday afternoon when two young Baptist men from a nearby church came knocking on the door. John invited them in, and they quickly got down to business sharing their Gospel message. I could see where this was heading. Excusing myself out the back door, I jumped a fence and made haste to my apartment, where I lit my pipe.

John and Gloria made commitments to Jesus that day, though, and it stuck with them. We continued in close friendship even though we had lifestyles on opposite sides of the spectrum. When we were transferred to our ship in Jacksonville, Florida, and had homes close to each other, they hosted a home Bible study on Friday nights. I would often show up in the middle of their Bible study, not really realizing this was a regularly scheduled event. I sat among all the couples while the Bible was being taught. Eventually I would excuse myself, go into the backyard, and light up. Then I would return and take my seat, no doubt reeking of weed. But they just continued to love me in my lost condition.

I found out later that I was their prayer project. Their prayers were drawing me to them. And of course, everyone there knew I was the neighborhood drug dealer, but they just loved and accepted me. The following Friday after receiving Jesus, I went to the Bible study to give my testimony. Needless to say, there was great rejoicing in the home that night. I will write later about the importance of prayer in effective soul winning.

Word traveled fast around my ship in the week following my salvation encounter. I had been dealing a lot of drugs to my shipmates. With my newfound faith, that supply line was about to dry up.

I was invited to attend a Catholic Charismatic meeting for young adults in the back room of a Christian/Catholic bookstore. It was a lively group, singing with clapping (my first experience with clapping in church), a message from Scripture, and a time of prayer. It was all right, with nice people and such. As the meeting was closing, John asked me if I wanted to be baptized in the Holy Spirit. I had no clue what he was talking about. I guess they tried to explain it, but it was all over my head. I finally responded, "I want whatever Jesus wants for me."

They gathered around me, put their hands on me (I did not understand that either), and started to pray. I could feel again that powerful presence of God I had felt less than a week earlier. I could not understand the words of their prayers, but then I started doing the same. I did not know what was going on, except I felt ready to explode. All I had said was, "I want whatever Jesus wants for me." I guess that was enough of an invitation. Perhaps this happened so easily for me because I really had formed no doctrines one way or the other about this gift called the baptism in the Holy Spirit. I just wanted whatever Jesus had for me.

I cannot recall if it was the next Sunday or the one after that, but another Christian I knew on the ship invited me to go to a church he was attending. When we entered, I was given a menu with the morning's agenda. This was new, as my only experience outside the Catholic church was in the back of a Christian bookstore. My friend told me this was a Baptist church. The music started, and there was singing and again clapping. After a few songs they started speaking in those strange tongues again. I joined in, and again it was a glorious experience.

It took me a few years to discover that this was not a typical Baptist church. The pastor had received the Holy Ghost baptism and introduced this gift to his congregation. I found this out in a most embarrassing way the second time I went to a Baptist church. At the beginning of the service, the pastor said, "Let us pray." I ripped off about a paragraph of tongue-talking before I noticed the rest of the church was quiet. When I opened my eyes, they were all staring at me. Sorry about that.

Well, this Sunday morning after we sang, clapped, and prayed in tongues, the pastor preached a sermon titled "The Lordship of Jesus." I had never heard anything like this before. Yes, I had heard the word Lord associated with the name of Jesus, but I had never heard this concept of His Lordship. The preacher clearly painted a picture of what His Lordship was and what it should mean to us. This was new terrain for me to cover.

Afterward, he invited people to respond at the altar to surrender their lives to Jesus's Lordship. Many left their seats and made their way to the front of the church. I did not. I could not. I needed to process this. I fully understood what I had heard, and I could see it as the relationship Jesus wants with us, but I also fully understood the seriousness of the commitment.

I went to my home that afternoon wrestling with this idea. I spent the rest of the day and continued into the evening struggling with this new notion. Finally, after hours of internal debate, I got down on my knees and said, "Jesus, I know everything you have done in my life this past week has been absolutely wonderful. So I trust you with this decision. Tonight, I make you Lord of my life. Thank you, Jesus." So in two weeks I had made Jesus my Savior, my Lord, and had been baptized in the Holy Spirit. Things were moving fast. What else was there that I did not yet know about?

Earlier I said I had an insatiable hunger for God's Word. I was reading that pocket New Testament every chance I had. I had read the Gospel of John, then Matthew, then Mark, then Luke, and then John again, and was somewhere in the middle of the Book of Acts when my next step was painted before me.

The city of Jacksonville covers a huge area, somewhere around 52 miles from the northern to the southern city limits. A week or two after I had surrendered to Jesus's Lordship, I was taking a bus from my ship to my home at the end of the day, which took 30 minutes or more. I only had enough change, or folding money for that matter, for a one-way bus ride. As I rode along, I noticed some Gospel tracts on the floor in the aisle of the bus. Then a man about my age reached down and picked one up and began to read it. I had learned from the beginning that the Holy Spirit is speaking to us continually, much more than we are usually listening. As I sat there, I heard the clear voice of the Spirit say, "Talk to him!"

"What, Me? I can't do that."

Again, the Spirit said, "Talk to him!" I guess He had not heard my previous protest. Again, I heard the words, "Talk to him!" I turned my face to the window and tried not to hear what I knew I was hearing.

Finally, I responded, "I don't know what to say."

As I sat there wishing I was somewhere else, the Holy Spirit stirred in my mind the passage in the eighth chapter of Acts, which I had read recently. Phillip saw a chariot riding along, and the Holy Spirit told him, "Go up and join this chariot." Next, Phillip ran alongside the Ethiopian's chariot asking him if he understood what he was reading. The imagery of this encounter has always intrigued me. Running alongside a chariot sharing the Gospel fascinates me. As I sat there entertaining the thought, again the Holy Spirit coaxed me, "Talk to him."

I reached across the aisle, tapped him on the shoulder, and like Phillip, asked him, "Do you understand what you are reading?"

He looked at me, shook his head, and responded, "No." I moved up into the seat next to him and began to share with him. I did not have any Scripture to share. All I had was the testimony of what Jesus had done in my life in the last three or four weeks. We passed my bus stop, and the bus continued on its route to downtown Jacksonville, 30 minutes farther than I had intended to go.

I shared with my fellow traveler as we entered the heart of the city. He was on his way to a job interview in the city center. I exited the bus with him on a city street corner. He still had 45 minutes until his interview. I knew I had to do more, but what? What now? The corner where we stood had an old southern church on it with about a dozen stairs up to the large front doors. The doors were propped open with a sandwich board on the stairs that said, "Come in and Pray." That was it, go in and pray! I had entered uncharted waters, but the Holy Spirit was painting the floor with all the dance steps. I asked my new friend, "Do you want to go in and pray?"

He said, "Yes!" We climbed the steps, walked to the altar railing, knelt down, and prayed. I remembered most of that salvation prayer in my Gideon Bible. We also prayed for his job interview, and he was off.

As I continued to kneel there, exhilarated and exploding inside, an elderly man tapped me on the shoulder from behind. He asked, "Would you pray for me too?" Of course, I did, and we too prayed a salvation prayer together.

Even today I cannot express the glory of this moment. I really had no idea what I was doing, but I was the guy in the place Jesus could use. I left the church in joy and rapture. As I walked along, I remembered that I had no money for the bus ride home. I crossed a main city intersection and saw someone I knew, one of the young men from the Catholic charismatic meeting. I shared with him what had just happened, and he was genuinely excited about it. Plus, he gave me bus fare to get home.

As a side note, I mentioned how I have always been intrigued by the imagery of Phillip's encounter with the Ethiopian and the idea of running alongside a chariot and sharing your faith. Years after those initial soul-winning experiences, I was walking along Main Street one Friday night in Longmont, Colorado, where I was living at the time. Every Friday and Saturday night for more than a generation, hundreds if not thousands of young people in really nice cars had descended upon Longmont to cruise Main Street. It was not unusual for people to come from all parts of Colorado, Wyoming, and Nebraska to cruise on those weekend nights. For six years, I shared Jesus's love and salvation there every Friday night. In just five years, I witnessed 600 young people give their lives to Christ. I handed out Bibles and New Testaments, tracts, and food. I broke up fights and helped some kids get home on nights when they could not find their way home on their own.

One night as I walked along, a car passed me, and I heard the Holy Spirit say, in essence, "Go up and join this chariot." I was still running long distances daily then, so I began to run along the street. Because of traffic and traffic lights, I was able to pass the car. I arrived at an entrance to a parking lot and stepped into the street in front of the car, waving it into the parking lot. They pulled over and rolled down their windows, wondering what was going on. I told them Jesus wanted me to tell them something.

There were four young people in the car, and I shared the Gospel message with them. Then I asked each of them individually if they would like to invite Jesus to be their Savior that night. Each of them replied, "Yes!"

Another night, I was crossing a street at a traffic light intersection. When I walked in front of the lead car, the Holy Spirit said to me, "Talk to them." I went around and knocked on the window. There were two young people in the front and one in the back. I told them Jesus sent me to tell them He loves them and has a plan for them. As we talked the traffic light changed, but I was not finished. The cars behind this lead car began to express their impatience. When I finished the Gospel message, all three occupants of the vehicle prayed with me to receive Jesus into their lives. God is good!

Back in the Navy, things in my newfound faith seemed to be moving at the speed of light, which I believe is 186,000 miles a second. After leading people to Christ, what was next on the horizon?

Not long afterward, a set of orders showed up on my ship to transfer me to Key West. I had finished my three and a half years of sea duty and was scheduled now for shore duty. But there was a hitch. In order to accept the orders to Key West, I had to extend my enlistment another 18 months. At that point I had less than a year and a half remaining in my active duty. "No way," I said, and I returned the orders to the personnel department. I really wanted to be out of the Navy. I liked the idea of returning to Key West, but the price was too great.

The next morning, during my personal devotions, I heard the Holy Spirit speak, "Why didn't you take those orders?"

"What?" I exclaimed, with a sense of shock and horror. I continued, "Well, you know why; I want to be out of the Navy!"

"How do you know I am not in them?" the Holy Spirit responded.

"Well, you can't be!" I countered. I was still growing in the Lordship thing. Thus began a two-week debate with God about my future. I understood the idea of His Lordship, but I was not walking it out yet in every part of my life. Every morning we had the same conversation.

Some mornings I even skipped my devotions because I did not want to hear it.

I tried to ply Him with bargains and deals. "Lord, if I get out of the Navy, I can go to Bible school." No response. I begged and whined, again with no response. After a couple of weeks, my ship was going out to sea for several weeks.

I had a rather good plan that might cause God to change His mind. I'd fast food and water for three days, in addition to prayer. Now I was young in Christ and did not know everything I should have known about fasting. I carried out my plan, sure that this would change everything. After three days it did: it changed me. I was completely broken by the ordeal. I cried out, "Okay, Lord, you win. I will take those orders and go to Key West!" I surrendered.

It was now three weeks since I had received the orders. With 5,000 men on the ship, I doubted the orders were still available. When I went to see the personnel officer, he asked, "What is your name?"

"Data Systems Technician Second Class Robert Gabelman, Sir," I replied.

Amazingly, he reached over to a pile of papers on the top of a basket, and the very top set of papers was mine. He handed the papers to me, and said, "Are these the orders?" Yes, they were. I shipped out to Key West in the late spring of 1979.

Over the next several years I realized it really was His plan and purpose for my life to go to Key West, even at the expense of another 18 months of enlistment. Several critical areas in my life took form during those next 10 years in Key West. Most importantly, I met my future wife and lifelong friend, Kathleen.

Shortly after arriving in Key West at my new duty station, some of my co-workers told me about some Christians who met every Friday night on the "Sunset Pier" to sing songs and share testimonies. "Sunset Pier," or Mallory Square, was really a dock facing the west on the Gulf of Mexico. Nightly, hundreds of tourists would gather to watch the sun set into the sea. It was also a haven for many street musicians and performers.

The next Friday night I went with my friends John and Gloria to check it out. Little did I know that I would be spending a lot of time in the next years on this pier growing in my giftings as a street evangelist. As we stepped onto the pier that night and approached the group of Christians we had heard about, I saw someone who literally captured my heart at first sight. Kathleen was sitting among the group on the edge of the pier. I am sure there was a halo around her head, but it could have been the sun setting just above the horizon behind her.

The Christian group was a fairly new ministry in the city called Street Church, with a focus on discipleship, evangelism, and community. Birthed out of the Jesus Movement of the late '60s and the 70s, they had been established for some time in Pennsylvania, Ohio, and even England. The Full Gospel Businessmen's group had invited them to establish their ministry in Key West, an ideal location for their vision to reach the lost. Even back in 1979, Key West had a thriving population of hippies, new agers, and other spiritual seekers, as well as young men and women my age.

I became involved with Street Church and spent a lot of time out on the streets witnessing, often with Kathleen. After about a year I rented a house near Duval Street, the main party street in Key West's central area. The home became our discipleship outreach center for the ministry. At times we had over 20 men living in the home. Each morning I would be up at 4:00 a.m. to pray and read the Bible. At 6:00 a.m. I would wake the entire house for morning devotions and then cleared out the house. One of the requirements for staying there was to be employed or at least be looking for work.

After finishing my Navy service, more than two years after arriving in Key West, I began full-time ministry with Street Church. I headed up the discipleship home, taught our discipleship curriculum every Tuesday night, and led home cell groups on Wednesday nights. Friday nights, I was on the pier, and I preached and taught our Sunday service on Sunday afternoons. I ministered in the county jail on Sunday evenings and spent time witnessing on the streets almost daily. Kathleen was by my side as all this progressed. We spent many nights together winning souls. I was head over heels in love with her, but it took me a year and a half to let her know this.

During this time, a friend named Matt was starting an electrical/construction contracting company. He would let me and several other Street Church volunteers work with him at times when we needed extra money. The ministry with Street Church, although more than full time, was unpaid. As time went by, Matt taught me the electrical trade.

On December 26, 1981, Kathleen and I were married. I turned over the leadership of the discipleship house to a couple of other single men and began to work full time in the electrical field to support my new family. Kathleen and I continued in Key West another seven years. During that time, our first three children, Jared, Shiloh, and Nathan, were born. We continued in street ministry and church leadership until we moved to Longmont, Colorado, in the fall of 1988. In the years after arriving to Colorado, we added two more Gabelmans to the quiver, Angela and Hannah.

Looking back on God's relentless urging to go Key West, I can see why He was so intent upon His purpose. Now I see how the very foundational areas of my life came together there. First and foremost, I met Kathleen, and we started our lifelong journey together there. Second, the gifting and calling in ministry as an evangelist were birthed and developed there. Third, it was there that I entered the electrical trade, which has allowed me to provide for my family for over 40 years. I can see why our faithful Father would not back down in getting me to take those orders.

The final 10 years in Colorado, from 1994 to 2004, I spent almost every Friday night witnessing on the streets in Longmont, Boulder, Fort Collins, and downtown Denver, Colorado. Many of the testimonies in the following chapters are from those years. I can say that, during those 10 years, I shared the Gospel 10,000 or 12,000 times. I know that by the number of "I.O.U. LOVE" ministry cards I had printed up and handed out on the streets. I.O.U. love comes from Romans 13:8. "Owe nothing to anyone except to love one another; for he who loves his neighbor has fulfilled the law." On one of those Friday nights in about 1995, as I walked along Main Street in Longmont, I heard the Holy Spirit say, "It is time to reproduce yourself." At that time, I began to write the Essentials of Personal Evangelism text, which I will be expanding on in the following chapters.

We were members of a large church in Loveland, Colorado, for 10 years. Kathleen and I were involved in a number of ministries there: working with children and junior high youth, leading a cell group in our home, and ministering at the altar each Sunday. While working with the junior high youth and our great friends Pastors Bob and Tammie, we made four trips to Mexico on youth mission trips. This was my first introduction to cross-cultural missions as well as my introduction to the mission organization we have worked with since 2004.

We left Colorado after 15 years for Laredo, Texas, on January 31, 2004, to work in full-time missions with Victorious Christian Harvesters (VCH) and our friends David and Donna Blanchard, its founders. Since its inception, the vision has been "one million Bibles for one million souls." On August 1, 2016, that vision was fulfilled. Today we continue with an expanded vision: "ten million Bibles for ten million souls."

We have worked extensively with VCH throughout Mexico and El Salvador, also spending time in Cuba and western China. I teach throughout the week in Nuevo Laredo, Mexico, at the International Harvesters Institute, the training school of VCH. Victorious Christian Harvesters has hosted more than 100 city-wide, weeklong evangelism seminars we call "Invasions" in all the major cities of Mexico and in El Salvador. Our national workers in Cuba are also equipping the saints there to win it for Christ. These following chapters are an expanded version of the material I teach on the opening night of an "Invasion" seminar.

In the next chapter we will press our ears to hear the heartbeat of God.

> *I have but one passion—it is He; it is He alone. The world is the field and the field is the world; and henceforth that country shall be my home where I can be most used in winning souls for Christ.*[6] *—Nicolaus Zinzendorf*

4

THE HEARTBEAT OF GOD: NONE PERISH, ALL SAVED

"Could a mariner sit idle if he heard the drowning cry?
Could a doctor sit in comfort and just let his patients die?
Could a fireman sit idle, let men burn and give no hand?
Can you sit at ease in Zion with the world around you
damned?"[7] —Leonard Ravenhill

WHY DO WE win souls? The primary purpose for winning the lost is that it honors God. Souls are our Father's primary purpose and desire. Winning the lost honors Him, pleases Him, and is the just reward for His Son's sacrifice. There are many secondary reasons, but the primary one is the glory of God. Let us look at Paul's letter to the Corinthians.

17 Therefore, if anyone is in Christ, he is a new creature; the old things passed away; behold, new things have come. 18 Now all these things are from God, who reconciled us to Himself through Christ and gave us the ministry of reconciliation, 19 namely, that God was in Christ reconciling the world to Himself, not counting their trespasses against them, and He has committed to us the word of reconciliation. 20 Therefore, we are ambassadors for Christ, as though God

were making an appeal through us; we beg you on behalf
of Christ, be reconciled to God. —2 Corinthians 5:17–20

In verse 20 we can see God's heart for lost souls. Through us, He is begging the lost to get right with Him or to be reconciled to Him. He desires every person on the planet to be right with Him, which He made possible through Christ. We are called to participate.

The Father cherishes His Son's sacrifice. One of my favorite Bible verses is Isaiah 49:6, my life scripture for more than 30 years. This verse summarizes my life's purpose.

> *He says, "It is too small a thing that You should be My Servant to raise up the tribes of Jacob and to restore the preserved ones of Israel; I will also make You a light of the nations so that My salvation may reach to the end of the earth."*

I love Isaiah 49:6 on many levels. First, I see it as a direct communication between the Father and the Son, hidden just for Jesus during His life and His ministry. During our years in Colorado, we participated in 22 summer and winter youth camps. Twenty of those were with junior high youth, and two were with elementary school children. When I served as a kids' camp counselor, several of the young children would each day unpack the clothes packed by their parents for them for that day. As they unrolled the clothes, they would find messages of encouragement from their parents. They obviously looked forward to finding these notes from home. In the same way, I could see the encouragement from the Father to the Son in Isaiah 49:6. This was a personal note from Father to Son, hidden for Jesus to find. Amazingly, I've noticed several similar communications in the Scriptures.

Secondly, I can see in this passage the Father's esteem for His Son's sacrifice. "It is too small a thing." He esteems His Son's sacrifice so greatly that it is not enough for a single group of people to benefit from such a great sacrifice. "I will make the benefits (salvation) of your sacrifice available to all people for all time." All nations here refers to Gentiles, so His sacrifice would reach the entire earth.

Thirdly, this verse is my life scripture because I can see the Father's heart for all people. It is too small a thing; it is not enough. This verse has continually motivated me to reach more lost souls. Whatever I have done is not enough, for more souls can be brought into the Father's kingdom. I mentioned earlier that I have shared the Gospel message 20,000 times. I never set out to do that. I have just lived with the Father's desire for more. I want to win one more soul, and after that one more soul, and after that one more soul. After more than 40 years living with this desire, I can look back and see tremendous results.

I recall the Friday night I had been out sharing the Gospel on what seemed like a fruitful evening. Seven people had prayed with me to surrender their lives to Christ. As I walked along feeling rather good about that, I saw a young man sitting on a planter on the side of Main Street. As I approached him, I could feel the Holy Spirit moving in me to talk with that young man. Instead, I walked on by. Later, knowing I had missed a Holy Spirit divine moment, I tried to go back, but he was not there. I could have won one more soul. I have never forgotten that single soul I missed by walking on by.

Another Friday night as I walked along, I sensed the Holy Spirit direct me to another part of town. I was walking through a pizza store's parking lot and noticed four young men chatting in the parking lot. These four young men all wore black trench coats, with their hair dyed dark black, and numerous piercings in their head and faces. The Holy Spirit directed me to speak with them, and I determined to do so.

As I approached them, though, my fears rose, and all I could hear in my head was, "Abort mission! Abort mission!" I veered away from the group at the last minute and walked around the corner. Less than a half block farther, I asked, "Holy Spirit, who would you like me to speak to tonight?"

Without hesitation, He responded, "Well, if you're not going to speak to the people I lead you to, you might as well go home!" Ouch! I did an immediate about-face, something I had learned well in Navy boot camp, and returned to those young men. It turned out they were in a heavy metal band and were open to my message. Three of the four young men prayed with me to receive Christ and His salvation. They were very thankful I had spoken with them and gladly accepted the pocket Bibles and New Beginners booklets I carried with me. Over the next few years, I saw those young men in different parts of town and developed a friendship with them. Lord, give me one more soul.

What is the Father's heart for nearly five billion souls who are without the blessed hope we have in eternity? In John 13, the Apostle John, probably a teenager at the time, is seated next to Jesus with his head on Jesus's chest. Have you ever laid your head on a person's chest? What did you hear? A heartbeat! John got to hear the heartbeat of God. Maybe Mary, His mother, also heard the heartbeat of God. But who else would have had such an incredible opportunity?

Well, to tell you the truth, I have. And you can too. I have laid my head on Jesus's chest many times in my daily devotions, and this is what I have heard: His heartbeat. And it sounds like this: "None perish...all saved." Let us look at Peter's second epistle:

> *2 Peter 3:9 The Lord is not slow about His promise, as some count slowness, but is patient toward you, not wishing for any to perish but for all to come to repentance.*

The Lord desires that none will perish. None perish! I would like to ask you a question to test your theological and mathematical skills. How many is none? It is zero, absolutely nada. He desires that none would perish.

Now let us look at Paul's first letter to Timothy:

1 Timothy 2:3,4 "This is good and acceptable in the sight of God our Savior, 4 who desires all men to be saved and to come to the knowledge of the truth."

God our Savior desires all to be saved. All saved! Again, I would like to ask you a question to assess your theological and mathematical proficiency. How many is all? Everyone. Each and every one. Every single one. All saved! This is God's desire!

Let us put them together: "None perish...all saved! None perish...all saved! None perish...all saved! None perish...all saved! None perish...all saved!" Can you begin to hear a heartbeat? I can. This is our Father's desire. Sometimes when I listen to people, I get the idea that the Father is wringing His hands impatiently to get down to some serious smiting. But I do not believe this is at the forefront of His heart.

Yes, there will be a day of judgment, but that day is not today. In chapter 1 I recounted the story in which Jesus omitted the phrase, "(To proclaim) The day of vengeance of our God" when reading from the scroll of Isaiah. He was clearly announcing what His ministry would look like. Later, when John the Baptist sent disciples to ask if Jesus was the "Expected One," Jesus's response showed how He was fulfilling those scriptures He had read in the synagogue in Nazareth.

2 Now when John, while imprisoned, heard of the works of Christ, he sent word by his disciples 3 and said to Him, "Are You the Expected One, or shall we look for someone else?" 4 Jesus answered and said to them, "Go and report to John what you hear and see: 5 the BLIND RECEIVE SIGHT and the lame walk, the lepers are cleansed and the deaf hear, the dead are raised up, and the POOR HAVE THE GOSPEL PREACHED TO THEM. 6 "And blessed is he who does not take offense at Me." —Matthew 11:2–6

God desires all to be saved, He desires none to perish. There is a day of judgment, but that day is not today. In this age we continue in the year of the Lord's favor. Isaiah calls judgment a strange work of God. God desires mercy before judgment.

> *Isaiah 28:21 For the LORD will rise up as at Mount Perazim, He will be stirred up as in the valley of Gibeon, To do His task, His unusual task, And to work His work, His extraordinary work.*

This verse speaks specifically of God's anger over the sin of His people and the imminent judgment for their sins. In context, we see that God's judgment connects with the ultimate objective of restoration. "Unusual task" can best be stated as a "strange task," and "extraordinary work" can best be translated "strange work." The coming judgment is not His ordinary work. It is strange to Him.

Let us look at Nineveh, the capital city of the nation of Assyria. Nineveh deserved to be destroyed. The word of the Lord to Jonah was, "Their wickedness has come up before Me." The prophet Jonah wanted Nineveh, the enemy of Israel, to be destroyed, so he was reluctant to warn them and thereby prevent their destruction. God dealt with Jonah, though, and he cried out to God for mercy while in the belly of the fish.

Jonah wanted a God who was merciful to him but not to his enemies. The key verse in the book of Jonah is chapter 4, verse 2. " For I knew that You are a gracious and compassionate God, slow to anger and abundant in lovingkindness, and one who relents concerning calamity." Jonah knew the character of God to be good and compassionate to Israel and to Nineveh. One of God's glorious attributes is His lovingkindness, which means He loves to perform acts of kindness for all people. This is still true today. Because of God's mercy over Nineveh after the people heeded Jonah's warning, the city prospered for another 140 years, until being destroyed by the Babylonian empire.

God did not somehow morph from one character to another between the Old and New Testaments. In both, He shows His goodness, His mercies, and His compassion. He is the same yesterday, today, and tomorrow. Look at the heartbeat of God for souls in these three verses from the prophet Ezekiel:

> *Ezekiel 18:23 "Do I have any pleasure in the death of the wicked," declares the Lord GOD, "rather than that he should turn from his ways and live?"*

> *Ezekiel 18:32 "For I have no pleasure in the death of anyone who dies," declares the Lord GOD. "Therefore, repent and live."*

> *Ezekiel 33:11 "Say to them, 'As I live!' declares the Lord GOD, 'I take no pleasure in the death of the wicked, but rather that the wicked turn from his way and live. Turn back, turn back from your evil ways! Why then will you die, O house of Israel?'*

Yes, there is a time of judgment coming upon the earth. Revelation chapter 15 speaks of the wrath of God filling seven bowls, and in them the wrath of God is complete. Seven angels exit the heavenly temple to pour these seven bowls of seven plagues out upon the earth. While this happens, the temple was filled with smoke from the glory of God and from His power. Significantly, verse 8 says that no one was able to enter the temple until the seven plagues of the seven angels were finished. While our Father's judgment is being poured out upon the earth, He sits alone in the heavenly temple.

> *Lamentations 3:44 You have covered Yourself with a cloud so that no prayer can pass through.*

Our Father in Heaven desires that none would perish and all would be saved. Do we have the same desire? Our merciful God desires His people, the Church, to participate with Him in worldwide evangelization.

Did you know that proclaiming this gospel of peace can be an act of worship?

> *Romans 1:9 For God, whom I serve in my spirit in the preaching of the gospel of His Son, is my witness as to how unceasingly I make mention of you.*

The Greek word here for serve is *latreuo*, which can be translated either to serve or as it is in other places of New Testament scripture, "to worship." It carries with it a dual meaning of serving with an attitude of worship. For Paul, preaching the gospel was an act of worship. If it is an act of worship, it will be a form of worship we can only experience while we sojourn on this earth. The day will come when we reach our eternal reward that we can never worship in this particular manner again.

Another Greek word translated as "to serve" in the New Testament is the word *douleuo*. It means to serve as a slave unwillingly. There is an amazing verse in Acts 7 where we see God's heart for His people:

> *Acts 7:7 (ESV): "But I will judge the nation that they serve,"* said God, *"and after that they shall come out and worship me in this place."*

Or another translation:

> *(MKJV) And God said, "I will judge the nation to whom they shall be in bondage," and "after these things they will come out and will serve Me in this place."*

Both *douleuo* and *latreuo* appear in this verse. Our Father is expressing His desire for us not to be unwilling slaves in our service but to serve Him willingly with an attitude of worship. That changes everything for me. It moves the work of soul winning from a forced activity to a desirable endeavor.

God desires all to be saved, but sometimes we meet some pretty unlovely, or even scary, people. But He loves the unlovely, even amid their unloveliness. About 18 years ago, I was in the center of Denver, Colorado, on a Friday night. At that time, around 400 homeless teenagers survived in the downtown area. As I walked along, the Holy Spirit moved me to cross to the other side of the street. Ahead I could see a group of about 10 young people in their late teens and early twenties. As I approached, a couple of them recognized me and drew near, excited to see me.

About a month earlier, I had met them and shared the Good News with them. The entire group had prayed with me that night to receive Christ and His salvation, and I had given each of them a pocket New Testament.

As they moved toward me on this night, they told the rest of the group, "There he is." Then they asked, "Hey, do you have any more of those little Bibles?" Apparently, when they took their Bibles to school and read them, their friends also wanted one. Imagine that, the Bible becoming fashionable in public schools. Well, I do not just hand out Bibles on the streets, but I gladly give them to those who respond to the Gospel.

I began to share the Gospel message with them. As I began, two young men backed away into the shadows. Once I finished the message and invited them to respond, they joined me in a prayer of salvation. Then I gave each a pocket New Testament, and they were all pleased to receive the Word of God.

When I finished with them, guess where I went. I approached the two young men who had backed away. One of my strategies in sharing with groups is to identify the strong personality in the group. This person is usually the most confident and able to lead others, for better or for worse. I direct my exchange toward that strong personality. Most of the time, if the strong one receives the message, the others will be receptive also. This strategy has succeeded more often than it has failed.

I moved toward these two and reached my hand out to the young man I felt demonstrated confidence and leadership qualities. As I extended my hand, I said, "Hey, my name is Bob, what is yours?"

His response came quickly. "It's Lucifer!"

"Hah hah, that's funny," I replied. "No, really, what's your name?"

Again, he answered, "It's Lucifer."

With that, the rest of the group drifted over toward us. "It really is Lucifer; you should see his driver's license."

"I would like to see that."

Lucifer got out his driver's license and showed it to me. His name really was Damien Lucifer.

"Wow! How'd you get a name like that?" I asked.

"From my parents," came the response.

"They sound interesting. Tell me about them," I responded.

Lucifer continued, "They are witches, they are heroin addicts, and they are both in prison."

I apologized to him for the uncertainty surrounding his life. Lucifer and I continued to talk in a friendly manner about his life, as well as the possibility of having hope and a future.

As I was preparing to leave, Lucifer asked me if he could have one of those Bibles. My response was, "You're not going to burn it, are you?"

Now, that may sound cold and harsh, but in just a few moments we had developed a friendship, and he knew I was only joking.

And so, I shared the Gospel with Lucifer and his friend, knowing and fully trusting that it is the power of God for salvation. Afterward, I asked Lucifer if he would like to invite Jesus into his life to be his Savior and Lord. He did! The rest of the group got really excited about that.

I extended my hand and said, "Let's pray." I had barely gotten out the first sentence of the sinner's prayer when Lucifer grabbed me and pulled himself into my chest, sobbing. It was some time before we could get through the rest of the prayer, but as Lucifer sobbed, I prayed that the Holy Spirit would heal his broken heart and soul.

After we prayed, I gave him his first New Testament. He was completely changed. We all talked a little more, especially about parents. Lucifer told me he would like to be a father someday. I acknowledged that he probably had a poor image of a good father, but now he had a Father in Heaven, who would show him what a good father is like. I asked if I could pray to break generational curses over his life and family. Now, he had no idea what that meant, but I did. Once again, we prayed, and once again, he held me tight. And that was the night I led Lucifer to Jesus Christ.

God really loves people; He really desires that none would perish and that all would be saved. I really love sharing this message of hope. I make it a point to have a good time with the people I encounter. I can have fun and be light with them. I have always maintained that, in everything I do, just like a doctor's Hippocratic oath, I should do no harm. I always hope that when I leave a person who may have rejected my message, I have done nothing to harm the next encounter they will have with the Gospel.

I was in Boulder, Colorado, one Friday night on what is called the Pearl Street Mall. It is an open area mall running about six blocks through the heart of downtown Boulder, just down the hill from the University of Colorado. On this night I chanced upon three college engineering students, a guy, and two gals, waiting to get into a restaurant. They had a restaurant pager which would go off with flashing lights when their table was ready. They were sitting on the ground under a tree when I came upon them. They invited me to sit down with them, which I could still do then. (I can still sit on the ground today; it is the getting up that is increasingly challenging.) We sat and chatted for a bit, and I shared the plan of salvation. They kindly declined my offer, and I realized this would not be the day of their good news.

So do no harm. I had spent 25 years in the electrical trade and seven years before that in the Navy working with analog and digital electronics. Somehow our discussion turned to how electricity flows through a conductor by the ionization of the atom's electrons in the valence shell of the atom. As we spoke, their restaurant pager went off, and it was time to go. As we rose to our feet to say goodbye, the young man said, "Thank you, I have never had a Christian talk to me like this," and he hugged me. The two young ladies responded in kind, thankful for my demeanor as I shared with them. I genuinely believe the next time a Christian opens a conversation with them about Jesus, these three young people will be open to hear their message. My prayer is that the next Christian will have the same attitude: "Do no harm!"

In the next chapter we will begin to look at seven essentials of effective evangelism. In my years of soul winning, I have discovered that these elements are vital in the process of winning the lost. The first essential we will look at is our relationship with Jesus.

> *Love your fellowmen, and cry about them if you cannot bring them to Christ. If you cannot save them, you can weep over them. If you cannot give them a drop of cold water in hell, you can give them your heart's tears while they are still in this body.*[8] *—Charles Spurgeon*

5

Essential #1: Passion—Our Relationship with Jesus

"While others still slept, He went away to pray and to renew His strength in communion with His Father. He had need of this, otherwise He would not have been ready for the new day. The holy work of delivering souls demands constant renewal through fellowship with God."[9] —Andrew Murray

Acts 4:13 Now as they observed the confidence of Peter and John and understood that they were uneducated and untrained men, they were amazed, and began to recognize them as having been with Jesus.

MANY PEOPLE HAVE asked me, "What is the most important essential in soul winning?"

My answer is always the same. "Your personal relationship with Jesus." Nothing is more important in any work in the kingdom of God than our relationship with Jesus. When the Pharisees confronted Peter and John regarding a healing that took place at the Gate called Beautiful, they considered them uneducated, untrained, and ordinary or common men, as some translations put it. But they were amazed at their confidence and boldness, and they realized these men had been with

Jesus. That is what makes the difference in our lives, being with Jesus. Just as John laid his head on Jesus's chest at the Last Supper, we need to be laying our heads on His chest daily as we wait in His presence.

I am sure that most of God's sons and daughters want to do great things for the kingdom of God. It is in our spiritual DNA to reach the world around us for the Kingdom of God. Who are those who will do great things?

Daniel 11:32b (NKJV) "...but the people that know their God shall be strong and do great exploits."

The people who *know* their God! That Hebrew word is *yada*, which means to know intimately and personally, not just scholarly. Jesus will take ordinary people like us and so change us that He will do great things through us. Great exploits will follow those who know Jesus.

In order to share our faith effectively, we must have a growing personal relationship with Jesus Christ. We must know our Savior's voice, we must know Him, and we must know His nature and His character. It is not enough to just know about Him. We must know Him. We grow in our relationship with Him in the secret places. Our prayer closets cannot remain empty day after day. It is in the quiet and secret places that we partake of the secret manna, the bread of life, Jesus, the bread of heaven. We also come to know Him through our devotion to His word, the Bible, and by our day-to-day walk with Him through our life experiences.

If we are not in personal relationship with Christ, the best we can hope for is give a book report about a historical figure. Our greatest aim should be to introduce those people in our realms of influence to the person—Jesus Christ. *Christianity is not just coming into an agreement with a system of beliefs* (a mental consent). It is not enough to just get the people we share with to agree with our doctrines. They need to have a head-on collision with Christ!

The Bible tells us they must believe with the heart. It is not enough to just receive the seed of the Gospel. In the parable of the seed sower, there were three types of soil that received seed, but only one which bore fruit. The seed must be received, and then we must take our stand upon it, that is put our faith in it. We must respond to the message. We will look more at this in a later chapter. People need to encounter Jesus through our presence because they need to have a head-on collision with Christ.

If I were to walk out on the highway tonight and step in front of a semitruck, it would change my life. If you were to come running out and peel me off the front grill, you might say, "Bob, you've changed! You're not the same person you were a minute ago." And you would be right. I would be different. I just got hit by a truck. The night I met Jesus Christ I had a head-on collision with Him. It did not just change my destiny in eternity, it changed my day-to-day destiny here on the earth. When I got down on that floor and cried out to Him from the depths of my heart, I was a lost sinner, a drug dealer, a liar, a cheat, and a thief. When I got up, I was no longer any of those things. I was changed.

I believe one reason we do not see lives change after conversion is the way we proclaim the Gospel message. Often our message sounds like this, "You do not want to go to that stinking hell, you want to go to Heaven. So if you believe in Jesus, you will go to Heaven. Now let us say this prayer together." Now this is a truth, but it isn't the whole truth. Yes, we are saved through our faith (believing) in His death and resurrection, through His grace, and not by anything we can do to earn or even deserve that grace. And it is totally God's doing. Our salvation does make us partakers in the blessed hope of Heaven. But there is more. Let's look at the message Jesus proclaimed.

Mark 1:15 "The time is fulfilled, and the kingdom of God is at hand; repent and believe in the gospel."

Jesus's invitation was this: the time has come; it is now. The kingdom is at hand; it is here. Repent and believe this Good News! That is, repent and change the way you are thinking about the kingdom of God. It is not just off in some distant future, but it is here and now. Believe it, it is Good News. Do you see that Jesus's invitation was to enter the kingdom, which is present and at hand? By sharing the invitation to enter into a relationship with Jesus and enter His kingdom here and now, and live by kingdom principles, we will see dramatic changes in new believers. Our invitation should sound like Jesus's invitation.

> *Matthew 11:28–30 28 "Come to Me, all who are weary and heavy-laden, and I will give you rest." 29 "Take My yoke upon you and learn from Me, for I am gentle and humble in heart, and YOU WILL FIND REST FOR YOUR SOULS. 30 "For My yoke is easy and My burden is light."*

Come to Me, connect with Me, and learn from Me. That is His first calling for all people. Connect with Me. That is the significance of the word yoke. He has a second calling for everyone who responds to the first calling. Follow Me! Get yoked with me!

> *If anyone serves Me, he must follow Me; and where I am, there My servant will be also; if anyone serves Me, the Father will honor him (John 12:26).*

> *My sheep hear My voice, and I know them, and they follow Me (John 10:27).*

In the four Gospels, this invitation is repeated 20 times. "Follow me." "My sheep, hear my voice," which indicates relationship. "I know them, they hear Me, and they follow Me." This is our calling, our invitation to pursue a relationship with Jesus day by day. It has been in my day-to-day relationship with Jesus, daily leaning my head on His chest, learning the sound of His voice, that He has prepared me to be a soul-winner.

We need to be ready in season and out of season, at any time, to share our faith.

> *But sanctify Christ as Lord in your hearts, always being ready to make a defense to everyone who asks you to give an account for the hope that is in you, yet with gentleness and reverence (1 Peter 3:15).*

For many years of my Christian life, I have set apart time specifically to go into public places to share this wonderful message. Before I go out on the streets to share my faith, I go to my room, lie on the floor, and wait on the presence of Jesus. I just wait, and rest, and soak in His presence. I want to, I need to, I must be filled with His presence. I believe it is my responsibility in soul-winning for people to have an encounter with the presence of Jesus. His presence is what will change them. Our message is important, and it has great power, but it really is a simple message. It is the presence of the Holy Spirit that empowers our message. As I go, I remain conscious of the Holy Spirit. I hear His voice, and I follow His voice. Sometimes He directs me where to go. Mostly I look for the people He is pointing out. When I see them, I know by the Holy Spirit's leading to approach and speak to them. It does not always mean they will be saved. But I always believe it will be significant.

One night as I walked down the street, I saw a young woman on a pay phone. You know it was long ago, as there are not many pay phones these days. The phone was in front of a real fleabag hotel where truly indigent people stayed. As I approached, I sensed the Holy Spirit moving in me to speak with her. But since she was on the phone, I did not want to be creepy and just hang out nearby. I walked the remainder of the block, intending to turn around and walk back. As I came back toward her, she hung up the phone and moved toward the entrance of the hotel. As she arrived at the threshold, I called out to her, and she stopped and started toward me.

I thanked her for waiting, and she said, "I wanted to talk to you." About five years earlier, she told me, I had engaged her and three others in a conversation on the streets. She told me they had just taken their $700 rent money and spent it on crystal meth. She said to me, "When we met you, we were really high, and we treated you shamefully with a lot of disrespect."

I did not remember that discussion. But then she recounted something I'd said to her that I often say to people in discussions that do not seem to end well. I will tell them, "Please remember this. Wherever you are, whatever you have done, whatever situation you may find yourself in in the future, if you will cry out to Jesus, He will hear you and save you."

She told me she noticed that no matter how badly they treated me, she could see I really loved and sincerely cared for them. Throughout the next day, she considered our meeting and thought about the things that were said. She received the seed but did not follow up with faith.

Life just went on from there, and she ended up pregnant by her boyfriend a few months later. About a year after our chance meeting, she had a baby girl. As time went by, she, her baby, and her boyfriend moved to Minnesota. After a few years, her relationship with him was failing. He was drinking a lot and was beating her regularly.

One Friday night, on his payday, in the dead of winter, he came home late, very drunk. He began to beat her and knocked her down onto the kitchen floor. As she lay on the floor, blood from the beating ran down her forehead into her eyes. In that moment she remembered what I had told her the night we met. "Wherever you are, whatever you have done, whatever situation you may find yourself in in the future, if you will cry out to Jesus, He will hear you and save you." So, she screamed, "Jesus, help me! Jesus, save me!" Her boyfriend freaked out and ran out of the house. As she lay there, something happened inside of her. Something changed in her. She gathered up her three-year-old daughter and the few things she could carry and ran out of the house. She caught a bus back to Colorado, and now here we were standing on the sidewalk talking. She told me she reached her younger brother, who was living in the same dysfunction, and the three of them were living in a room at this hotel. Upon getting a job at 7-Eleven, she intended to change things for her family.

I was in tears. We talked about what she had felt after calling out to Jesus, and I affirmed that what she had felt was His presence and the new birth. Oh, and by the way, just before I saw her on the pay phone that night, I was wondering to myself if I was making a difference out there on the streets.

I have always tried to rely on the leading of the Holy Spirit in street ministry: where I should go, whom I should speak to. I spent three and a half years witnessing on Colfax Avenue in Denver, near the Colorado State Capitol. It was an area full of homeless people, drunkards, pushers, pimps, prostitutes, 24-hour dirty bookstores, murderers—yes, murders—and about anything else you could imagine or not imagine. The people there came to know me, and I came to know them. They called me "da Preacher."

One night I encountered a drug dealer I knew, who was walking with a nicely dressed gentleman in a fine leather black jacket and pants. I reached my hand out to greet him, asking how he was doing. I walked behind the two for a few steps, and the guy in the leather jacket asked, "Who is that dude?"

The pusher man said, "Oh he's all right, he's da Preacher." Others around there called me Jesus Man. Yeah, people would say all the time, "Jesus Man, would you leave me alone!" Or "Jesus Man, would you get outta here!" So I was Jesus Man.

Well, on this Friday night, as I walked along, I heard the Holy Spirit say, "Turn around now and go the other way." I turned around and began to walk the way I had just come. The buildings along there were two or three stories, mostly old commercial buildings with a lot of nightclubs and bars, as would be expected in this environment. As I walked by an alley between two buildings, a man exited and bumped into me. I handed him my I.O.U. LOVE ministry card and told him, "Jesus sent me here to tell you He loves you."

The guy went off like a bomb. He cursed me, cursed God, and screamed like a madman. Then he swung at me and landed a punch in my jaw. Now this is a very public street, and lots of people were out that Friday night. And "da Preacher" just got punched. So, being a pretty smart fellow, I stood back about five feet while he continued to rant and rave. I figured that should be a good buffer, seeing as he had about a three-foot reach and maybe a two-foot lunge. At some point he had to pause for a breath. When he did, I said, "Man! God sent me here to help you!"

The atmosphere changed drastically again, but I was bewildered by what was taking place. Now he stood there and began to cry, I mean really weep, repeating over and over, "I don't want to go to hell! I don't want to go to hell."

He finally calmed down enough for me to ask, "Man, what's going on?" Then he told me his story. About a year earlier, he was living in Wyoming. He and his buddy were out partying in a wilderness area on a Friday night. Liquor was flowing, and they got into a fight. He pushed his buddy down, breaking his head open. His buddy died, and he had been on the run ever since.

Wow, that was quite a story, and it shed some light on the range of emotions he had just experienced. I began to share with him the Good News, and he calmed down further. I asked him if he could feel peace right then, and he said he did. He could not remember when he had last felt peace. We prayed, and I told him Jesus could forgive his sin, but he still owed a debt to society. He would have more peace in a prison cell, I told him, than out here on the run. He refused my offer to take him to the police station where he could begin to make things right. Clearly, the Holy Spirit had a sense of great urgency in turning me around. God our Father had not given up on this man.

I teach that there are three elements in proclaiming the Gospel, and I call them "the three Ps": presence, proclamation, and persuasion. We have been talking about the first "P," presence, the presence of Jesus. It is of greatest importance that people encounter the presence of Jesus in our witnessing. Presence also includes our actions, which should reflect those of our Heavenly Father and of His Son Jesus. We should ask ourselves, What did Jesus do? Our actions can be a great benefit or a great harm to our message. Remember one of the glorious characteristics of God is His lovingkindness. Lovingkindness is attributed to God 171 times in the Old Testament.

> *Then the LORD passed by in front of him and proclaimed, "The LORD , the LORD God, compassionate and gracious, slow to anger, and abounding in lovingkindness and truth" (Exodus 34:6).*

> *For the LORD is good; His lovingkindness is everlasting And His faithfulness to all generations (Psalms 100:5).*

He abounds in lovingkindness; His lovingkindness is everlasting. This means God loves to perform acts of kindness toward us. It is His glory to do kind things for us. As representatives of His kingdom, we ought to do the same, letting our actions proclaim the practical aspect of His presence. Let us make sure our message includes acts of kindness.

Our relationship with Jesus should be our greatest passion in life. Let us look at the Apostle Paul's example in those famous verses found in Philippians 3:

> *10 ...that I may know Him and the power of His resurrection and the fellowship of His sufferings, being conformed to His death; 11 in order that I may attain to the resurrection from the dead. 12 Not that I have already obtained it or have already become perfect, but I press on so that I may lay*

hold of that for which also I was laid hold of by Christ Jesus. 13 Brethren, I do not regard myself as having laid hold of it yet; but one thing I do: forgetting what lies behind and reaching forward to what lies ahead, 14 I press on toward the goal for the prize of the upward call of God in Christ Jesus. 15 Let us therefore, as many as are perfect, have this attitude; and if in anything you have a different attitude, God will reveal that also to you. —Philippians 3:10–15

Paul's passion is evident in these statements: "that I may know Him; I press on; reaching forward; and again, pressing on." I can hear the heart of the Apostle. "I want to know Him; I am pressing on to know Him; I'm straining to know Him." I see a passionate pursuit of Jesus.

Consider that Paul was not a new believer, a novice Christian, displaying hunger for more of Jesus. This is Paul the aged, the longtime faithful servant. This is Paul who was fundamental in expanding the Church of Jesus Christ throughout Asia Minor and Europe. This is Paul who wrote a large portion of our New Testament. This is Paul who worked powerful miracles, including raising people from the dead. When Paul wrote this letter to the Philippians, he was in Rome, under house arrest, awaiting his trial. He was near the end of his life. History tells us he had two or three years left before his martyrdom. And here we find his passionate plea, "I want to know Him!" We need to maintain this same passion for Jesus. Each and every day we need this same hunger for His presence. I want to know Him!

Street church of Key West on the Sunset Pier, 1984.

Street church of Key West.

Bob the Evangelist, 1982.

Finishing Miami marathon, 1985.

Evangelizing Mazatlán Carnaval.

Gabelman family on the mission field in Mazatlán, Mexico.

One-on-one evangelism, Mazatlán.

Soul-winning in Mexico City.

Soul-winning in Mexico City 2.

Witnessing to Mixteco children using Evangecube.

Witnessing to indigenous Nahuatl man in Mexico City.

Poza Rica Veracruz indigenous Totonacan people.

Praying for the sick in Tulancingo, Mexico.

Several years ago, I was in Cuba working with our ministry leaders in illegal churches in the center of the island, the city of Camaguey. I had been arrested and interrogated for four and a half hours over two days after speaking to a gathering of 120 pastors. I was teaching the contents of this book. After a two-and-a-half-hour morning session, a government agent from the Ministry of the Interior came to arrest me. I was not arrested because of the poor quality of my teaching but for teaching this material.

After the second day of interrogations, three of our ministry's Mexican staff and I were ordered to return to Havana and report to a high-ranking official. Then we were ordered to leave Cuba as soon as possible, which would take four days. Initially, we were put under house arrest in our hotel. I requested permission for us to tour Havana while we waited deportation. The official's only stipulation was that we could have no further contact with the pastors we had been working with. We gave him our word. Over the next three days, we left our hotel each morning and walked through the city. I wore my camera slung over my shoulder, having stuffed my camera bag full of Spanish New Testaments, tracts, and other literature. Off we went, to see the city and the people in it. But okay, we were actually hitting the streets in groups of two to share the Gospel.

On one of those mornings, we walked along the Malecon, which means the waterfront. It was breathtakingly beautiful. We met a man who was crippled and began to share with him. He told us he had been crippled when he was hit by a bus while riding his bike.

I asked him if getting hit by a bus changed his life in any way. He said it changed his life in every way. I asked him if he would like his life to change like that again, in every way. He said yes, he would. We shared Jesus with him and introduced him to Christ. He was a new person standing right in front us, deeply thankful to receive the hope of Heaven and a Bible. We take for granted all the Bibles in our homes that are so easily available to us. Many people in this world do not have the luxury of a readily available Bible.

On the same day, a little further along the waterfront at the entrance to the Havana harbor, a group of young men in their early twenties asked us for money. Everyone asks you for money in Cuba. It is apparently a custom in Cuba to give a coin to someone on their birthday. Everywhere we went, people told us it was their birthday. I wondered how so many people had the same birthday. I eventually realized it was their strategy to get a coin from us.

Well, I told these young men we really did not have any money, but we had something better. "What do you have that is better than money?" asked a young man in behalf of the whole group.

"We have Jesus Christ," I answered. The group was a bit rowdy when we approached, but when I responded to their question, they quickly calmed down and got profoundly serious with us.

The young spokesman looked me squarely in the eye and said, "I have heard of Jesus, but I do not know how to have him in my heart." Whoa, what an invitation to share Christ. The whole group of around nine young men listened attentively and respectfully to our message. Afterward, eight of the nine prayed with us to receive Him as Savior and Lord. We gave out the rest of the Bibles we had with us that day. Over three days, we prayed with 25 people to receive Christ as Savior. Not only that, but I also recall four or five divine healings in which people gave testimony and evidence of their healings.

Next, we will look at the second essential in soul-winning: compassion—a burden for lost souls. This essential is a direct fruit of the first essential, passion for Jesus. Compassion for the lost springs out of our passion for and relationship with Jesus.

> *We need men so possessed by the Spirit of God that God can think His thoughts through our minds, that He can plan His will through our actions, that He can direct His strategy of world evangelization through His Church.*[10] — *Alan Redpath*

6

ESSENTIAL #2: COMPASSION—OUR BURDEN FOR THE LOST

"Perhaps if there were more of that intense distress for souls that leads to tears, we should more frequently see the results we desire. Sometimes it may be that while we are complaining of the hardness of the hearts of those we are seeking to benefit, the hardness of our hearts and our feeble apprehension of the solemn reality of eternal things may be the true cause of our want of success."[11] —Hudson Taylor

A BURDEN FOR lost souls is essential in leading the lost to Jesus. We must have a genuine concern for people and their destiny. We must care for the people around us. Where does this burden come from? It comes from Christ. With each new day as we lay our head on Jesus's chest in our secret places, as we listen to His heartbeat, none perish, all saved, we will begin to feel what He feels for a world of lost souls. Jesus had compassion for lost people. He wept over Jerusalem because they did not recognize the time of His appearance. He looked at people and saw they were helpless and harassed, like sheep without a shepherd. He had compassion for the blind, the lame, and the sick. He had compassion for a mother when she lost her only son to death. When He saw people in their brokenness and their great needs, He stopped.

Sometimes that is the first step we need to take, that is, not to take another step, and stop, and meet the person in their need. When you are living with Jesus's compassion for the world and the people in it, you become better tuned in to the hurt and pain in the people you pass by. Most of the time, we live our lives at a speed of about ten miles an hour over the speed limit. We have places to go and things to do, and we are too busy to notice the needs of the people around us. Sometimes we just need to stop.

I have found that I cannot work up this compassion or burden. I have to ask the Father, "Let me touch your heart for the world around me. Let me feel what you are feeling. Let me see what you see. Let my heart break with yours." I recognize I am feeble in this area of compassion, of caring. But our Father cares, and I need His help. Often, I recognize the hardness of my heart when I do not feel compassion for the world, so I must ask Him to once again break my heart for a world of lost souls. When I do this, He is faithful to answer. He desires to answer. And often it is at a time and place when I least expect it to happen. Many times in my life, I have felt an overwhelming sense of burden and compassion that can only come from God. And when it comes, it breaks me.

I have been in public places with many people coming and going about their business, such as airports, restaurants, and even amusement parks, when I become overwhelmed by the lostness of the people around me. I am suddenly aware of the horror of the destinies of multitudes of people who are heading into eternity without Christ, without hope. It breaks me. I begin to weep in this public place, and I ask, "Lord, why here, why now?"

"Because you asked," is His reply.

Although it can be ugly and inconvenient from my perspective, it is precious and wonderful to touch such an intimate place in the Father's heart. I encourage you to ask Him, "Father, let me touch your heart for the people around me. Let me feel what you feel. Break my heart for the lost." He will, and it will change you. It will move you, compel you, to reach the world around you.

For a number of years, I managed the electrical contracts at an international business that manufactured data storage equipment. I managed up to fifty electricians at times. The campus of this company had nine large manufacturing buildings, two and three stories tall, with a number of smaller support buildings. One morning I was in the cafeteria of the main corporate office building where the CEO, CFO, high-ranking executives, and other administrative people worked. I was working on some paperwork and noticed it was about time for the morning break to begin. In a matter of moments, the cafeteria would be invaded by hundreds of corporate personnel. I gathered my belongings and headed for the exit that led into the main hallway. Then as I walked down the main corridor, I found myself moving against the flow of the oncoming masses.

In an instant I had an overwhelming vision of myriads of people walking along a road that led to the gates of hell. These people were walking straight into the fires of hell, and as they approached the entrance, the fires and flames would reach out and grab them, pulling them in. All the people had an object in their hands that attracted their attention, and they did not see the approaching peril. They just continued upon that road directly into their impending doom. Also, they did not see the demonic forces standing on both sides of the road, keeping them from wandering off the road.

My heart began to break, and I began to weep, not just a tear or two but with uncontrollable grief. Here I was walking into this sea of people with tears running down my face. As I approached the main electrical room on that floor, I quickly entered the room and continued to weep uncontrollably. Again, I asked, "Father, why here, why now?"

"Because you asked Me, son," was the answer.

As you can see, receiving a burden for the lost can be dangerous, but it is something precious. Few of God's people have ever truly touched that place in His heart for lost souls. You ask how I know that? Because if more of His children carried His burden for the lost, there would be fewer people walking down that road I described. Touching the Father's heart for lost souls will compel us to go to them.

> *13 For if we are out of our mind, it is to God; or if we are in our senses, it is for you. 14 For the love of Christ constrains us, judging this, that if one died for all, then all died; 15 and He died for all, that the living ones may live no more to themselves, but to Him who died for them and having been raised. —2 Corinthians 5:13–15 (MKJV)*

The love of Christ constrains us, which is the opposite of being restrained. It means to compel, oblige, force. Sensing God's love for lost souls will move us beyond our fear and pride to do something, to get in the way of people heading into eternity without the hope of Heaven. A burden for the lost produces the boldness we need to unashamedly proclaim the salvation of Jesus Christ. I am not naturally outgoing, nor am I a bold person, but hearing the heartbeat of the Father, and with Christ in me, I am compelled to go.

I was preparing one Friday night to go into the streets to share the Good News of Jesus Christ. As I said before, I would go to my room to lie upon the floor, rest, wait, and soak in the presence of the Lord. While waiting in His presence, He spoke into my heart, "Bob, you have no urgency for the people you are going to tonight." When He speaks to me like that, I have learned to not try to hide from His presence or make an excuse but to simply agree with Him. Putting His finger on attitudes of our hearts is not for the purpose of rejecting or humiliating us; it is an extension of His love for us. He wants to heal our broken attitudes and restore us.

I confessed to Him, "Yes, Lord, I have no sense of urgency. Heal me, change me, let me feel what you feel."

He was right, of course. I was approaching this night without an urgency for souls. My attitude was that this was what I did on Friday nights. That needed to be fixed. He is faithful.

As I was finishing my time in His presence, He spoke into my heart again, "First Peter 4:5." That is all He said: "First Peter 4:5." I could not remember what the verse said, so I looked it up.

> But they will give account to Him who is ready to judge the living and the dead (1 Peter 4:5).

The people I would meet that night were headed into judgment without Christ. The part which was highlighted in my mind was, "Who is ready to judge..." He is ready! This gave me an immediate sense of urgency for the people I would meet that night. A fresh burden, a fresh touch of the Father's heart.

The Father really loves people, all people, regardless of how unlovely they may seem to us. One cold winter night, I was in Boulder, Colorado. As I walked along, I felt the Holy Spirit directing me to go to the bus station. I walked several blocks to the station and walked around it. No one was around. Since it was cold out, I decided to check out the inside. I went in, but it was also empty. I went back outside and sat on a bench. I felt a sense to just stay put. After a while, a man appeared in front of me, a homeless man, appearing very disheveled. He was a big man, with a heavy overcoat reaching to his knees. His long hair and beard were unkempt, and he stood in front of me swaying in the cold winter breeze.

Now I was sitting on a bench, and he was standing directly in front of me, when it hit me. There was a stench like none I had ever encountered in my life. The odor was a mixture of urine, feces, body odor, foot odor, and Listerine. I guess he was drinking Listerine to get drunk. I do not know how that works. How much Listerine does it take to drown your sorrows? This was the most unpleasant, disgusting, overpowering stench I had ever smelled. I was honestly gagging, trying to hold back from vomiting, but also trying to hide my olfactory discomfort. As I sat there in my distress I prayed, "Lord, I cannot love this man the way you do unless you help me here."

With that prayer, the air instantly cleared. It was truly miraculous. The Father loved this man, more than I ever could, and He was faithful to alter some natural circumstances to pour His love over him. I invited him to sit down next to me, and we talked and laughed and carried on for a while. I spoke to him of God's great love for him, demonstrated by sending His Son, Jesus, from Heaven, to make a way for us to have right relationship with the Father and the hope of eternity. We prayed together, and I gave him a Bible and a parcel of food I had in my backpack. We hugged, yes, we hugged, and he ambled off into the cold winter night. God really, really, loves people, even the unlovely. How needy I am to know this great love! My feeble apprehension of the depths of His love cry out for His intervention in my humanness.

As time passed in my ministry and I saw the great needs of the people of the street, I started filling and carrying a backpack with practical needs. This is presence evangelism, meeting the obvious and immediate needs of people. My backpack had to grow bigger as time went on. I had always carried Bibles, New Testaments, tracts, Gospel literature, and "New Believer" booklets, along with local church information to give to the people I would meet.

I established a wardrobe that was functional for ministry, and it has essentially been my wardrobe for more than 25 years: cargo pants. Cargo pants eventually became popular, but I started wearing them years earlier. I could purchase them from sporting outfitters, and they held six English pocket New Testaments on one side and six Spanish pocket New Testaments on the other side. I wore two-pocket button-down shirts so I could carry English tracts on one side and Spanish tracts on the other. In cold months I wore an olive drab military jacket. My backpack held extra Gospel literature and food packages I had prepared before I went out.

In the spring and summer, I bought winter gloves, hats, and wool socks at department stores when they went on clearance. Then I gave them away in the cold Colorado winter months. It was typical for my backpack to weigh 40–50 pounds at the start of the night on the streets. I would pray, "Father, help me to meet people quickly, so I can lighten this load on my back."

I also carried bottles of "Smart Water," because it has electrolytes. One night I gave a homeless teenager a bottle of "Smart Water." As he surveyed the label, he asked me if it would cause him to want to read books. I chuckled and replied, "Yes, and if you drink enough, you will want to read this book," as I handed him a New Testament.

It became clear to me on one occasion that I looked like I was homeless, with the huge backpack, the olive drab military jacket, and bulging pants pockets. One night in downtown Denver as I headed to my VW van at about 2:00 a.m., I got stuck in the middle of the intersection of Colfax and Broadway streets. This is the corner of the Colorado State Capitol building. It is amazing how much traffic can be on the streets at that time of night.

A fellow sojourner was trapped with me in the middle of the inter-section. He was ex-military, a Vietnam vet, and when he noticed my military jacket, he asked me if I had a place to stay that night. I told him I was good, and then he said, "I've got a gallon of vodka at home." Again, I declined. I began a conversation with him about Jesus. He quickly dismissed me, waved me off, and turned to walk away, but traffic still held us hostage in the middle of the intersection. He took a step or two, turned around, and said to me, "But do you know what? I am tired! No, man, I mean it, I'm just really tired of it all." What a game changer. Or a conversation changer anyway. We had a great chat there in the middle of the street, and then prayed together before we parted ways as the traffic parted.

For three and a half years, I spent nearly every Friday night wit-nessing in downtown Denver. These were the years before we left to work on the mission fields of Mexico, El Salvador, and Cuba. I would

71

park my old VW van in the neighborhood behind the Capitol building and spend the early hours of the night working in the area around Colfax Avenue. Around nine or ten o'clock, the mood in the area got pretty wild and crazy, like a New Orleans party atmosphere. At that time, I would move down into the heart of the city where there was about a ten-block open mall, a number of nice restaurants, and up to 400 homeless teenagers.

About 1:00 or 2:00 a.m., I would head back to the Colfax area, where by then the scene on the street had died down a bit. As I made my way back to my van, I always found more people still out on the streets. You may wonder what kind of people are hanging out on the streets at 2:00 a.m. Well, I found that many of them were lonely.

On one of those nights, I ran into a young Navajo man, younger than me anyway, who was an alcoholic. His wife had thrown him out of the house until he got sober. We sat down on the curb and had a chat. He asked me for a Bible, and I handed him a New Testament. "No," he said, "do you have a whole Bible?" I reached into my backpack and found a Bible for him. He thumbed the pages and asked me, "Will this help?"

"Help with what?" I asked.

"Help me get my life together," he replied.

In that moment, the Holy Spirit gave me an illustration I had never considered before. "Suppose you were ill with an incurable disease," I began. "You were dying, and there was no hope. One day your doctor called you and said he had great news; he had a medication that was 100 percent effective to cure your disease. You hurried down to his office, and he gave you the medication. You hurried home and opened the medication and poured it out on the table. All that came out of the bottle was directions for taking the medication, but there was no medication. Would you be cured by just reading the directions?"

"Why, no," he responded.

I continued, "The fact is you are sick with a deadly disease. It's called sin and death, and it is going to kill you. That Bible gives directions for the cure of your sickness, and mine, and the whole world's. But you must take the medicine to have the cure. The medicine is Jesus. Surrender your life to Him, and invite Him to be your Savior and Lord. Then read this Bible and follow the directions God has given us."

"Okay!" he said. We were already sitting on the curb, so I asked him to kneel on the sidewalk and pray with me. As we knelt on the street, and people passed us by, this man surrendered his life to Christ.

One of the great things about personal evangelism is you get to be there the moment the Holy Spirit reveals the truth of our message in the listener's heart. You can see it in their eyes, in their countenance. I have also seen the moment the truth of the message is revealed in the eyes of people I have spoken with, as well as the moment they reject it.

Another Friday night I was on Colfax early in the evening, and I felt led to sit down on a bench with two women, one in her twenties and one maybe in her forties. As I spoke with them, they told me they were a mother and daughter. They also told me they were both prostitutes working together on the street. They told me they were trapped in this lifestyle and saw no way to escape.

We talked a bit, and I presented the Gospel. They listened intently; afterward, we prayed for them to receive Jesus as Savior and Lord. I gave them New Testaments and told them, "Now, your Father in Heaven is going to open doors for you to leave this lifestyle. You will need to be fearless to go through those doors to leave this lifestyle. He is faithful and will perform His word for you." With that, I prayed for them, for their futures, and for protection on the streets.

About an hour later, I was walking on the opposite side of the street. There was a knee-high block wall almost exactly across the street from where I had spoken to the two women a little earlier. As I approached the wall, a man jumped off the wall, stepped into my path, and halted me. He was not pleased. "Who do you think you are, coming on my turf and talking to my women?" he spewed at me.

"God has sent me here to reach all of these people who are lost and broken," was my reply. I love to say, "God has sent me here" because it is the truth. With that I stepped by him and continued to walk. He caught up with me and continued to walk between me and the street. He continued his rant about me invading his territory.

When we approached some buildings on my left side, he started to shoulder me into the brick building. About a half block farther, I stopped with my back to a 24-hour sleaze merchant and faced my antagonist. He said he ought to rip my head off. At times like this, you really need to rest in the Holy Spirit and hear His voice. What came up out of my spirit was, "Yeah, but you're not going to do that."

"What do you mean, I'm not going to do that?" he snarled.

Again, the Holy Spirit inspired my response, "Because I like you."

"What do you mean, you like me?" he growled.

"Because if you are good enough for Jesus Christ who died for you, you are good enough for me!" I replied. And then, I saw it. I saw in his eyes that the Holy Spirit had driven home the truth of the message into his heart. And then I saw something else in his eyes. He rejected the truth.

With that, the spirit of an Old Testament prophet rose up in me, and the dance changed. With all authority, waving my finger at him, I said, "Who do you think you are messing with the man of God? You mess with me, and you are messing with God. You don't own this street, and you don't own those women, and I am telling you right now, if you don't get right with God tonight, you will be in jail before morning!"

Suddenly, the seas parted, the traffic light right behind him changed, and I made great haste to cross that street, and then cross the next street, standing kitty-corner from the man. I stood there with my index finger still extended in the pointing position, and a most amazing thing happened. First, a red jeep with a black top came screeching to a halt next to where the man stood. A policeman jumped out of the jeep and brought the man down to the sidewalk and cuffed him. Then, a police cruiser with lights a-flashing roared up. Two policemen rushed to the man, scraped him off the concrete, shoved him into the back of the cruiser, and thundered off down Colfax.

I quickly closed my index finger and put it in my pocket, thinking, "I need to put this away. It's more dangerous than I thought." I also remembered the prayer and the word I had spoken to the two women on the bench earlier, that God would open doors for them to exit this lifestyle. I thought getting this knucklehead out of their lives was probably the first door to open.

Living with this compassion for the world around us originates with Jesus. A burden for lost souls is derived from our relationship with Him. Our passion for Jesus will bear the fruit of compassion for souls. Our compassion for the lost, living in our realm of influence, may result in varied actions.

During my years on Main Street in Longmont, I crossed paths with a young man several times over a period of months. It took me several months to notice I was talking with the same young man every couple of weeks. In retrospect, I remember the first time I met him. He was sitting in a family station wagon in a parking lot facing Main Street to watch the cruising. He had driven in from a nearby farming community about 30 miles away.

I approached his driver's side window and started a conversation with him, sharing the Gospel message and inviting him to respond. He told me he was a Christian, so I asked the passenger with him if he would like to respond, and he said yes. I walked around the car and prayed with him to receive Christ and then gave him a New Testament and parted ways.

A month or two later I saw the same family station wagon sitting in the same spot on a Friday night but did not recall the previous meeting at that time. Again, I approached the driver's side window and initiated a conversation leading to the Gospel message and invited the young man to respond. Again, he responded that he was a Christian, so I directed my invitation to his passenger. Yes, he did want to invite Jesus to be his Savior and Lord. We prayed, I gave him a New Testament, and we went our separate ways.

A month or so later, the same thing: the station wagon, the same nice young man, and the passenger who needed Christ's salvation. It was this encounter when I put it all together. It was a month or so before I saw him again, with a different passenger in the front seat. I was with a friend that night and asked him to go around and lead that young man to Jesus. Then I knelt down by the side of the car to speak to the young man. I asked him why he came so often, each time with a different young man who needed Jesus. He responded, "I come here with my friends, because I know if I bring them here, they will have an opportunity to hear the Gospel and be saved." I saw him a few times after that, each time with the same results.

Sometimes, like this young man, we may really care for the world around us, but do not know how to lead people to Jesus. I hope as we continue this book, we will learn more of the essential elements of effectively sharing our faith. In the next chapter, we will look at the importance of knowing the destiny of the person who goes into eternity without Christ.

Give me one hundred preachers who fear nothing but sin and desire nothing but God, and I care not whether they be clergymen or laymen, they alone will shake the gates of Hell and set up the kingdom of Heaven upon Earth.[12] — *John Wesley*

It takes a man of God, with the Word of God, and the Spirit of God, to make the children of God, for the glory of God.[13] *—Jack Wellman*

7

Essential #3: Knowing— The End of the Lost Soul

"Oh, to realize that souls, precious, never dying souls, perishing all around us, going out into the blackness of darkness and despair, eternally lost, and yet feel no anguish, shed no tears, know no travail! How little we know the compassion of Christ."[14] —Oswald Smith

"12 And I saw the dead, the great and the small, standing before the throne, and books were opened; and another book was opened, which is the book of life; and the dead were judged from the things which were written in the books, according to their deeds. 13 And the sea gave up the dead which were in it, and death and Hades gave up the dead which were in them; and they were judged, every one of them according to their deeds. 14 Then death and Hades were thrown into the lake of fire. This is the second death, the lake of fire. 15 And if anyone's name was not found written in the book of life, he was thrown into the lake of fire." — Revelation 20:12 – 15

HELL! HELL IS real. How do I know? Jesus had much to say about hell. There are many people who do not believe in hell. However, the Bible does not support the idea of universalism, that is, the concept that all people will be saved regardless of whether they have put their trust in the saving act of Christ on the Calvary cross. This would invalidate the necessity of world evangelism and a large part of Christ's commands to go into all the world. The truth is: Hell awaits the lost soul who enters eternity without hope, that is, Jesus Christ.

> *16 For God so loved the world that He gave His only begotten Son, that whoever believes in Him should not perish but have everlasting life. 17 For God did not send His Son into the world to condemn the world, but so that the world might be saved through Him. 18 He who believes on Him is not condemned, but he who does not believe is condemned already, because he has not believed in the name of the only begotten Son of God. —John 3:16–18*

Jesus is the only way to eternal life, and there is no other door to Heaven but through faith in the finished work and in the person of Jesus Christ. Believing in Jesus grants us access to Heaven. And we must believe in the heart and confess with our mouth that Jesus is Lord. This is more than an intellectual assent; it is faith in our hearts.

So why should we know about this place called hell? You may say, "I'm not going there." Well, here's why: because billions of people on the earth are rushing headlong toward that terrible place. In the first chapter, I shared some world population statistics. The final analysis stated that every second, an eternal soul enters an eternal hell. Not for a week, or a month, or a year, or a million years, but forever. God did not create hell for man; hell was created for the devil and his demons. God created man to be with Him in Heaven for eternity. He created Heaven for man.

1 Do not let your heart be troubled; believe in God, believe also in Me. 2 In My Father's house are many dwelling places; if it were not so, I would have told you; for I go to prepare a place for you. 3 If I go and prepare a place for you, I will come again and receive you to Myself, that where I am, there you may be also. 4 And you know the way where I am going. 5 Thomas said to Him, "Lord, we do not know where You are going, how do we know the way?" 6 Jesus said to him, "I am the way, and the truth, and the life; no one comes to the Father but through Me." —John 14:1–6

If hell is then real, and people are heading there every second, and hell can be shunned by faith in Jesus, we had better get this message out to as many people as we can. This is our responsibility, to proclaim the message of hope to the world around us.

13 for "WHOEVER WILL CALL ON THE NAME OF THE LORD WILL BE SAVED." 14 How then will they call on Him in whom they have not believed? How will they believe in Him whom they have not heard? And how will they hear without a preacher? 15 How will they preach unless they are sent? Just as it is written, "HOW BEAUTIFUL ARE THE FEET OF THOSE WHO BRING GOOD NEWS OF GOOD THINGS!" — Romans 10:13–15

We have been given the remedy to guide the world of unbelievers away from hell. Preach Good News. If we will proclaim it, they can hear it, they can believe the message and call upon the name of Jesus.

Before we continue, I would like to ask you to perform an exercise. Right now, wherever you are, close your eyes and imagine hell. Take a few moments and consider everything you may have heard or read about this terrible place.

In your thoughts of hell, what did you see or imagine? Fire? Darkness? Burning? Demons? Were there outcries of pain? Or despair? Or cursing? Did you see the forms of people? Or their faces? Often when we consider hell, we may know there are people there, and we may imagine the forms or shadows of people, but we do not see their faces in our mind's eye. It is uncomfortable for us to recognize the face of a person or the name of a person in hell. When people remain nameless and faceless, it all remains impersonal to us. But the reality is, people in hell have names and faces. When we recognize this, it will provoke us to do something about it. That is, to stop as many people as we can from going there. Living with this vision of hell will increase our burden to reach the lost. It will move us to action.

Several years ago, I was leading this exercise in a YWAM (Youth with a Mission) school with international students in Mazatlán, Mexico. After a moment of contemplation, I posed the question, "What did you see in hell?"

A young lady from a Scandinavian country responded to the entire class, "I saw my brother." She told us her brother had died before she had departed for this school. She was convinced that when he died, he had never heard the Gospel, let alone responded to it. That really made us all feel extremely uncomfortable, and I really needed the Holy Spirit's guidance to help the group process this. He is faithful, and I was able to acknowledge to her and the class that the uncomfortable feeling we all had in this moment is the way we should feel about everyone we know who is without Christ.

Right now, I would like to take a trip into hell through the words of our Lord and Savior.

> *Now there was a rich man, and he habitually dressed in purple and fine linen, joyously living in splendor every day. 20 And a poor man named Lazarus was laid at his gate, covered with sores, 21 and longing to be fed with the crumbs which were falling from the rich man's table; besides,*

even the dogs were coming and licking his sores. 22 Now the poor man died and was carried away by the angels to Abraham's bosom; and the rich man also died and was buried. 23 In Hades he lifted up his eyes, being in torment, and saw Abraham far away and Lazarus in his bosom. 24 And he cried out and said, "Father Abraham, have mercy on me, and send Lazarus so that he may dip the tip of his finger in water and cool off my tongue, for I am in agony in this flame." 25 But Abraham said, "Child, remember that during your life you received your good things, and likewise Lazarus bad things; but now he is being comforted here, and you are in agony. 26 And besides all this, between us and you there is a great chasm fixed, so that those who wish to come over from here to you will not be able, and that none may cross over from there to us." 27 And he said, "Then I beg you, father, that you send him to my father's house—28 for I have five brothers—in order that he may warn them, so that they will not also come to this place of torment." 29 But Abraham said, "They have Moses and the Prophets; let them hear them." 30 But he said, "No, father Abraham, but if someone goes to them from the dead, they will repent!" 31 But he said to him, "If they do not listen to Moses and the Prophets, they will not be persuaded even if someone rises from the dead." —Luke 16:19–31 19

Hell is real. How do I know? Because Jesus had much to say about hell. When Jesus uses the word Hades, it means hell. He does not use the term Gehenna here, referring to the Lake of Fire described in Revelation 20. Hades is the local jail holding cell waiting for the day of judgment. Gehenna, or the Lake of Fire, is the eternal habitation of the lost soul. Both places are places of torment, agony, and fire.

Of the two men in this text one is a rich man whose name is not given. The other is a sick beggar named Lazarus, whose name in

Hebrew means "God surrounds" or "God protects." I personally believe these were two actual men, and this is not a parable. These men were on the earth over 2,000 years ago, and one even now remains in the conditions described in these verses, awaiting the day of judgment. On the other hand, Lazarus, was released from that place of repose, known as the bosom of Abraham, on the day Christ set those captives free during the days His body lay in the tomb. Both then and today, the believer who dies in Christ is taken soul and spirit to be in Christ's presence.

Who is the unnamed rich man? Often, when we consider hell, it is comfortable for us not to give the inhabitants of hell a name or a face. Let us give him a name and a face. Let us give him the name and the face of someone we know without Christ.

Both men die. Lazarus is immediately attended to by angels. The word is plural. One moment he was in this world suffering and dying and the next he is surrounded by angels and taken to Abraham's bosom, a place of rest and repose. The rich man also dies and is buried. Nothing is said about his funeral, but it was no doubt quite lavish. He was rich, so surely many friends were in attendance. I expect there were wonderful eulogies given about his great accomplishments in the community. He probably had an impressive grave memorial for all to remember him by. But there is no mention of that here. It simply says, "He died, he was buried, and he is in hell."

Hell is a place of torments, a word that is also plural. The fire in hell burns forever, yet never consumes. Every sense—sight, sound, taste, smell—is tormented, as well as every thought and every memory. Five times, the words *torment*, *agony*, and *fire* are used to describe the man's condition. Three times, the rich man himself uses the terms *torment*, *agony*, and *fire* to describe his circumstance. The scripture says he looks, sees, and hears. Everything he sees and hears torments him. He smells burning flesh. He sees Abraham and Lazarus, which does not comfort him. It torments him as he remembers the opportunities he once had to improve his eternal destiny. He calls out, "Father Abraham..."

He hears in response, "Child!"

He reflects, "I am a son of Abraham, with all of the benefits and blessings of a son, and I have forfeited those benefits and blessings." And it torments him.

What I believe is the greatest torment is the despair of knowing he will never leave. He is there for eternity. Consider, he asks for a single drop of water to be placed on his tongue. A single drop that will bring a moment of comfort for all eternity. Think about it. Why not ask for a glass, or a bucket, or a river? If you had one wish in hell, what would it be? "Get me out of here!" Do you see that he knows he cannot have a single drop of water? He also knows he will never leave this place. This is the torment of eternal despair.

Then there is the torment of every memory, thought, and emotion. He thinks of his family at home, which does not comfort but brings more torment. These family members will soon be here with him, and that will add torment upon torment, being surrounded by his family and hearing their cries of agony and pain.

I once read this passage of scripture in my morning devotions while we lived in northern Colorado. I pondered the thought of being surrounded by your family in hell. It was winter, and I left for my office around five o'clock each morning to open the office for the work crews who would be arriving an hour later. As I sat at a traffic light, with no one on the streets, I had a vision in which I was in a terrible car accident. My two daughters were in the back seat, and we were all seriously injured, trapped in our places in the car, and conscious. In great pain, I heard my daughters crying out, "Daddy, help me!" "Daddy, please, it hurts." "Daddy, please help!" As I heard their cries, my own pain and suffering were multiplied.

My friends, people are heading to hell at the rate of one soul every second. What are we going to do to stop them from going there? My purpose in writing this in such detail is to move us to action and to increase our burden and compassion for the lost. I have rarely preached about hell to the unbeliever, only a handful of times, and usually when someone has asked me about hell. I teach this description of hell to believers so that we may fully grasp the end of the soul who goes into eternity without Christ. We must stop people from going to this place. We must spend and be spent in this soul-winning endeavor.

Another time I was teaching this lesson at the YWAM Mazatlán base, and a young lady from England was present. Afterward, she went to the base office and called her brother in England and led him to Christ over the phone. This lesson moved her to action. That is the purpose of this teaching, to move us to action in seeking and saving the lost.

There is a world of lost souls crying out for someone to save them. We must train our ears to hear the cry of the lost all around us. Those who are going out into eternal darkness and eternal damnation are crying out to us, "Save our souls!" One night, as I walked along Colfax Avenue in Denver, I saw a young woman, a prostitute, talking on a pay phone. Next to her, a man was waiting impatiently. I had spoken with her on several occasions out there on the streets. She was a prostitute. As I waited to cross the street, I looked toward her, and our eyes met. I could see it in her eyes then, and I can still see her eyes in that moment today. I could hear her cry, "Will somebody save me?"

I once read a book about the Reverend John Harper, a Scottish evangelist who was traveling to America on the *Titanic* to speak at The Moody Church in Chicago. The book *The Titanic's Last Hero*, a very inspirational read, gives an account of his actions. When the ship was sinking, with many people already in the water, he swam back and forth to groups of people to tell them about Jesus's salvation. One man clinging to debris in the water gave record of Reverend Harper asking about the condition of his soul. When the man assured John that all was well with his soul, that he did indeed have the hope of eternal life, John turned to swim to another group of drowning people. It was the last record of John Harper. In the book were a few quotes of the survivors of the tragedy.

Sir Archibald Gracie, survivor of the Titanic: "The most pathetic and horrible scene of all. The piteous cries of those around us still ring in my ears, and I will remember them to my dying day."[15]

Eva Hart, survivor of the Titanic: "The sound of people drowning is something I cannot describe to you. And neither can anyone else. It is the most dreadful sound. And there is a dreadful silence that follows."[16]

We must learn to train our ears to hear the cries of those all around us to save their souls.

One night in Denver, the Holy Spirit guided me through streets where I had never ministered before. I passed an old house built up on a grassy bank with a knee-wall in front. I was led by the Spirit to sit there and wait, for what I did not know. As I sat there, I noticed the house was a museum. It was the house of Molly Brown, also a survivor of the *Titanic*.

I sat there for some time waiting for the Holy Spirit to move me on.

I noticed a homeless man stumbling along the street about two blocks away. The lots surrounding the Molly Brown home had been cleared for new construction, and it was possible to see several blocks away. Well, I watched this man bend over and pick up something in the street. He walked my way and then crossed to my side of the street. As he approached me, I greeted him and struck up a conversation, so he sat down on the wall with me. As the conversation turned to Christ, he looked at me with wonder in his eyes and told me, "Just over there, I bent over to pick up a quarter in the street. When I stood up, I asked God if He was real, and would He show me He is real." This was a divine moment orchestrated by God, a setup. It is so essential to be led by the notions and motions of the Holy Spirit. Needless to say, the man received salvation through Jesus Christ that night.

Many times, while out witnessing, the Holy Spirit just pushes the pause button, and I wait for Him to move. One comfortable Friday night, an old friend and I walked together from my home to Main

Street in Longmont. As we walked, we passed through a housing project where three or four groups of men were playing what is called gym-rat basketball on the court. Gym-rat basketball is where several groups of guys form impromptu teams and play to a certain point, such as 11 or 15 baskets. The losing team sits down, and a team-in-waiting takes the court to play the winning team. The winning team stays on the court as long as it wins.

As we passed by, I felt the Holy Spirit push the pause button, so I stopped and watched the ensuing couple of games. My friend was getting a bit impatient, but I was not going to move until the cloud of the Spirit moved. I really had no plan but to wait. After about 40 minutes, the ball came rolling across the court and stopped at my feet. I picked it up and walked out to center court. With all eyes on me, I introduced myself and initiated a conversation. As I said, there were 15–18 guys there. When I began to speak about Jesus, some left immediately, leaving about 10 or 12. We ended up sitting down at center court and sharing the Gospel with these guys. Everyone who stayed prayed with us to receive Jesus as Savior and Lord. Afterward, I handed out New Testaments, and we held a little Bible study until the sun went down and we could no longer see the small script in the New Testaments. There are times when the Holy Spirit will just hold you in a place to fulfill His plan and purpose.

Sometimes we just do not know how small the window is after someone receives Jesus until they are called into glory. One autumn night in 1995 in Longmont, I walked through a supermarket parking lot. Over the years I had been witnessing in Longmont, I spent many hours in this parking lot talking to the young people. It was a place where many of the cruisers would park and hang out together. On this particular night, I came upon three young men standing around a Jeep with no wheels. Another young man, the Jeep's owner, was furious. The whole group was from a town about 15 miles north of Longmont.

The angry young man worked in the supermarket and had just purchased the Jeep and bought a new set of off-road tires for it. Upon finishing his shift, he came out to find his Jeep on blocks, stripped of the new wheels. Just before I walked up, his three friends had revealed to him that it was a practical joke. They had come into town, removed the wheels, placed them in their pickup, and then waited for him to see his reaction.

Needless to say, the air was thick with emotion. Somehow, I was able to steer the conversation toward Jesus. I directed my discussion toward the three delinquent "friends" who had stripped the vehicle. They stood on my left side while the young Jeep owner stood on the right. As I concluded our exchange, I invited the three to decide for Christ right there. Each of them responded positively.

Then I turned to the other young man. You could see the Holy Spirit's presence all over him. He responded immediately that yes, he did want to invite Jesus to be his Savior and Lord. We all prayed together, and I distributed pocket New Testaments. I assured the young man that now his friends were going to get his tires back on his Jeep, and the three young men heartily agreed.

Fast forward now to Super Bowl Sunday 1997, the first of the Denver Broncos' Super Bowl wins. The following morning, I read in the morning paper about a young man who had died in a rollover accident early Sunday on his way to work at the supermarket where I had met the four young men about one and a half years earlier. Over the next few days, further details about the accident and the young man were published. Apparently, an animal had run into the street in front of the young man. He swerved to miss the animal but hit a tree, killing himself.

The newspapers had visited the local high school where he was a senior. What I read indicated that this was a nice young man, a man of faith. Students reported that he had a religious awakening about a year earlier. He had started and led a Bible club in his high school. A number of students were interviewed, and each gave testimonies of a transformed life.

On Wednesday, I returned home from my work to a phone call from a friend with whom I often spent nights witnessing on the streets.

He asked me whether I had seen the newspaper reports about the young man who died in the car accident. I told him I had, and I was very delighted that the young man had faith in Jesus. Then my friend told me, "You led him to Christ." I guess he had one of the I.O.U. LOVE ministry cards I have given out over 12,000 times over the years. He had shown it to many others at his high school and credited me with leading him to Christ.

I guess we need to understand that each person we lead to Christ will someday be called into eternity. What a great joy it is for me to be involved in a ministry that will have eternal outcomes for those who hear the message of hope. It is my sincere hope that you too will experience the tremendous satisfaction of being a soul-winner.

In the next chapter we will look at the starting point in the marvelous journey into soul-winning.

> *His authority on earth allows us to dare to go to all the nations. His authority in heaven gives us our only hope of success. And His presence with us leaves us no other choice.[17]*
> *—John Stott*

> *What a compelling motive we have for prayer, for preaching, for soul winning when we learn that every responsible human being who leaves this world without a definite change in heart immediately lifts his eyes in Hell, tormented in flame![18] —John R. Rice*

8

Essential #4: Beginning—
Praying for the Lost

"Oh, my brothers and sisters in Christ, if sinners will be damned, at least let them leap to hell over our bodies; and if they will perish, let them perish with our arms about their knees, imploring them to stay, and not madly to destroy themselves. If hell must be filled, at least let it be filled in the teeth of our exertions and let not one go there unwarned and unprayed for."[19] —Charles Spurgeon

"Our prayers lay the track down which God's power can come. Like a mighty locomotive, his power is irresistible, but it cannot reach us without rails."[20] —Watchman Nee

Brethren, my heart's desire, and my prayer to God for them is for their salvation.' —Romans 10:1

NOW WE HAVE already seen that the most important element in being effective in soul-winning is our personal, growing relationship with our Lord Jesus. We must have a passion for His presence. Each day, day by day, as we seek Him and His presence, laying our heads on His chest in the secret places, listening to His heartbeat, that "None would perish," and "All would be saved," we will grow in compassion for the world around us. As our Christ-given burden for the lost increases, we will be constrained and compelled to go into the world. We have seen the horrors of hell and the future of those who enter eternity without the hope of eternal life. The agonies of hell should move us to get in the way of as many people as possible to stop them from going to that horrible place.

Now, what is our next step? Where do we start in our venture into soul-winning? Well, let us start here at the first of all:

> *1 First of all, then, I exhort that supplications, prayers, intercessions, and giving of thanks be made for all men, 2 for kings and all who are in authority, so that we may lead a quiet and peaceable life in all godliness and reverence. 3 For this is good and acceptable in the sight of God our Savior, 4 who will have all men to be saved and to come to the knowledge of the truth. —1 Timothy 2:1–4*

Where do we start? First of all, with prayer, supplication, intercession, and thanksgiving. For whom? All men and women. Every noble work in the kingdom of Heaven begins on our knees. Prayer lays the groundwork for soul-winning. It is our indispensable weapon. Praying for the lost will alter the atmosphere around them. Praying for the lost can change a person's receptiveness to the Gospel.

Are the names of the people living within our realm of influence being announced in heaven regularly? Are their names echoing repeatedly throughout the courts of heaven? Are those 24 elders who surround the Father familiar with the names of our unsaved family, friends, co-workers, and classmates? Do the four living creatures who minister before the throne of heaven know their names? Are angels being sent out on assignment on behalf of the lost around us because of our frequent prayers, supplications, intercessions, and thanksgivings? Our regular prayers announce these names in the throne room of Heaven.

Over the years, I have established what I call prayer campaigns for lost souls who are living in my realm of influence. A prayer campaign is when I determine I am going to pray for someone until one of three events occur in that person's life. Number one: the person is born again by the Holy Spirit of God. This of course is the preferred outcome. Number two: the person dies. If that happens, I can no longer pray for their salvation. This is the undesirable outcome. Number three: I die. If I die, the prayer campaign ends also. But do you see? A prayer campaign is a serious commitment to pray a person through to salvation. Yes, they still must hear the Gospel message, and we will talk about this later. And they still must personally make a decision to receive Jesus's salvation. But prayer is, as Paul puts it, the first of all. It is our starting point.

When I married Kathleen, she had two brothers, Mike and Jerry, and a brother-in-law, Randy, who were unbelievers. What a great joy it is to report that today they are genuine believers in Christ. For several years, I taught the original outline of this book, which I had titled "The Seven Essentials of Soul-Winning," at our church's Men's Advance weekend during Saturday afternoon breakout sessions. As I taught, I looked up into the tiered seats where Kathleen's two brothers sat together, laboring intensely to hold back the tears. Through many prayers over a number of years, we saw each of them come alive in the kingdom of Heaven. Today, both Mike and Jerry are amazing men of God.

When I first met Randy, he was a devout unbeliever. The first time I spoke to him about Jesus, he quickly quieted me, telling me he did not want to hear it. Somehow, somewhere, someone had really affronted him in their zeal to impart the Gospel. Randy and I did become great friends. I really enjoyed being around him. We went hiking together in the northern Georgia forests, ran road races together, and spent as much time together as we could even though we always lived at a distance from each other. I determined I would honor his request to not be preachy.

For 17 years, I never spoke another word to Randy about the Gospel. But daily I announced his name in Heaven. Randy's name echoed in

Heaven regularly. When our mutual father-in-law was close to death in Longmont, Randy and his family came to pay their final respects. Dad was in hospice care at home. After two days, our father-in-law continued in a semi coma and had not awakened since Randy and his family had arrived.

On the third day, I came to the house from work and entered the room where our father-in-law lay. Randy was the only person in the room. I went to the bedside and quietly prayed. As I concluded my prayer, I placed my hand on Dad's chest, and he immediately sat up in bed. Only Randy was there to witness it.

Dad was awake and lucid the rest of the night. All his family was present, and he visited with us throughout the evening. Randy was comforted that they had been able to say goodbye. Dad died the next afternoon. Over the next couple of days, we made the funeral arrangements and held the funeral.

Several days later, Randy and his family were preparing to return home to Georgia. The night before they left, I heard the Holy Spirit speak into my heart to go and visit with Randy. "He's ready to listen." We sat together in the garage on folding chairs as Randy listened, sincerely interested in what I had to say. He told me he was not ready to make a decision that night, but he welcomed me to send him Gospel literature, which I did.

With this turn of events, Kathleen and I raised our prayer campaign to a new level. Each morning we would take each other's hand and pray for him. Shortly thereafter, Randy made plans to move his family to California, and he went there alone first to set things up for the arrival of his family. As I understand the story, he was driving his car in the city of Irvine, part of the Los Angeles metropolitan area, when it broke down in front of a gated community. At the entrance of the community was a guard in a guard house. He approached the guard and asked for permission to leave the car overnight and retrieve it in the morning.

In the guardhouse, he noticed a Bible and struck up a conversation with the guard about the Bible and Jesus. Randy's wife, Cheryl,

Kathleen's sister, had told him he should check out Greg Laurie's Harvest Church, also in Irvine. Randy asked the guard if he knew where Harvest Church was. The guard responded, "Yes, I'm a member there." Randy went to church that Sunday and continued to attend a few more Sundays. Finally, after several visits, a salvation invitation was given to anyone who wanted to get right with God. Guess who responded. Randy surrendered his life to Christ. Prayer campaigns are vital!

Randy grew in his love for the Lord and became a wonderful husband, father, and man of God. Several years ago, Randy contracted a rare aggressive cancer that was attributed to his contact with jungle defoliant Agent Orange when he served in the Air Force in Vietnam. He died less than a year after his diagnosis. In the weeks before his death, I spent an all-night prayer watch in his hospital room. I was glad to spend that time with him. He faced his death with great courage and great hope in eternity. I will see him again—of this I am sure. When I see him on the other side of eternity, do you think I will wish I had not prayed so long and hard for him? Will I feel that I wasted 17 years praying for him? No, I will be delighted to have been a part of his eternal story.

I want to tell you about a neighbor I once had named Doug. Doug, a functioning alcoholic, was a real neighborly type of guy. We would often meet in the street in front of our homes to have a chat. Doug had made it clear that he was not interested in my Jesus message, but he did not know I was announcing his name in Heaven almost daily. Neighbors for many of the 15 years we lived in Longmont, we often left for work about the same time in the early hours of the morning. Doug worked in a building supply store, and it was on the route I took to my office each day. For a time, I did not see Doug, nor did I see his car at the building supply store. Then one day I saw Doug heading my way upon arriving home with my family. Guess it was time for our mid-street get-together.

Doug started up the conversation. He asked if I had noticed his absence. I said I had and that I had not noticed his car at work either. I asked, "What's up?" He said he had gotten extremely sick while visiting family in the east. He had almost died. I asked him if that gave him a sense of his mortality, thinking I could turn the conversation into something of eternal value.

His response was a shock, for he said, "No, it gives me more of a sense of immortality. Do you see, I have realized through this that there is a purpose for me here on earth. I will not die until I fulfill that purpose; I do not know what it is. Perhaps you do."

Prayer campaigns are powerful in preparing hearts and also attracting the people to the one praying for them. Well, this opened a tremendous door of opportunity. We had a long talk about God's purpose for each of us in this life we live. And that purpose is found in Jesus. When I finished, he looked at me and said, "Hmm, I never thought of it that way." And he turned and went home. Although I continued to pray for Doug, I never was able to get any further with the message. He moved away a short time later, and I still hope and pray that others have entered his life to continue the Gospel story.

Praying for the lost in our realm of influence is essential, and so is praying for our communities. I would like to share some stories of various community prayer campaigns I have been involved with. While living in Longmont in 1999, a prayer initiative was organized by a group of local churches to pray over every home in the city before the arrival of the new millennium, the year 2000. Neighborhoods were divided up among the prayer participants. Kathleen and I spent many evenings walking through our neighborhood and praying over each individual home. Before the advent of the year 2000, every home and family in the city had been prayed for.

Each Saturday, the local Longmont newspaper would contain a crime report with a map of the city and assorted crimes committed during the previous week. Different symbols identified specific categories of crime. When I saw a high concentration of crime in a specific area, I would go out for a prayer walk. Armed with a spray bottle of anointing oil, I would walk, pray, and spray around the borders of the neighborhood touched by crime.

I believe the Bible when I read, "For we wrestle not against flesh and blood, but against principalities, against powers, against the rulers of the darkness of this world, against spiritual wickedness in high places" (Ephesians 6:12). I also believe, "The effectual fervent prayer of a righteous man can gain much" (James 5:16). You see, dark forces create dark influences over nations, regions, cities, and neighborhoods. I believe we are called to be watchmen over these places. And I also believe we have weapons to engage those dark powers, the greatest of which is prayer. I must tell you that each time I would walk, pray, and spray, the following week the criminal activity on the crime map would diminish significantly in that area, sometimes altogether. Prayer is powerful to pull down strongholds of violence and crime.

So now you are probably thinking, "This guy's a hyper spiritual nutcase." And maybe I am, but I tell you I have seen the powerful results of prayer. Here is one more dose of my Holy Spirit extremism. Please understand that I did not come up with these endeavors on my own. I am not that creative, or crazy. It was through prayer and waiting upon the voice of the Holy Spirit that I was introduced to these pursuits. Hanging out with the Holy Spirit can be dangerous, and hanging out with people who hang out with the Holy Spirit can be equally dangerous.

This story involves a bucket of oil. My home church in northern Colorado holds an annual "Men's Advance." I guess "Advance" is more positive than "Retreat." Around 700 men would "go up the mountain" each spring for the weekend to get filled with the mighty presence of God. It is a sight to see when a hundred or so men are dancing wildly and shamelessly before the presence of God. Like David danced, except I do not remember anyone's clothes falling off.

A powerful speaker would address us, and our senior pastor would bring an anointed, powerful message to the men. And the worship time was not three songs and out but would go on for what seemed like forever. For many years I was invited to teach the curriculum in this book during the Saturday afternoon breakout sessions.

One particular year an evangelist named Dave Roever was the guest speaker. Dave, a Vietnam veteran, was a riverboat gunner in Vietnam. A phosphorous grenade exploded next to his head, which burned him beyond recognition. Now he has a tremendous evangelistic ministry and speaks extensively in public schools. During the weekend Men's Advance meetings, he announced his ministry schedule for the next two weeks at schools in cities along northern Colorado's Front Range. He would be speaking at two junior high schools in Longmont on a Tuesday two weeks later.

Each Monday night I met with a group of men in Longmont. It was a very informal group, and we would encourage and pray for each other and pray for the city. On a number of occasions, we would prayer-walk through the city on those Monday nights. The Monday night after the Men's Advance, we talked about Dave Roever speaking at the two schools in Longmont. While we prayed that night, I lay on the floor when I had a vision of a line of oil surrounding the schools. Each student and faculty member would have to step over the line of oil before entering the school on that day. As they did so, attitudes and influences would have to be left behind.

As I lay there on the floor, I asked the Holy Spirit how to apply the oil. The first thing I saw was a carpenter's blue chalk line being snapped on a piece of wood. Next, I saw a saturated line of oil being snapped on the ground surrounding the school. Upon receiving this direction, I announced that we would go to the two schools the following Monday to anoint them with oil. Then I went home and concocted the oil bucket.

First, I got a five-gallon paint bucket. Second, I drilled half-inch holes on either side of the bucket about two-thirds up from the bottom. Third, I ran a half-inch pipe through the drilled holes. Fourth, I drilled a bolt hole in the bottom of the bucket and attached a small pulley using two rubber sealing washers to keep the oil from leaking. Fifth, I purchased a 1200-yard spool of twine, placed it on the half-inch pipe, ran it down through the pulley and up through the opening on the top of the bucket. Then, I waited for Monday night.

On Monday night, I showed the guys my contraption. When I explained what we were going to do with it, a loud silence fell over the men. We were going to pour about a gallon of olive oil into the bottom of the bucket and then pray for the anointing upon that oil. We would run the twine from the spool down through the pulley and then go to the first school. One person would go to each of the corners of the school and hammer a long nail into the earth. Then we would tie the twine onto the first nail and walk to each successive nail, wrapping the oil-saturated twine around the nail. We would continue until we had run the twine around the perimeter of the building. Next, we would walk along the line and snap it like a carpenter's chalk line. Then, we would gather up our supplies, gather at the flagpole, and pray over the next day's school assembly.

As we drove to the first school, the silence in the car was deafening. No one said a word. They were probably wondering how they let me get them into this. We went to each school and pulled it off without raising the attention of any authorities. It really did leave a line of oil around the school, especially noticeable on the concrete walkways. On the drive home from the second school, the van was filled with excitement. We all had a sense of accomplishment.

The next morning at the first school, which was in my neighborhood, the principal permitted our homeschooled children to attend the assembly, so my family and several others joined in. In the parking lot before the assembly, I saw Dave Roever, and he recognized me from the Men's Advance. I told him what we had done and pointed out the visible line of oil on the concrete at the entryway. He gave me the funniest look and said, "I ain't never heard anyone do that before." And went in.

Dave's public-school assemblies begin with a secular presentation. He tells his story and how he was able to overcome the unfortunate event. Then he opens it up for questions. During this time, if a question is asked about the specifics of his story, he can give details of God's hand in his life. The meeting went really well, the students were attentive, and they participated in the question-and-answer time.

These assemblies were the last of his scheduled meetings in the area. On Wednesday night, a rally was held at our home church. On the platform with Dave Roever were the two principals from the Longmont junior high schools he had visited the day before. When Dave began to speak, he introduced the principals and stated the assemblies in these two schools were the best school assemblies he had ever participated in. I believe prayer and obedience were the reason. Prayer is powerful and will produce a shift in the spiritual atmosphere.

I have not written these things so you will all run out and construct an oil bucket or grab an oil spray bottle and go out for a walk, pray, and spray. I am merely relating some of the things the Holy Spirit has inspired me to do in this area of community prayer campaigns. Listen to His voice, and possibly He will lead you into significant prayer actions in your community.

We have looked at the importance and the power of prayer campaigns for the lost, for nations, cities, regions, and even public schools. Never minimize the importance of this type of prayer.

In our next chapter, we will look at the essential of continuing this journey in prayer and specifically focusing our prayers for the lost.

How long will it take us to learn that the shortest route to the man next door is by way of God's throne?[21] *—A. T. Pierson*

You must go forward on your knees.[22] *—Hudson Taylor*

9

ESSENTIAL #5: CONTINUING—
WHAT DO WE PRAY FOR?

"Go for souls. Go straight for souls and go for the worst."[23]
—William Booth

*"It is possible for the most obscure person in a church, with a
heart right toward God, to exercise as much power for the
evangelization of the world, as it is for those who stand in
the most prominent positions."*[24] *—John R. Mott*

WE HAVE ALREADY seen that the most important essential in effective evangelism is our passion for Christ. We must continue in our
day-to-day lives with a hunger for the presence of Jesus. Each day as
we lay our head on His chest in our daily quiet time and listen to His
heartbeat of "None perish! All saved!", we will be stirred with His compassion for a lost and dying world. A burden for the lost comes through
our relationship with Jesus. We have seen Hell through Jesus's own
words and understand the dreadfulness of that place. Now we know
the vital importance of praying for the lost in our realms of influence
and the significance of praying for our communities. In this chapter,
we will look at specific areas of focus while praying for those who are
without Christ.

Those who oppose him he must gently instruct, in the hope that God will grant them repentance leading them to a knowledge of the truth and they will come to their senses and escape from the trap of the devil, who has <u>taken them captive</u> to do his will. —2 Timothy 2: 25, 26 NIV

The god of this world <u>has blinded the minds of the unbelievers</u>, so that they cannot see the light of the Gospel of the glory of Christ who is the image of God. —2 Corinthians 4:4 NAS

Who is our enemy? Some may get the idea that our enemy is that difficult person we must deal with at our work. Or a deranged neighbor. Or maybe that political party whose ideologies oppose ours. Or foreign national governments not aligned with our system of government. The true enemy of God and humankind is the devil, Satan, aptly named as the adversary, and the broken world system he has imposed on broken man. We live in a broken world ruled by broken people who have been taken captive by the devil to do his will. When people hurt and offend us, we need to see the deeper cause of their actions. Satan is the one behind all of this sin and brokenness. Jesus tells us Satan comes only for the purpose of robbing, killing, and destroying.

10 The thief comes only to steal and kill and destroy; I came that they may have life, and have it abundantly. 11 I am the good shepherd; the good shepherd lays down His life for the sheep. —John 10:10, 11

Look at another description of Satan, again in Jesus's words:

You are of your father the devil, and you want to do the desires of your father. He was a murderer from the beginning and does not stand in the truth because there is no truth in him. Whenever he speaks a lie, he speaks from his own nature, for he is a liar and the father of lies. —John 8:44

The devil is the enemy of God, and the enemy of humankind. As Paul writes in Second Timothy, it is the devil who has taken broken man captive to do his will. What is his will? Killing, stealing, destroying, lying, hurtful behavior, and so forth. When we understand that it is Satan who is our adversary, we can begin to look at people and their hurtful actions in a different light. Let us look at another of Paul's letters to gain further understanding of humankind's brokenness.

3 And even if our gospel is veiled, it is veiled to those who are perishing, 4 in whose case the god of this world has blinded the minds of the unbelieving so that they might not see the light of the gospel of the glory of Christ, who is the image of God. 5 For we do not preach ourselves but Christ Jesus as Lord, and ourselves as your bondservants for Jesus' sake. 6 For God, who said, "Light shall shine out of darkness," is the One who has shone in our hearts to give the Light of the knowledge of the glory of God in the face of Christ. —2 Corinthians 4:3–6

The god of this world. Who is that? Again, it is our adversary, the devil. Satan has blinded the mind of the unbeliever. He has taken away the sense of discernment of spiritual truths such as, "The light of the Gospel of the glory of Christ, who is the image of God." Satan has blinded the minds of men and women so they cannot understand spiritual reality. Many years ago, I wrote in the margin of my Bible next to verse four, "Warfare Focus!" When we pray for the unbeliever, we must bind up the darkness the devil has covered them with. They do not see the truth because they cannot see the truth.

I have come to realize that people believe that which they believe is the truth. It may be obvious to you and me that it is not the truth, but to them it is the truth. No one willfully accepts a lie as the truth unless they are out of their mind. I have also come to realize that the devil's undertaking is to dress lies up as truth to make them believable to the unbeliever. Remember, he is the father of lies, and there is no truth in him. It is his nature to lie. That is why it is so important to recognize the Bible, in its entirety, as our source of truth. Regardless of what this fallen world system tries to impose upon us as truth, we need to distinguish truth by what is revealed to us in God's Word.

Here is a brief description of how we have moved away from Biblical truth into humanistic ideology. In the past 150 years, the scale of absolute truth has been sliding, and it continues to do so today. There was a time in Western civilization when God's Word, the Bible, was considered absolute truth, and rightly so. During the modernistic movement, the idea of absolute truth was revised to include humans' ability to reason, which came about due to humanity's advances in science and industry. The postmodern thinking of today includes humans' ability to reason as modified by their feelings and experiences. Today truth is based upon what you have experienced and what you feel is right, which is humanistic, placing humans, their reason, and their feelings above the truth of God's Word. Now, who do you think is the instigator of this sliding scale of truth? Satan, the father of lies.

Let us look a little closer at the previous scripture. Verse 4 says, "The god of this world has blinded the mind of the unbeliever." Verse 6 says, "For God, who said, 'Light shall shine out of darkness,' is the One who has shone in our hearts to give the Light of the knowledge of the glory of God in the face of Christ." The truth is, God desires to have relationship with humans. The problem is that the adversary, the devil, has blinded humankind from seeing the light of this truth.

God's solution for this problem is Christ. He is the light of the world, the bright morning star shining through the darkness. He is shining the light of the character and nature of our good heavenly Father, according to the Father's plan and purpose.

We may look at this and see that the battle for humans' souls seems to be between the Creator Father and the adversary Satan. We may reason, "Maybe we should withdraw ourselves from the conflict and let these two spiritual forces resolve the problem." It seems like the Father has it all under control. But how many of you know that verse 5 comes before verse 6? This is some high theology we are considering here. Let us look at verse 5, "For we do not preach ourselves but Christ Jesus as Lord, and ourselves as your bondservants for Jesus' sake." The Father's plan includes you and me. He has commissioned us to share the Gospel.

Let us review: Our Father in Heaven desires relationship with men and women everywhere. Remember, "All saved, none perish." The problem is humankind's sin and the blinding lies of the enemy, Satan. The Solution is the saving life, death, and resurrection of Jesus. The necessary action includes our participation: we preach Jesus Christ as Lord.

Praying for the lost in our realms of influence involves engaging the enemy of our souls in a battle. I have called it a prayer campaign because it is a militaristic endeavor. We must be relentless for the souls of the lost. We have an enemy who has blinded them and wants to keep them in darkness eternally.

> *Many do not recognize the fact as they ought, that Satan has got men fast asleep in sin and that it is his great device to keep them so. He does not care what we do if he can do that. We may sing songs about the sweet by and by, preach sermons and say prayers until doomsday, and he will never concern himself about us, if we don't wake anybody up. But if we awake the sleeping sinner, he will gnash at us with his teeth. This is our work to wake the people up.*[25] —*Catherine Booth*

In our battle for lost souls, we must pull down the strongholds of darkness in the hearts of the unbeliever. We must expose the lies the enemy has blinded them with, and we must bind those lies from operating in their minds and hearts. As those lies are impeded by the truth of the Gospel message, they will recognize it as truth, and the Truth will set them free. All of this in prayer, first of all. Also, as you prepare to go with the Gospel message of truth, ask for the keys—the words or actions—that will open hearts to and endorse the message you bring.

In a future chapter, we will discuss the gifts of the Spirit in our witnessing. I believe and expect all the gifts of the Spirit in soul-winning, and I have walked in those gifts throughout my years in the harvest fields. I also like to believe that I can pray what I have called BAP prayers when praying for or with the lost. A BAP is a big, audacious prayer. Our Father loves to show Himself big and powerful when reaching out to the lost. I have learned to say and pray things that are huge and audacious when speaking to the lost. When I do, I feel I am kind of bragging on how big and awesome my Father in Heaven is.

I have prayed big, audacious prayers when out on the streets with the people I meet. Oh, and by the way, when you are praying on the streets with people, you do not have to close your eyes to pray. I love to pray with eyes wide open and every head raised. One of the great things about praying this way is how often I see in their eyes the moment the Holy Spirit empowers the message, revealing its truth in the heart of the hearer. This is the exact moment they are being born of the Spirit. It is absolutely wonderful to be a part of the moment of new birth.

On a very cold night in downtown Boulder, with below-freezing temperatures, I was talking to a group of two or three college students when I heard from behind me a most pitiful cry. An elderly man cried out, "I can't see! I ain't lying! And I'm scared!" I was finishing my witness with the group when I heard the cry a second time.

As I turned around, there arose in me a warlike spirit. Without much time to even assess the situation, I commanded with authority, "In Jesus's name, I take authority over you, you spirit of alcohol." I was kind of surprised to hear myself speak those words and in such an aggressive manner.

We approached the elderly man, and again he cried out, "I can't see! I ain't lying! And I'm scared!" He was a very thin homeless street person wearing a dirty white trench coat that seemed like it could wrap around him two or three times. His hair and beard were long, unkempt, and white. He looked like Santa Claus on a weight loss workshop diet plan.

As I have said previously, I try in these situations to fall in behind the Holy Spirit and follow His lead. Remember, Jesus declared that He only said what He heard the Father say, and He only did what He saw the Father do. As I read the Gospels, I can almost see a pause in Jesus as needs were presented to Him. I believe the pause is to see what the Father is doing. When I find myself in a position where such a great need is presented to me, I have learned to take that pause myself.

As I stood in front of this unfortunate soul, I saw in my spirit the image of placing my thumbs in His eyes. I asked the man if I could pray for his eyes, and he gave me permission. I pressed my thumbs into his eyes and prayed what I thought was a fairly good prayer, taking authority over the spirit of alcohol. I commanded his sight to be restored, along with his body and mind. When I finished, he announced, "I peed my pants!"

"What?" I exclaimed.

Again, he responded, "I peed my pants!" Oh man, I was thinking, Jesus laid his thumbs on the blind man's eyes, and his sight was restored. I laid my thumbs on the blind man's eyes, and he peed his pants. And he did not just spring a small leak, it was a deluge. The ground below the man was now a puddle soon to freeze. And he still could not see. I did mention that the temperature was at or below freezing. Have you ever had wet pants in the freezing air?

Again, he said: "I peed my pants!" adding: "You are not mad, are you?"

Okay, this was really getting weird. I did not know what to think. After asking if I was mad, I responded, "No, I'm not mad, they aren't my pants, maybe if they were my pants, I might be a little mad."

His response was, "That's not funny."

After a brief moment, though, he started to blink his eyes and say, "Hey, it's coming back." His sight was being restored, and in a few more moments his sight was normal. He pulled a bottle of some sort of liquor, about two-thirds empty, out of his trench coat and then asked me if I thought he should get rid of it. I told him I thought it would be a good idea. He threw it into a nearby trash can.

I shared the Gospel story with him, and we prayed to invite Jesus to be his Savior and Lord. I gave him a Bible and a sack of food. He was grateful and appreciative, thanking me repeatedly for restoring his sight. Then he shuffled off into the cold, cold night, wet pants and all. I stood there confused. I had absolutely no idea what had just happened.

I did not think much about what had taken place with the old guy the rest of the weekend. But on Sunday morning, I was in the prayer room of our church before the early morning service. As a family, we would arrive at church an hour before service every Sunday to pray for the service, and especially for the salvation of souls. In 10 years, I cannot remember many Sundays, if any, when someone did not respond to the salvation invitation at the end of the service.

Well, on this Sunday morning as I prayed, the Holy Spirit began to speak to my heart about the old man. The Holy Spirit told me when I prayed for the man and took authority over the spirit of alcohol, He, the Holy Spirit, had squeezed the man's liver and kidneys, forcing out the alcohol that had made him "blind drunk." That is why he peed his pants. I have heard the phrase "blind drunk" before, but I never realized it can be a real consequence of hard drinking.

I guess we do not always know exactly what God is doing through us. Had the Holy Spirit not clued me in on what had taken place when I prayed for the man, I probably would have never known what happened there, and you would not be reading it now.

Keeping a tight connection to the Holy Spirit in this type of street ministry is vital. It is also a lot of fun to see what God does in so many situations. There are many times when the circumstances can get very tense, but keeping a calm spirit makes it possible for you to clearly hear the directions of the Holy Spirit.

One Friday night on Colfax, a couple of blocks from the state Capitol, I happened upon a wiry street guy and started talking to him. I shared the way of salvation, and he seemed open and genial. After praying together for his salvation, I provided him with a New Testament and a food bag from my backpack. At that point, things turned for the worse. He looked at the sack of food and said he did not want it. Instead, he wanted me to give him some money to go buy a hamburger. I did not carry money with me out on the streets, and I told him I was sorry but could not oblige that request.

He continued to insist that I buy him a hamburger, and I continued to decline. He took the bag of food I had given to him, walked over to a trash can on the street, and with great ceremony dropped the food in the trash. I walked over, retrieved the food, and again asked him if he wanted it. With great contempt, he spurned the offer.

When I started to return the food to my backpack, he became enraged. It was quite the transformation from this warm friendly fellow into a fuming irritated madman. He grabbed me by the arm, and the atmosphere became foreboding. I said to him, "If you are wise, you will let my arm go."

He let my arm go and became "OOC," out of control. His body tensed up, and with clenched fists and hunched shoulders, he started shouting, "What are you going to do? Hit me! Come on, hit me." This was all taking place on a very public street corner. Immediately, a crowd started gathering for the quickly approaching storm. People were coming up out of manholes and sliding down building downspouts to see da Preacher get punched.

This is where it pays to keep a calm spirit, expecting the Holy Spirit to move. In my spirit, I saw myself laying my hand on his chest. So I took the necessary steps to approach him, extending my open palm. In that moment, these words came up in my heart, "In Jesus's name, I speak peace to your heart." When I touched his heart, he went limp, like a ragdoll. I quickly did an about-face, that little maneuver I learned in Navy boot camp, and walked toward the crowd. Approaching the crowd, it parted like the Red Sea did for Israel. I marched through the crowd and skedaddled. Amazingly, in the months that followed this momentous occasion, I spoke with a number of people who witnessed the occurrence and recognized a powerful presence of God. I became sort of an urban folk legend on the streets because of this incident.

On another night, just around the corner from the previous episode, I had another exciting, but less threatening, encounter. I sensed the heavens were open that night. Often, after consistently working in an area, I find the atmosphere becomes increasingly fruitful for the harvest. Working regularly in an area, I believe, seeds the heavens with the Gospel truth. Powers and principalities of darkness over the area are disrupted by the word that goes forth. The concepts of sowing and reaping for the harvest come into play as we proclaim the truth recurrently in an area. As we go about sowing, we are preparing to reap, and even as we reap, we are sowing for a future harvest. Thus, over time, the results increase exponentially.

On this particular evening, I sensed a great anointing on the ministry. Everyone I had stopped to share with had surrendered their lives to Christ, with seven or more salvation responses in just the first hour of ministry. I could sense the power of the Holy Spirit's presence, so I decided to test it.

I walked around the corner, where I had encountered the wiry guy previously, and I saw a group of people about halfway down the block. The group that caught my attention included a big menacing-looking character and four young ladies. I quickly surmised this was a souteneur and his ladies of the night. Oh, if you did not know, a souteneur is a pimp. I concluded that he was giving the young women their instructions for the night.

Since I was really sensing a powerful presence of the Holy Spirit, I approached the group without hesitation. I introduced myself and distributed my I.O.U. LOVE ministry card. The size of a business card, it folded over to make four sides. "I.O.U. LOVE" was printed on the front side, with the plan of salvation and supporting scripture printed on the two inner leaves. This card was my first point of contact with people as I approached them on the streets.

I introduced myself and asked them if they knew where they would spend eternity when they died. I had their attention immediately. They stopped their conversation, genuinely attentive to everything I was sharing. As I continued to share the message of salvation, a man—probably a potential customer—approached the souteneur and whispered in his ear.

The big ominous fellow responded to the man by saying, "Right now we are listening to this man," (who was me) "so if you could just wait over there until we are finished, I will talk to you then." I was right, there was a special Holy Ghost anointing on the night. I continued with my message, and after a short while the potential client returned and whispered in the big guy's ear again. Well, that really aggravated the big guy, and he roared back at the man, "Listen, I told you, right now we are listening to what this man has to say. Now you stand over there until we are through here!"

I thought to myself, "This is awesome!" and continued sharing the Gospel. When I finished, I invited the group to make a decision for Jesus. They all decided they would like to pray a prayer of salvation together. We all prayed, there on the street. I gave them pocket New Testaments and follow-up booklets. Then I prayed for their safety and for doors to open to escape this lifestyle.

When I finished with the ladies, I approached the big guy. His countenance had transformed dramatically since I had first arrived. I felt a holy boldness to confront him. I exclaimed to him, "Man, you are going to die out here if you don't leave this way of life!"

Holding back tears, he answered back, "I know. I am trapped out here. I don't know of any way out of this." Pimps, prostitutes, drug addicts, alcoholics, and others are prisoners of their own choice but captives nonetheless. We do not know their history or the events that led them into their captivity. Jesus came to set the captives free, and as the Father sent the Son, so the Son sends us.

So Jesus said to them again, "Peace be with you; as the Father has sent Me, I also send you." —John 20:21

In this chapter, we developed the foundation of the prayer campaigns we establish for the people in our realm of influence who are without Christ. We examined what the Word of God declares about the condition of lost souls: They have been taken captive by our adversary, the devil, to do his will, and he has blinded their eyes. In our prayer campaigns we must bind the enemy and his lies in the minds of the unbeliever through intercessory warfare prayer.

But no one can enter the strong man's house and plunder his property unless he first binds the strong man, and then he will plunder his house. —Mark 3:27

In the next chapter, we will look at what we can expect from our prayer campaigns.

The greatest form of praise is the sound of consecrated feet seeking out the lost and helpless.[26]—Billy Graham

You can take nothing greater to the heathen world than the impress and the reflection of the love of God upon your character. That is the universal language.[27] —Henry Drummond

10

Essential #6: Action—What to Expect from Our Prayers

"To be a soul-winner is the happiest thing in this world. And with every soul you bring to Jesus Christ, you seem to get a new heaven here upon earth."[28] *—Charles Spurgeon*

"I know that some are always studying the meaning of the fourth toe of the right foot of some beast in prophecy and have never used either foot to go and bring men to Christ. I do not know who the 666 is in Revelation but I know the world is sick, sick, sick and the best way to speed the Lord's return is to win more souls for Him."[29] *—Vance Havner*

"1 Now after this the Lord appointed seventy others and sent them in pairs ahead of Him to every city and place where He Himself was going to come. 2 And He was saying to them, "The harvest is plentiful, but the laborers are few; therefore, beseech the Lord of the harvest to send out laborers into His harvest. 3 "Go; behold, I send you out as lambs in the midst of wolves." —Luke 10:1–3

WE HAVE SEEN that the most important essential in effective evangelism is our passion for Christ. The world needs Jesus, and we must be so full of His presence that He literally drips off us wherever we go, just as sweat drips off me in Mexico's summer heat. We must continue in our day-to-day lives with a hunger for the presence of Jesus. Each day as we lay our heads on His chest in our daily quiet times, listening to His heartbeat for the world, we will be stirred with His compassion for a lost and dying world.

We have seen that a burden for the lost comes through our relationship with Jesus. We saw hell through the words of Jesus and understand the reality of the torment, agony, and fire filling that place. Now we know the vital importance of praying for the lost in our realm of influence and significance of praying for our communities.

In the preceding chapter we examined what the Word of God declares about the condition of lost souls: They have been taken captive by our adversary, the devil, to do his will and he has blinded the eyes of the unbeliever. Our prayer campaigns bind the enemy and his lies from operating in the minds of the unbeliever through our intercessory warfare prayer. By engaging in prayer, we foster an atmosphere such that when people hear the truth, they will recognize it, and it will set them free. In this chapter, we will look at what we can expect from our prayers for lost souls.

In the conclusion of the previous chapter, I shared some stories about people feeling trapped in lifestyles with no ability to escape. The devil had taken them captive, but Jesus came to set captives free. We do not always know people's stories. True, some have made bad decisions. Someone, somewhere, once said, "Sin will take you farther than you ever expected to go; it will keep you longer than you ever intended to stay, and it will cost you more than you ever expected to pay."

Jesus desires to deliver people who have been taken captive by the consequences of their sin. In His home synagogue in Nazareth, Jesus read from Isaiah 61:1:

The Spirit of the Lord GOD is upon me, Because the LORD has anointed me To bring good news to the afflicted; He has sent me to bind up the brokenhearted, To proclaim liberty to captives And freedom to prisoners.

I want to draw attention to two groups here: captives and prisoners. Captives are held against their will, but they have done nothing to deserve their current plight. Prisoners are confined due to poor decisions they have made. Jesus has come to give liberty and freedom to both groups.

I sat on a wall in the open area mall in downtown Denver one Friday night. After carrying my 40-pound backpack for the past three hours, I was resting. I noticed a young man of about 18 years of age walk by. A few minutes later, I noticed him pass by again. Then he passed by a third time and sat about 10–15 feet away on the same wall.

I finished my breather, walked over, and sat next to him. His name was Joshua, and he was a homeless heroin addict. Recognizing me as the street preacher, he hoped to speak with me. As we talked, he swayed back and forth, which he said was caused by coming down off a heroin rush. More than once, he just laid his head on my shoulder and sighed.

I asked him how he had become addicted to heroin. He told me his parents were heroin addicts. On his fifteenth birthday, his father came into his room and announced, "Well, you'll probably start doing this someday anyways, so you might as well learn how to do it right." With that, he shot his son up with heroin for the first time. Joshua enjoyed the rush so much that he tried it again, then again, until he was addicted and homeless.

So, I ask, is Joshua a prisoner or a captive to heroin addiction and homelessness? Sometimes we look at a person in a deplorable circumstance and think they got themselves into the situation. But we need to hear their stories. Whether captive or prisoner, Jesus came to set them free. He sends us to do the same, and often it can be messy, even stinky.

Remember when Jesus raised Lazarus? The story contains an image of setting prisoners and captives free:

39 Jesus said, "Remove the stone." Martha, the sister of the deceased, said to Him, "Lord, by this time there will be a stench, for he has been dead four days." 40 Jesus said to her, "Did I not say to you, if you believe, you will see the glory of God?" 41 And so they removed the stone. And Jesus raised His eyes, and said, "Father, I thank Thee that Thou heard Me. 42 "And I knew that Thou hears Me always; but because of the people standing around I said it, that they may believe that Thou didst send Me." 43 And when He had said these things, He cried out with a loud voice, "Lazarus, come forth." 44 He who had died came forth, bound hand and foot with wrappings; and his face was wrapped around with a cloth. Jesus said to them, "Unbind him, and let him go." —John 11:39-44

Of course, I love the King James Version dialogue between Jesus and Martha where she says in verse 39, "Lord, by now he stinketh." Here we see Jesus calling Lazarus from the grave. How was Lazarus dressed when he came out? In grave clothes. On the other hand, when Jesus rose from the dead, he left his grave wrappings neatly folded and lying in the tomb. The first thing Jesus did when He rose from the dead was make His bed. Obviously, part of the resurrection miracle included new street clothes.

But not so with Lazarus. And it is possible that those wrappings did indeed stinketh. Jesus said to the people present, "Unbind him and let him go." They then proceeded to unwrap Lazarus one layer at a time. That is what setting captives and prisoners free can look like: the tedious effort of removing the grave clothes layer by layer. And yes, at times it can be unpleasant. That is what Jesus came to do and what he sends us to do as well. When new believers enter our churches, they come wrapped in their grave clothes. Our responsibility as the Church is likewise, "Unbind them and let them go."

As we pray for the lost in our realm of influence, we must prepare ourselves to go. Let us look at what Jesus said about praying and going.

> *3 Now after this the Lord appointed seventy others and sent them in pairs ahead of Him to every city and place where He Himself was going to come. 2 And He was saying to them, "The harvest is plentiful, but the laborers are few; therefore, beseech the Lord of the harvest to send out laborers into His harvest." 3 "Go; behold, I send you out as lambs in the midst of wolves." —Luke 10:1-3*

Here we see Jesus admonishing His disciples to pray for the harvest, specifically, for laborers who would go to the harvest. The harvest is indeed plentiful, and praying for the harvest is in the center of our Father's will. After we pray for the lost, what can we expect?

Verse 3 says, "Go! I am sending you." Praying is the first step, and going is the next necessary step. We must be willing to be the answer to our own prayers, and this is true of all things we pray for. So often, we pray to the Lord of the harvest to bring in the harvest Himself. How often I have heard prayers like this, "Oh Lord, bring the lost to our church" or "We call in the lost from the north, south, east, and west." We want God to bring them to our doorstep.

I often imagine that God hears prayers like these and sighs to Himself, "Didn't I tell you to go and bring them in?" Many church marquees say, "Visitors Welcome!" in an effort to fulfill the evangelism mandate. I was once speaking with a fellow when I noticed a sign in front of nearby church, which read, "Sinners Welcome!" I wonder if those sinners show up each Sunday.

Studies show that only about 10 percent of lost souls come to salvation within the confines of a church. I am not talking about children growing up in the church who commit to Christ in their youth but unchurched people who come to Christ later in their lives.

Jesus told His disciples to *go*! Without *"go"* there is no *Gospel*. Now consider this. Have you ever seen a farmer go out to his barn during harvest, throw wide the barn doors, and holler at the crops in the fields, "Come! Get in the barn!" Imagine him turning to the wheat field and shouting, "Wheat! Come! Get in the barn." When the wheat does not respond, he steps closer and repeats, this time a bit louder, "Wheat! Come on! Get in the barn." When it still refuses the offer, he shouts, "You rebellious wheat!"

That is our response at times when the lost do not respond to the offer to come to church. Now, would that farmer see his field harvested? Probably not. If the farmer wants to see the harvest, he must go out and work the field, gather the crop, and bring the harvest into the barn.

It is the same with the church. If we desire to see the harvest, we need to go to the harvest field and work among the lost to bring in the harvest of souls. The lost seldom show up at church on Sunday morning. Unbelievers who enter the church often find that it does not make any sense to them. They feel uncomfortable with the goings-on and do not return. And to tell you the truth, the lost are not supposed to come to church. The church is supposed to Go to the lost! I believe church is primarily for the saint. It is the place we gather to worship God, grow in Christ and His Word, be discipled, become more like Him, and be equipped for the work of service. This is made clear in Paul's letter to the Ephesians:

> *11 And He gave some as apostles, and some as prophets, and some as evangelists, and some as pastors and teachers, 12 for the equipping of the saints for the work of service, to the building up of the body of Christ; 13 until we all attain to the unity of the faith, and of the knowledge of the Son of God, to a mature man, to the measure of the stature which belongs to the fulness of Christ. 14 As a result, we are no*

longer to be children, tossed here and there by waves, and carried about by every wind of doctrine, by the trickery of men, by craftiness in deceitful scheming; 15 but speaking the truth in love, we are to grow up in all aspects into Him, who is the head, even Christ, 16 from whom the whole body, being fitted and held together by that which every joint supplies, according to the proper working of each individual part, causes the growth of the body for the building up of itself in love. —Ephesians 4:11–16

I have been involved in the work of soul-winning my entire Christian life. I have the gifting of an evangelist, but I do not believe I stepped into that gifting until I started equipping the saints for the work of service to be soul-winners. These fivefold gifts listed above are for the equipping of the saints for works of service, to the building up of the body of Christ, until we all attain to the unity of the faith and of the knowledge of the Son of God, to a mature man, to the measure of the stature that belongs to the fulness of Christ.

One night in downtown Denver I came across a church youth group out doing some sort of scavenger hunt. As I spoke with the group, a young lady asked me, "Are you an evangelist?"

I responded, "I don't know if being out here sharing my faith is evidence that I am an evangelist or if it is just evidence that I am a Christian."

Remember to ask God to open doors of opportunity to witness to those we desire to come to know Jesus. Earlier, I spoke of my brother-in-law, Randy, whom I prayed for diligently for 17 years. Finally, the night came when I heard the Lord of the harvest speak to me, "Now go! I am sending you."

"Pray the Lord of the harvest to send laborers to the harvest." The disciples were instructed to pray in this manner. Who then were the "laborers" who were sent to the harvest? The disciples! Whenever or whatever we are praying for, we must be willing to be used as the answer to that prayer. We not only need to pray for the lost in our realm of influence but also for the opportunity to share Jesus with them. Watch and see as the Lord brings those lost neighbors and friends and family to your doors. Listen to the voice of God in your inner man when He tells you to go to them, and you will see that He has prepared the way for you.

> *And He said to them, "Go into all the world and preach the gospel to all creation." —Mark 16:15*

"Go into all the world." Some are called to go across the oceans with the Gospel, while others are called to go across the street. But we are all called to go someplace and proclaim the good news of salvation. And wherever we go, there are people waiting to hear the good news.

I read a missionary account of a man who went to an unreached indigenous group of people. After several years of living and working with the group to learn their language and their culture, he began to share the Gospel story. Unlike our Western individualistic culture, where individual decision-making is encouraged and celebrated, this was a collective culture. In such a setting, individual decision is considered treasonous and a betrayal to communal standards.

Collective cultures require unique strategies of evangelization where the missionary guides the group into what is known as a people movement, where the group shares an interest in moving toward Christ. This missionary did not immediately push for personal decisions but listened as the people deliberated among themselves regarding this new idea. The end result was a community decision comprised of individual decisions and a collective group decision.

The new believers in the tribe were thrilled with their newfound belief. Afterwards, the tribal chief thanked the missionary for bringing the Good News. He then asked the missionary, "How long have you known this message?"

The missionary responded in some puzzlement, "Well, we have known this message for several thousand years now."

With a distressed look, the chief asked, "Why did it take you so long to get here? Our fathers and grandfathers died without ever hearing this Good News." It is not Good News if it arrives too late. There are people in our culture, living on our streets, who are waiting to hear the Gospel message. We must go to them before it is too late.

God has put into place the principle of reproduction. All things reproduce after their own kind, as it says in Genesis chapter 1. This same principle of reproduction is an active principle for Christians as well. Consider a couple who marry and try to have a baby. After the first year, no baby. No big deal, they will keep trying. After the second year, no baby. By this time, the wife cries at that certain time each month. After three years, no baby. After year four and year five, no baby. At some point, the couple will seek medical help. Why? Because it is not normal.

God created humans to reproduce, and it is not normal when they cannot. Now, in the Church, a believer can go one year, two years, five years, ten years, twenty years, and more without ever reproducing another believer. Some can go this long without ever speaking a word about Jesus outside of the walls of the church. And yet we never consider this abnormal. I have come across many people who have been sincerely thankful that I shared this Good News with them.

El Salvador Salvation Prayer.

Clowns for Jesus, El Salvador.

Soul-winning, Mazatlán Carnaval.

Street evangelism, Mazatlán, Mexico.

Kathleen ministering to family near Mexico City.

Ministry in El Milagro, El Salvador.

Ministry in El Milagro, El Salvador.

Mixteco Children, Oaxaca, Mexico.

High Mountain, Mixteco children, Oaxaca, Mexico.

Group devotion, Mexico City, when the fire fell.

Group devotion, Mexico City, when the fire fell.

Indigenous door-to-door soul-winning.

Indigenous Totonac people, Poza Rica, Veracruz, Mexico.

Indigenous Mixteco people, Oaxaca, Mexico.

126

Mexico City, Jorge, who came to Christ in the Northern Prison with family.

I walked along the 16th Street open area mall in downtown Denver one cold winter's night. The air smelled like snow. I noticed a young man leaning against a building. When I stopped to converse with him, I learned he had been saved in a street mission that week. He gladly accepted my offer of a New Testament. Then I offered him a hat and some gloves, and finally a sack of food, which he also received happily.

As I handed him the items, I realized he was only using one arm to gather the items, while the other arm was withered and frozen up against his shoulder. He told me he had a muscle disorder; during the Iraqi war, Desert Storm, in 1991, exposure to chemical warfare had caused this condition. I asked him if I could pray, and he said yes. After praying, I could see that his hand and arm were still frozen and withered.

But then he started to wiggle his fingers on the withered hand. I realized this young man had faith for healing, which inspired faith in me. I prayed again, but this time in an unorthodox manner. The Holy Spirit rose up in me, and I began to repeat, "Oh Lord, just bring it, bring it, bring it!" At that point, the young man stretched out his withered hand, looked at it, and fell in a heap on the ground, weeping uncontrollably. I was somewhat embarrassed to stand over him and witness this amazingly intimate moment with Jesus.

After a while, he gathered himself and stood up. He invited me to spend some time with him, so we walked several blocks to some steam grates feeding off the US District Courthouse building. Twenty or more people were camped out over these steam grates, which provide a warm place of refuge. It was lightly snowing as I sat down with the crowd and began to share the Good News message. I gave out New Testaments, and we had a Bible study while sitting on the grates with the snow falling from above. The people squatting there were genuinely thankful for my time, and I visited them several times over the next weeks.

As I walked away from the young man and the homeless community, I thought to myself, "I should have called Kathleen or one of my friends to confirm this miracle." But the Holy Spirit spoke, "Bob, it's not about you. It is about my love for this young man. He has nothing to offer Me. But I love him and healed him because I love him."

When I started preparing for my first junior high ministry Mexico mission trip in the spring of 1998, we were given an assignment to learn some Spanish. We all received a handbook with several pages of Spanish phrases and the plan of salvation in English and Spanish. My initial thought was, "I don't need to do this. This is for the students." The next morning during my quiet time, the Holy Spirit challenged my attitude, making it clear that I did need to do this.

I did not see how this would change the way I witnessed, but He did. I took index cards and wrote out English and Spanish phrases, one to a card, and I did the same with the plan of salvation and the salvation prayer. A friend of mine made a cassette tape for me so I could learn the proper Spanish pronunciation. At that time, I knew no Spanish whatsoever. Despite memorizing those index cards, I did not use those phrases or plan of salvation a single time on the mission trip.

And yet, I began to carry the phrase cards with me on the streets of Longmont on Friday nights. One night I approached a group of three people, a father, his teenage daughter, and his twenty-something nephew, none of whom spoke English. Somehow, I was able to initiate a conversation using the Spanish phrases I had memorized. While sharing the plan of salvation in Spanish, I totally forgot the remainder of the salvation message. The Holy Spirit gently reminded me, "You have the index cards in your pocket."

My initial thought was, "Yeah, but it would be lame to get the cards out and read from them."

The Holy Spirit responded, "What is more important? Your feelings or the salvation of these people?" Jesus is so patient with me! I got the cards out, finished the Good News message, and invited them to pray with me. We read the salvation prayer off the index card together. Afterward, I gave them Spanish New Testaments and Spanish tracts.

For many years, I have carried a small multipage booklet in English and Spanish from the Billy Graham Evangelistic Association called "Steps to Peace with God." A number of times, I led Spanish-speaking people to Jesus with the tract, using the pages in English to help me guide a Spanish-speaking person to salvation. Whatever it takes, right?

A few days after sharing with that Mexican family, I received a phone call from the friend who had been with me that night. At work that morning, a Mexican co-worker, who was a Christian, came to his cubicle and asked if he had been on Main Street Friday night sharing the Gospel. He acknowledged he had. His co-worker said, "You need to come back to the mail room. Hector, whom you guys led to Christ, is sharing his testimony to the entire mail room. There is a revival in the mail room!" The nephew we had shared with on Friday night worked at the same company as my co-laborer in the Gospel. He had been transformed by the Gospel message, and he wanted to share that transforming message with his friends and co-workers.

And to think, I was hesitant to learn the Gospel message in Spanish. In those early years of learning it, I was just making sounds with my mouth, but they happened to make sense to those I talked to. This taught me about the power connected with the Gospel message. If we can just share it, it will accomplish what it is sent forth to do. Today, after 18 years in the harvest fields of Mexico, El Salvador, and Cuba, I have shared that plan of salvation thousands of times. By the way, I still have those index cards 22 years later. I do not have to use them any longer, but they remind me that a soul is more valuable than whether or not I may feel lame about my Spanish skills.

Before moving on, let me share with you one more experience of my growth in my Spanish proficiency. In downtown Denver is a little park I used to visit frequently on Friday nights. It was known for drug dealing, especially among the Hispanic population. On this night, a group of about eight young Honduran men in their twenties were peddling their trade. They did not speak English. Undocumented immigrants, they had come to the land of promise, only to find out it was not as promising as they were promised. They were unable to gain employment and didn't take the drugs themselves but had to resort to selling drugs on the street: heroin, cocaine, and meth. Because I really liked these guys, I stopped by every Friday night to share the Gospel message with them. Understand, I could not speak Spanish except for the words on my index cards.

Every Friday night, then, I dropped by and shared the same Spanish Gospel message with them. None would respond, but while I was there, they would stop their trade and listen respectfully to the Good News message. One night, they found a guy among them who could speak some English. He greeted me with great respect and said, "Sir, would you please leave? None of us will sell our drugs while you are here with us." I said goodnight and told them I would see them the following week.

I connected with one young man in the group. His girlfriend worked in the McDonald's on the mall, and he brought me there to introduce me to her. She was an American of Mexican heritage, and I got to know her pretty well. I occasionally stopped by to see her at the restaurant. One late night, she exited the McDonald's in front of me, so we walked to the light-rail mass transit system together. I shared the Gospel message with her as we approached her station and was at the point of invitation when her train arrived, and the door opened. I asked her quickly if she would like to invite Jesus into her heart to be her Savior and Lord, and she said yes. There was no time to pray, so I asked if she could confess Jesus as her Savior and Lord. She nodded yes. I said to her, "Then say it." She confessed, "Jesus is my Savior and Lord." With that, the door slid shut. As the train pulled away, I waved to her, and she waved back, with tears running down her face.

Some weeks later I was at home with Kathleen and my family on a weeknight when the phone rang. It was the young lady from the train, who asked if I could come to Denver to speak with her and her Honduran boyfriend. Sure, I told her, and Kathleen and I loaded up in the van and headed for Denver. We found the house, an ancient house bordering the downtown area. They lived in the cavern of the basement with the centerpiece of their little lodging a century-old boiler used to heat the home.

The night this young lady had confessed Jesus as her Savior had transformed her life. She had repeatedly discussed her newfound faith with her boyfriend. He asked her to contact me to come and tell him more. We talked for hours, and he was reluctant to make a decision for Christ, due to his work as a drug dealer. He knew drug dealing was not compatible with a life in Christ.

After some further conversation, we did pray with him and provided a Spanish New Testament. Then we loaded up in the van and drove to a nearby church I had seen many times while ministering in the area. It seemed like a church geared to the street culture. The people in the church welcomed them in and provided information regarding their services and ministry.

In the following chapter, we will look at our powerful soul-winning tool, the Gospel message. We will look at what the message is and the power hidden within the message.

It is the greatest pleasure of living to win souls to Christ.[30]
—Dwight L. Moody

Let our voice be heard and not be afraid nor intimidated by those who try to get us to shut up and dry out. Real ambassadors publish the Good News and the good tidings and get as many people saved as they can. Going soul winning regularly will make the difference in our society.[31] — Shelton Smith

11

Essential #7: Power—The Message

"Some wish to live within the sound of church and chapel bell. I want to run a rescue shop within a yard of hell!"[32] —*C.T. Studd*

"One Way: Jesus! One Job: Evangelism!"[33] —*T.L. Osborn*

"I'm all for lifestyle evangelism, but I'm also in favor of intentionality, where we seek out opportunities for spiritual conversations and are equipped to explain the Gospel and why we believe it."[34] —*Lee Strobel*

"1 Now I make known to you, brethren, the gospel which I preached to you, which also you received, in which also you stand, 2 by which also you are saved, if you hold fast the word which I preached to you, unless you believed in vain. 3 For I delivered to you as of first importance what I also received, that Christ died for our sins according to the Scriptures, 4 and that He was buried, and that He was raised on the third day according to the Scriptures, 5 and that He appeared to Cephas, then to the twelve. 6 After that He appeared to more than five hundred brethren at

one time, most of whom remain until now, but some have fallen asleep; 7 then He appeared to James, then to all the apostles." —*1 Corinthians 15:1–7*

LET US REVIEW. We started with the understanding that the first essential in effective evangelism is our personal relationship with Jesus. We must know him personally, not just know about him. Evangelism should be introducing someone to our dear friend Jesus Christ. Few people struggle with introducing their friends to their other friends. Passion for Christ is the greatest and most important essential in soul-winning.

The second essential comes from the first. Our passion for Jesus will lead to His compassion for the world of lost souls. As we lay our head on His chest day by day, we will hear His heartbeat of "None lost! All saved!"

Thirdly, we have seen the end of the lost soul in eternity, eternally lost in a hell created for the devil, not for man.

Fourth, we have seen the power in praying for the lost in our realm of influence. We have begun prayer campaigns and determined we will pray for those we know who are without Christ until (1) they are saved, (2) they die, or (3) we die.

The fifth essential is knowing what it is we need to focus our spiritual warfare on for the lost. (1) The devil has taken the lost captive, and (2) our adversary, the devil, has also blinded their minds to the truth of the Gospel, making lies appear as the truth. This is our warfare focus in prayer, to bind the enemy, to bind his lies, to expose his lies, so that when the truth is made known, it will be recognized as truth, and truth will set the captives and prisoners free.

And the sixth essential as we saw in the previous chapter is that we can expect to *go* with the Gospel message. After we have prayed, we must be ready to be the answer to our prayers. We can expect to hear the voice of the Lord of the harvest as He says to us: "Now go, for I am sending you." Now that we have heard His voice to go, what tool do we possess to bring in the harvest of souls?

In this chapter we will look at the greatest tool we have been given to win the lost: the Gospel message. We will see what the message is and the power that accompanies our message when we faithfully share it.

> *For I am not ashamed of the gospel, for it is the power of God for salvation to everyone who believes, to the Jew first and also to the Greek. —Romans 1:16*

The Gospel is the power of God for salvation to everyone who believes. There is an inherent power in the Gospel message. Remember the Word of God is alive, it is living and active, and it will accomplish what it is sent forth to do. There is a power in the Gospel greater than our ability to express it. There is something powerful that takes place between the moment the words leave our lips until they reach the ears of the hearer. In that interim of time and space the Holy Spirit applies His power. I strongly believe there is a place in our witnessing for our testimonies, illustrations, and apologetics. But after all of this, it is the Gospel message that carries the power needed to penetrate the heart of the hearer. Remember, our message is aimed at the heart, not the head or intellect. Believing the message in the heart leads to salvation. Let us look at the next verse:

> *17 For Christ did not send me to baptize, but to preach the gospel, not in cleverness of speech, so that the cross of Christ would not be made void. 18 For the word of the cross is foolishness to those who are perishing, but to us who are being saved it is the power of God. —1 Corinthians 1:17, 18*

Let us pare this verse down a bit to see where the emphasis lies. "The word (or message) of the cross is the power of God for salvation." Again, Paul repeats here that there is a power inherent in the message of the cross. If this Gospel message is the power of salvation, we had better proclaim it. We must understand that, as we are faithful to proclaim the message, it is the Holy Spirit that is revealing the truth of the message in the hearts of the hearer. We must learn to depend on the Holy Spirit to bring about the new birth in those who are hearing our message.

I once was witnessing in a mall with my son Shiloh. Shiloh and I were both missionaries in different parts of Mexico at the time. We happened to be together in northern Colorado at the same time, so we went out to share our faith. We happened upon a young man, about my son's age. This fellow had several tattoos, one being a bar code on his neck. Shiloh also was laden with tattoos, so they hit it off pretty well. After a time of discussing the personal significance of each of their tattoos, I asked the young fellow if I could ask him a question.

"Sure," he responded.

I asked, "If you were to die tonight, can you be sure where you would spend eternity?"

His response was one I do not think I had ever heard before. He said: "Probably hell because I'm not a Christian or anything."

My response was, "Do you want to become a Christian tonight?'"

"Sure!" was his reply.

I reached out my hand and invited him to take it and repeat a prayer with me. When he took my hand, I heard the Holy Spirit say to me, "The Gospel is the power of God for salvation." I slammed on the brakes and retraced my steps. Then I shared the Gospel message. When I was through, guess what happened. He still wanted to become a Christian then and there. I clearly understood in that moment how important the message is for salvation.

I would like to share something that I hope will not get too many stones thrown at me. It is the Gospel message that Paul delivers to us. Paul tells us he received the Gospel he preached through a revelation of Jesus Christ. We have now looked primarily at the Apostle Paul's statements concerning the Gospel and its power in this chapter and will continue to focus on the Gospel Paul delivered to the Church throughout the remainder of the chapter. Let us establish that fact:

> *11 For I would have you know, brethren, that the gospel which was preached by me is not according to man. 12 For I neither received it from man, nor was I taught it, but I received it through a revelation of Jesus Christ. —*
> *Galatians 1:11,12*

So Paul's Gospel is by a revelation of Jesus Christ. The Epistle to the Galatians referenced above was written in Ephesus at the time of Paul's two-year stay there during his third missionary journey.

I am not exactly sure when Paul had this revelation, but I believe it may have happened during his travel from Athens to Corinth during his second missionary journey. Something significant took place between the time Paul left Athens and arrived in Corinth.

First let us look at Paul's message on Mars Hill in Athens. You can find this in Acts 17:22–34.

Paul Addresses the Areopagus

> *22 So Paul stood in the midst of the Areopagus and said, "Men of Athens, I observe that you are very religious in all respects. 23 "For while I was passing through and examining the objects of your worship, I also found an altar with this inscription, 'TO AN UNKNOWN GOD.' Therefore what you worship in ignorance, this I proclaim to you. 24 "The God who made the world and all things in it, since He is Lord of heaven and earth, does not dwell in temples made with hands; 25 nor is He served by human hands, as though He needed anything, since He Himself gives to all people life and breath and all things; 26 and He made from one man every nation of mankind to live on all the face of*

the earth, having determined their appointed times and the boundaries of their habitation, 27 that they would seek God, if perhaps they might grope for Him and find Him, though He is not far from each one of us; 28 for in Him we live and move and exist, as even some of your own poets have said, 'For we also are His children.' 29 "Being then the children of God, we ought not to think that the Divine Nature is like gold or silver or stone, an image formed by the art and thought of man. 30 "Therefore having overlooked the times of ignorance, God is now declaring to men that all people everywhere should repent, 31 because He has fixed a day in which He will judge the world in righteousness through a Man whom He has appointed, having furnished proof to all men by raising Him from the dead." 32 Now when they heard of the resurrection of the dead, some began to sneer, but others said, "We shall hear you again concerning this." 33 So Paul went out of their midst. 34 But some men joined him and believed, among whom also were Dionysius the Areopagite and a woman named Damaris and others with them. —Acts 17:22–34

First and foremost, I would like to affirm that every word of this sermon is divinely inspired truth. Paul does well in identifying with his listeners through the things they were familiar with, "an altar to an unknown God." They were philosophers and intellectuals, and Paul speaks to them on the level of their education and experience. This level of identification with our listeners is of immense importance in conveying our message, and the Apostle Paul imparts to us valuable communication skills in his effort here. The issue here is not what Paul said, it is what he did not say. Look closely at this address. Nowhere will you find references of Jesus's name, sin, or the crucifixion of Christ for the sins of humankind. While his message contained truth, it fell short of what he will later call the Gospel he preaches. Okay, so please stay with me here, Paul is going to teach us the importance of certain elements of the Gospel message; these elements are indispensable and are where the power of the message is derived from. Acts 17 ends with the names of two people who believed in Athens, Dionysius and Damaris. Acts 18 begins with:

> *After these things he left Athens and went to Corinth.*
> *—Acts 18:1*

Paul leaves Athens for Corinth, about a 65-mile journey, so maybe three days travel on foot or beast. Something transpires along the way. I believe Paul was not afraid to evaluate his ministry, and during this journey he assessed what transpired in Athens. Now let us look at Paul's first letter to the Corinthians and see his conclusions of his evaluations.

> *17 For Christ did not send me to baptize, but to preach the gospel, <u>not in cleverness of speech, so that the cross of Christ would not be made void.</u> 18 For the word of the cross is foolishness to those who are perishing, but to us who are being saved it is the power of God. —1 Corinthians 1:17, 18*

In coming to Corinth Paul came determined to preach not with cleverness of speech, like at Mars Hill. He understood that merely appealing to human wisdom would void the power of the message of the cross of Christ. That word, void, means to diminish in its ability to accomplish its purpose. The message of the cross of Christ has the power and ability to accomplish its purpose. By our presentation we can diminish the inherent power of the message. We must trust in the Gospel message and the power that God has instilled in it and depend on the Holy Spirit to deliver the truth of the message. I believe Paul recognized the futility in appealing to human intellect and human wisdom and recognized there is a power beyond our abilities in the message. He continues:

19 For it is written, "I WILL DESTROY THE WISDOM OF THE WISE, AND THE CLEVERNESS OF THE CLEVER I WILL SET ASIDE." 20 Where is the wise man? Where is the scribe? Where is the debater of this age? Has not God made foolish the wisdom of the world? 21 For since in the wisdom of God the world through its wisdom did not come to know God, God was well-pleased through the foolishness of the message preached to save those who believe. 22 For indeed Jews ask for signs and Greeks search for wisdom; 23 but we preach Christ crucified, to Jews a stumbling block and to Gentiles foolishness, 24 but to those who are the called, both Jews and Greeks, Christ the power of God and the wisdom of God. 25 Because the foolishness of God is wiser than men, and the weakness of God is stronger than men. —1 Corinthians 1:19–23

The Gospel message is foolishness to the human intellect. The Gospel must be grasped by the heart of man. God is well pleased that man in his wisdom cannot come to know Him. We must enter the kingdom as little children. Paul realized his aim was about 18 inches too high in Athens. That is about the distance between the heart and the head. He was aiming at the head and not the heart. And we as the bearers of the message are considered as the message itself:

For consider your calling, brethren, that there were not many wise according to the flesh, not many mighty, not many noble; 27 but God has chosen the foolish things of the world to shame the wise, and God has chosen the weak things of the world to shame the things which are strong, 28 and the base things of the world and the despised God has chosen, the things that are not, so that He may nullify the things that are, 29 so that no man may boast before God. 30 But by His doing you are in Christ Jesus, who became

to us wisdom from God, and righteousness and sanctifica-
tion, and redemption, 31 so that, just as it is written, "LET
HIM WHO BOASTS, BOAST IN THE LORD." —1
Corinthians 1:26–31 26

As the message is considered foolish to the intellectual mind, so the messenger is considered foolish for proclaiming it. God chooses to confound the wise. He uses the foolish things, the weak things, the base and despised things, and the things that are not to accomplish His purpose. That is all right with me. I do not mind being considered as these things by this world to bring glory to my Father. Often witnessing to people on the streets confirms how this world considers the messengers of God. It is hard to harbor pride if you regularly witness to people in public places. Now recall in Paul's address to the Areopagites he made no mention of Jesus Christ, sin, or the crucifixion. Look at the message he determined to bring to Corinth:

1 And when I came to you, brethren, I did not come with
superiority of speech or of wisdom, proclaiming to you the
testimony of God. 2 For I determined to know nothing
among you except Jesus Christ, and Him crucified. 3 I was
with you in weakness and in fear and in much trembling,
4 and my message and my preaching were not in persuasive
words of wisdom, but in demonstration of the Spirit and
of power, 5 so that your faith would not rest on the wisdom
of men, but on the power of God. —1 Corinthians 2:1–5

I determined to know nothing, nothing, except Jesus Christ, and Him crucified. I did not come with superiority of speech or wisdom. Can you see the difference in Paul's presence in Athens and his presence in Corinth? Paul recognized there is an inherent power in the Gospel message, and he determined he would trust in that power alone. I do not know when the Gospel Paul received through the revelation of Jesus Christ occurred, but there was certainly a transformation that took place on his way to Corinth. I am grateful for Paul's pliability in the Holy Spirit's hands to be taught of Him and then to impart to you and me this great treasure of learning where the power in the Gospel lies.

Now let us continue to look in Paul's first letter to the Corinthians to see what exactly Paul's Gospel is. I think you will find it is much simpler than expected.

> *1 Now I make known to you, brethren, the gospel which I preached to you, which also you received, in which also you stand, 2 by which also you are saved, if you hold fast the word which I preached to you, unless you believed in vain. 3 For I delivered to you as of first importance what I also received, that Christ died for our sins according to the Scriptures, 4 and that He was buried, and that He was raised on the third day according to the Scriptures, 5 and that He appeared to Cephas, then to the twelve. 6 After that He appeared to more than five hundred brethren at one time, most of whom remain until now, but some have fallen asleep; 7 then He appeared to James, then to all the apostles. —1 Corinthians 15:1–7*

Here we will find out the elements of Paul's Gospel. But first he tells of the results of preaching the Gospel message. First, it must be preached, it must be proclaimed in some form whether speech, printed, or even dramatized. Being proclaimed in some form gives the hearer the opportunity to hear the voice of God. Faith comes from hearing, and hearing by the word of Christ (Romans 10:17). The Greek word used here for "word" is rhema: the present, uttered, spoken word of God. When we proclaim the Gospel, the voice of the Holy Spirit confirms its truth in the heart. So it is proclaimed so that it can be heard and then it must be received, and finally we must take a stand on it, that is, believing it and putting our faith in it.

Only receiving the word is not the point of salvation. In the parable of the sower, three types of soil received the seed, but only one bore fruit. Remember the story I told previously about the young woman on the pay phone whom I had talked with years earlier. The night I spoke to her, she received the seed, but it did not spring to life until years later, the night she lay on the floor having been beaten by her boyfriend. That night she took her stand on the message preached years earlier. Do you know there are people in our churches today that have received the message but have not taken their stand on it? They may like the message, even agree with it, but have never put their unwavering faith in it. See, Paul tells us that salvation is this process: the message must be proclaimed so that it can be heard in the heart; then it must be received, and a resolute stand on it is taken. Then verse 2: "By which you are saved." So that is the process.

But what is the Gospel? Verses 3 and 4: (1) Christ died (2) for our sins and (3) was buried and (4) He rose again. All of this according to scripture, specifically Old Testament scripture. Each of these four elements can be elaborated on as we share the message as the Holy Spirit leads. Such as He died on the Cross of Calvary. He was buried in the tomb, and after three days he rose again. Paul adds here his resurrection can be attested to by over 500 witnesses.

Acts chapter 10, verses 34 through 48, is the account of Peter's sermon in the Gentile Centurion, Cornelius's home. I encourage you to review it. His sermon only lasts about two minutes, the moment Peter encompasses all four of these points, the power and presence of the Holy Spirit falls on the listeners and all are saved and filled with the Holy Spirit. Paul in his communications throughout the first letter to the Corinthians presents the indispensable elements of the Gospel. First, Christ died; second, he died for our sins; third, he was buried; and fourth, he rose again. That fourth element is especially important, sometimes we neglect the resurrection in our Gospel presentation.

Without the resurrection our story is about a good man, who went about doing good and died for a good cause. The resurrection changes everything, it adds the dimension of divine power, confirming the deity of Christ. The resurrection confirms everything Jesus proclaimed about Himself and His mission here on the earth. It supports the concepts of our resurrection to new life and the bodily resurrection of the believers in the end of all things. Do not forget to declare the resurrection in soul-winning.

I have found it helpful to follow various outlines in sharing my faith. Remember the indispensable elements that the Apostle Paul has taught us in your outline. A Gospel outline will help you to follow a pattern to ensure you cover all of the elements of the Gospel, and it can help you to return to your presentation when you turn aside to answer questions or give an illustration. In our citywide "Invasion" conferences, which we have hosted in more than 100 cities throughout Mexico, we teach a plan of salvation in four steps. They are: Plan, Problem, Solution, and Decision.

We start with Plan: God has a plan for us to have a relationship with Him.

Problem: But there is a problem, and that is our offenses toward a Holy God. He is Holy. We are sinners, and our sins separate us from God.

Solution: God sent His Son, Jesus Christ. Jesus is the Son of God and God the Son. Jesus died on the Cross of Calvary to pay our debt for sin and restore our relationship with the Father. He died and was buried. He was in the grave for three days, but the story does not end there. On the third day Jesus rose again to new life and He is alive today and would like to live within you through the Holy Spirit.

Decision (this is also the persuasion element I shared with you earlier): Would you like to decide to accept God's plan for your life and accept His forgiveness through Jesus Christ? Of course, if they say yes, we pray a prayer of salvation with them. I feel this prayer will identify a definite point in time for them when they made this decision, and it will be the moment where they made the confession with their mouth that Jesus is Lord. If you confess with your mouth Jesus *as* Lord and believe in your heart that God raised Him from the dead, you will be saved (Romans 10:9).

One of my favorite Gospel outlines is the Gospel acronym: G.O.S.P.E.L. For many years we taught this to our junior high youth group and would take them to the local mall to share their faith. Over the years these young men and women became quite proficient in winning souls. It is an easy outline to learn and quite suitable for young men and women. It goes like this: <u>G</u>od created us to be with Him. <u>O</u>ur sin separates us from Him. <u>S</u>in cannot be erased by good deeds. <u>P</u>aying the price for sin Christ died, was buried, and rose again. <u>E</u>veryone who trusts in Him alone has eternal life. <u>L</u>ife that's eternal means we will be with Him forever.

There are several other Gospel outlines such as: "The Four Spiritual Laws." Or "John's Road to Eternal Life," which follows the Plan, Problem, Solution, Decision outline: Plan: John 3:16; Problem: John 10:10 and John 8:34; Solution: John 1:29 and John 3:3; Decision: John 1:12.

The Romans Road to Heaven also follows the Plan, Problem, Solution, Decision outline:

> *Plan (Romans 5:8): "But God demonstrates His own love toward us, in that while we were yet sinners, Christ died for us."*

> *Problem (Romans 3:23): "For all have sinned and fall short of the glory of God."*

> *Solution (Romans 6:23): "For the wages of sin is death, but the free gift of God is eternal life in Christ Jesus our Lord."*

> *Decision (Romans 10:9,10): "If you confess with your mouth Jesus as Lord, and believe in your heart that God*

*raised Him from the dead, you will be saved; 10 for with
the heart a person believes, resulting in righteousness, and
with the mouth he confesses, resulting in salvation."*

For many years I have followed an outline in my Gospel presentation. As I share the Gospel message, I am also sensitive to the Holy Spirit regarding illustrations, stories, or testimonies I might share to highlight each point. One night on Main Street in Longmont I approached two young men hanging out in a parking lot. As I engaged them in a conversation one of the young men told me I had spoken with him about eight or nine months earlier. I could not remember the meeting. I asked them if I could share my message with them, nevertheless. They said I could. As I began to share the Gospel points, I would have a sense to share different illustrations. Now I do not share the same illustrations and stories with each person I meet. But here, each illustration I was led to share, the young man I had spoken to months earlier would tell me: "Yeah, you said that last time we spoke." I mean three or four times he interrupted to tell me "You said that last time we met." I realized the Holy Spirit was re-emphasizing certain points He wanted the young man to hear.

At the end of the presentation I asked him if he would like to invite Jesus to be his Savior and Lord tonight. He declined the offer. I turned to his friend, and I could see the Holy Spirit's presence on him. He accepted the invitation without hesitation. As I was leading this young man in a prayer of salvation, I could hear the first young man praying with us. Finishing the prayer, I turned to the first young man and asked: "Did you just invite Jesus into your heart?" Grinning, he nodded yes.

For ten years I worked with my good pal Pastor Bob with the junior high youth. One of the powerful regular activities of the ministry that produced disciples, and a lot of excitement, was sharing their faith. Every other month or so we would take the youth to the local mall for what we called the "Mall Outreach." We would have a time of training and prayer on the youth bus and then turn them loose in groups of three. One member of the group was designated as the group's intercessor while the other two witnessed. These outreaches were greatly productive both in the student's lives and in the souls won to Christ. They really became proficient in sharing their faith. We used the G.O.S.P.E.L. acronym with the students, which became a powerful tool among the youth. Following the outreach as we boarded the bus, we would have a time of testimonies, and they were incredible. After the outreach, the atmosphere on the bus was electric.

One Saturday afternoon after we had dropped the students off in a parking lot across the street from the mall, Pastor Bob and I were closing up the bus before heading into the mall. After securing the bus I noticed a group of four young people walking away from the mall in the parking lot where we had parked. I felt a strong leading from the Holy Spirit to follow them. The group crossed the parking lot to a smaller shopping mall with us following them. As they walked along the sidewalk next to the smaller shopping center a city bus pulled up and they boarded it and sped away. I was puzzled by this turn of events, having clearly sensed we were supposed to speak with them.

We turned around and headed toward the mall where the youth group had gone. Approaching an intersection of the street that circles the mall we saw a group of four young people walking along coming from the direction we had just come from. I called to them, and they waited for us to cross over to their side of the street. We began a conversation with them and found out they had just gotten off the same bus the first group of four had boarded. Now we knew why we felt we were supposed to follow the first group. As we spoke to the group, I received a word of knowledge from the Holy Spirit. Words of knowledge are part of the nine gifts of the Holy Spirit found in Paul's first letter to the Corinthians in chapter 12. We will look closer at these gifts in the following chapter. The word I heard from the Holy Spirit concerned one of the young girls. I sensed that she had been sexually violated in her early youth. Now a word like that cannot be just blurted out, so I asked the Lord, What do you want me to do with this?

We continued to impart the Gospel message with the group, and they were very attentive; at the conclusion of our presentation they all agreed to receive Jesus as their Savior and Lord. We prayed with them, and as we completed our witness, I turned to the girl the Holy Spirit had highlighted to me and said to her, "Something happened to you years ago that robbed you of your sense of acceptance by others. You feel unworthy, undeserving, and rejected by people around you. Jesus wants to touch you and heal you in this area you have been broken." Immediately tears began to flow. One of the young men went to her quickly and it was evident he had a gift of compassion in leadership. We prayed for that young girl and could see freedom come to her in her captivity. We commended the young man for his compassion toward others and had a word of knowledge for him regarding a pastoral gift in him. He thoroughly acknowledged that word and its truth for his life. What occurred there was a divinely inspired moment. Souls were saved, captives set free, and destinies set in place. I guess when you learn to be led by the Holy Spirit, He will manage to keep you in His timetable.

A number of years ago I was leading a youth mission trip in Mexico City. We hosted two church youth groups from Texas for a week. Each youth group ministered throughout the city in parks, plazas, and several men's, women's, and juvenile prisons. I was with a group that went to a men's prison in the northern area of Mexico City's metropolitan area. There are twenty-one to twenty-four million inhabitants in this region. After getting our team of maybe twenty people through screening and processing to enter the prison we walked through the prison yard to the prison auditorium.

As we walked through the yard, thousands of men dressed in off-white prison uniforms crowded us on either side requiring us to walk in a single file line. One of our staff workers led the team while I followed at the rear of the line. Honestly, it was a bit intimidating walking through that sea of men.

We entered the auditorium where over 500 prisoners had gathered to await our arrival. As I have often noticed while working in Mexico's prisons, there were no guards present. Our Mexico City staff co-worker, Alma, was with me and introduced me to the prison pastor. He was a prisoner himself. Typically, when we are hosting mission teams, we have a program using dramas to portray the Gospel message, followed by an invitation for salvation, followed by prayer and distribution of Gospel literature.

The prison pastor asked me if I was going to preach.

"Sure!" was my response. "How soon?" I asked.

"Ten-minutes," was his response.

I stepped back while Alma continued her discussion with the pastor. I had not come prepared to preach, so I asked the Holy Spirit, "What do you want me to speak to your people?"

He said to me, "Teach them what I have been teaching you in your quiet times during the past several weeks."

For several weeks I had been meditating on Acts chapter 27, Paul's shipwreck on his journey to Rome as a prisoner. I had seen a series of clear-cut events that took place that led to the shipwreck. I saw in this chapter seven distinct steps that were taken resulting in the loss of the ship. I looked around the auditorium and saw hundreds of men who had shipwrecked their lives, and the message I had been given over the course of the last weeks would be relevant to my captive audience. I had no notes, but I had something better, fresh bread.

Our team went up onto the stage of the auditorium, and we presented our Gospel dramas first. Several hundred men responded to the invitation for salvation. After praying with them we distributed New Testaments to each new believer. Then I took the pulpit, and Alma translated for me.

I named my teaching there on the spot: "Seven Steps to Shipwreck your Life and One Step to Avoid Shipwreck." After sixteen years working throughout Latin America my Spanish is still too deficient to preach or teach. Linguistics is not my gift. The message was suitable for the audience. It came across beautifully; often you know when you are moving with the anointing and hitting your target. The congregation was open and enthusiastic regarding what they were hearing.

As we finished the ministry, we invited the prisoners who would like prayer to come forward to the platform. About a hundred men responded. We went out with our team to pray for the men. Kathleen and I prayed for several men when we came upon a particularly distraught man. He was married, had two children, and there was no one to take care of his family. He was afraid his wife would leave him while he was in prison. Kathleen and I began to pray for him. Together we spoke three words of knowledge over his situation. The first was that he would find great favor from the authorities in the next couple of months. The second was that God will take care of his family and send others to take care of them as well. The third was his family will be there to meet him when he walked out of the prison. And that was that, or so I thought. Often, we can speak such things over people and never expect to hear the outcome.

Fast-forward three-years. I was leading another youth mission trip in Mexico City. We had gone into a neighborhood called La Prensa in the midst of the city. We were working with a satellite church of the main church we have worked with for 25 years, Restoration Church. The young woman Alma, whom I mentioned previously, is the daughter of the pastor, Victor, who oversees about 35 satellite churches throughout the region. It was market day in La Prensa. Almost every neighborhood has one day a week that is market day. On market day armies of vendors set up in the streets to sell. Some sell fruits and vegetables, some hardware, some electronics, some stolen goods. It is a potpourri of mercantile goods available. We set up in several locations throughout the morning and presented the Gospel dramas. There were a good number of responses.

At the final ministry site before lunch, a man approached me and asked if I had been in the northern prison three years ago. I told him I had. He asked if my wife has long white hair. I told him she has. Then he told me his story. This was the man we had prophesied over three years ago. He told me first of all, on that day, all the prisoners were surprised that you all would leave the platform and come down to us to pray for us. No one ever does that. Next, he told me the day after we left, he went out into the prison yard and sat down and determined he would not move from his spot until he personally heard the voice of God speaking in his heart. I had spoken about this the day I preached from the platform in the prison auditorium. He spent the entire day waiting to hear the voice of the Spirit. As the day was ending, he recognized that still small voice deep in his spirit. This event solidified his resolve to go after Christ. He became active in the prison congregation. He devoured the Word of God we had given him. He began to pray fervently for his family and share his faith with them when they came to visit him. His family all received Jesus as their Savior and Lord. He received an emergency call one night, from his daughter about 12 years old. His young son had crashed his bicycle and severely cut his leg open. He was bleeding to a point where he was close to bleeding out. After being rushed to the hospital they were able to stop the bleeding, but he had lost a lot of blood and doctors were not sure of his prognosis. The father told his daughter to go into the son's hospital room, lay hands on him, and in the name of Jesus speak life and healing over him, which she did. The son survived. A little while later his wife became extremely ill. She was bedridden for weeks up to a month. There was no one to take care of her or the children. There was no income. He prayed for his family. Several days into this sickness two women from a nearby church came to visit her and saw her condition. They took care of her and the children until she became well. The two women were from the same Restoration Church we were working with that day. The church was two and a half blocks from the family's home. Then, four months after our visit, the man was called to the prison administrator's office. He was told the officials had made a terrible mistake and he could go home right now. He was sent to gather up his belongings and was released immediately. As he walked out of the prison, having had no time to call his wife and family, his family was walking toward the prison. Three prophetic words we spoke over him that day three-years earlier. The first was that he would find great favor from the authorities in the next couple of months. The second was that God will take care of his family and send others to take care of them as well. The third was his family will be there to meet him when he walked out of the prison. He remembered those three words and saw the results in his life. Again, this strengthened his faith.

I went to visit his home and wife and family after the ministry site. It was a celebration atmosphere. His son showed me the scars on his leg from the bicycle injury. His wife cried, and the man was honored I would come into his home. He took a picture of Christ seated over Jerusalem off his wall and presented it to me; it hangs in my home office today. Afterward, he and his family joined us at the church a few blocks away for lunch. Twenty-one to twenty-four million people in Mexico City—only a divine appointment could arrange this.

In the next chapter we are going to look at signs, wonders, miracles, the gifts of the Holy Spirit, and angels, yes angels in evangelism ministry.

We talk of the second coming, half the world has never heard of the first.[35] —Oswald J. Smith

You have nothing to do but to save souls. Therefore, spend and be spent in this work. And go not only to those that need you, but to those that need you most it is not your business to preach so many times, and to take care of this or that society; but to save as many souls as you can; to bring as many sinners as you possibly can to repentance.[36] —John Wesley

12

THE CHARISMATA—SIGNS, WONDERS, AND SPIRITUAL GIFTS IN SOUL-WINNING

"15 And He said to them, 'Go into all the world and preach the gospel to all creation. 16 'He who has believed and has been baptized shall be saved; but he who has disbelieved shall be condemned. 17 These signs will accompany those who have believed: in My name they will cast out demons, they will speak with new tongues; 18 they will pick up serpents, and if they drink any deadly poison, it will not hurt them; they will lay hands on the sick, and they will recover.'"
—Mark 16:15–18

"Christian signs and wonders are beyond rationality, but they serve a rational purpose: to authenticate the gospel. The gospel is opposed to the pluralistic lie that says all religious experience is equally valid. Signs and wonders validate Christ's sacrifice on the cross and His lordship over every area of our lives."[37] —John Wimber

"We don't seek God's power; we seek His presence. His power & everything else we need is always found in His presence."[38] *—John Wimber*

"God has given believers the responsibility of spreading the Gospel to all the world, and we need to use all at our disposal to accomplish this task."[39] *—Theodore Epp*

TODAY, THERE IS a lot of conversation within the church in relation to prophetic evangelism. An increasing number of God's people are going into public places and moving in the prophetic gifts to engage the lost in Gospel conversations. This excites me, mostly because I see a fresh movement of soul-winning as people move in the gifts of the Holy Spirit. Much has been said about spiritual gifts in evangelism over the past 35 years, and I am delighted by that. Pastor John Wimber, one of the founding leaders in the Vineyard Movement, along with Kenn Gulliksen, who actually planted the first Vineyard churches before turning over the leadership to Wimber, began to bring attention to this subject of power evangelism in the mid-1980s. It was a young firebrand revivalist from the Jesus Movement named Lonnie Frisbee who introduced John Wimber to the power available through the Holy Spirit.

For over 25 years, I have expected spiritual gifts, signs, and wonders as I evangelized. In fact, I have had the privilege of moving in spiritual gifts in soul-winning thousands of times. Hearing the Holy Spirit's voice leading and guiding me adds the dimension of power in soul-winning. His leading assists our effectiveness greatly in winning the lost to Christ.

In this chapter, we are going to look at this topic. Jesus has placed spiritual gifts at our disposal to accomplish our task of world evangelization. The world needs to encounter the powerful presence of Jesus, for when it is manifested, supernatural things happen. We carry this presence on the earth.

One Sunday morning, when I was lost in the presence of Jesus during worship, the Holy Spirit spoke to my spirit, "I will be to you as an armor bearer and give to you the weapons of the battle in the moment you need them. But you need to be quick to take them and use them." I understood He was talking about the gifts of the Holy Spirit that He would impart to me on the streets in the midst of ministry.

> *7 But to each one is given the manifestation of the Spirit for the common good. 8 For to one is given the word of wisdom through the Spirit, and to another the word of knowledge according to the same Spirit; 9 to another faith by the same Spirit, and to another gifts of healing by the one Spirit, 10 and to another the effecting of miracles, and to another prophecy, and to another the distinguishing of spirits, to another various kinds of tongues, and to another the interpretation of tongues. —1 Corinthians 12:7–10*

Spiritual gifts—word of wisdom, word of knowledge, faith, healing, effecting of miracles, prophecy, distinguishing of spirits, various kinds of tongues, and interpretation of tongues—are all gifts furnished by the Spirit and especially helpful in the task of evangelization. I have experienced most of these, especially during ministry to the lost. On that Sunday, He promised to assist me by providing His gifts for the benefit of lost souls, and I have experienced it repeatedly. The stories I have shared document my dependence on the guidance of the Holy Spirit in soul-winning.

Jesus has commissioned us to "go into all the world and preach the Gospel." He does not send us out without His power. Signs and wonders indeed authenticate and validate the Gospel. As referenced in the previous chapter, Paul depended on the Spirit and power of God to confirm his message to the Corinthians. We have the same Holy Spirit and power of God as our provision to accomplish the task given to us.

3 I was with you in weakness and in fear and in much trembling, 4 and my message and my preaching were not in persuasive words of wisdom, but in demonstration of the Spirit and of power, 5 so that your faith would not rest on the wisdom of men, but on the power of God. —1 Corinthians 2:3–5

Miracles, signs, and wonders were an integral part of Jesus's ministry. Jesus tells us in Luke chapter four that His ministry would restore humankind in body, soul, and spirit, all the areas in which sin has broken us. Then He tells us in John 20:21, "As my Father has sent me, so I am sending you." Clearly, we too are to operate in miracles, signs, and wonders in carrying out His commission.

Jesus's ministry was bursting with signs, wonders, and miracles. Look at a summary of His ministry:

24 Jesus was going throughout all Galilee, teaching in their synagogues and proclaiming the gospel of the kingdom, and healing every kind of disease and every kind of sickness among the people. 24 The news about Him spread throughout all Syria; and they brought to Him all who were ill, those suffering with various diseases and pains, demoniacs, epileptics, paralytics; and He healed them. —Matthew 4:23, 24

35 Jesus was going through all the cities and villages, teaching in their synagogues and proclaiming the gospel of the kingdom, and healing every kind of disease and every kind of sickness. 36 Seeing the people, He felt compassion for them, because they were distressed and dispirited like sheep without a shepherd. —Matthew 9:35, 36

Why did Jesus do these things? Because He felt compassion. Seeing people in their brokenness, He met them in their great needs. Jesus's ministry was one that was carried out "on the way." Often the Gospel narratives states, "And while He was on His way." When He encountered a person with great need, Jesus stopped and ministered to the person.

His first response was to stop. We need to learn to stop when we encounter people in their needs. I have noticed that when He stopped, He paused. Why? I believe He paused to ask, "Father, what are you doing here?" He only did what He saw the Father do. He only said what He heard the Father say. We need to adopt this moment of pause to sense in our spirits what the Holy Spirit wants to do.

Have you noticed that Jesus's miracles were diverse in manner? He didn't perform His miracles as some sort of formulaic process. Each miracle was unique. "Father, what are you doing here? Oh, spit in the man's eyes." He spit in the man's eyes, and his sight was restored. "Oh, make mud from my spit and smear it in the man's eyes." He made mud from His spit and rubbed it in the man's eyes. The man's sight again was restored.

Now the disciples who witnessed these occurrences did not go and set up healing spitting tables. This is the sort of thing people tend to do today. They see a method that works and develop a formula for healing out of it. The key is simply dependence on the Holy Spirit, which is why we must maintain a tight connection with Him.

When a leper approached Jesus for healing, Jesus could have merely commanded the leper to be healed. Instead, He paused. "Father, what are you doing here? Oh, place My hand on the leper." That shook up some religious spirits. According to the Law of Moses, if you touched an unclean leper, then you were unclean. Not so with Jesus. Rather than Jesus becoming unclean, the unclean leper became clean.

Some of our workers in Cuba would remove their sport jackets and swing them at people coming forward for healing, hitting them with their jackets. When asked why they did that, they responded that they had gotten a DVD from a healing evangelist who used this method. They figured the power was in the swinging of the jacket. Well, maybe it was for the healing evangelist in the moment he used that method, but it should not have become a formula for healing. The key is our dependence on the Holy Spirit in the moment we are faced with a person's need.

The disciples followed this pattern from Jesus's ministry. At the Gate called Beautiful in Acts 3 and 4, Peter and John passed a lame man over 40 years old who sat at that gate daily. When the lame man asked them for an offering, they responded, "Look at us." I believe this was the pause where they asked, "Father, what are you doing here?" What they heard or maybe saw in their spirits was taking the man by the hand and raising him up. It was in the moment of raising him up that his feet and ankles were strengthened.

Something else about this story intrigues me. Jesus had passed by the same gate many times before and during His three and a half years of ministry as He attended the appointed feasts. Remember, every male was to appear in Jerusalem during the three annual feasts of Israel. Jesus had surely passed this man many times, but He never stopped to heal him. Possibly, Jesus knew this man's healing was for another time and another purpose. In any case, He must not have seen the Father healing this man when He passed him by.

In the Gospel of John, chapter 5, Jesus visits the pool of Bethesda, which means "House of Kindness." It was a place where a multitude of sick, blind, lame, and withered people gathered daily. On this Sabbath day, the infirm were present. Among them was a man who had been ill for 38 years. We do not know exactly what his infirmity was, but he was carried on a pallet, and he needed help to get into the pool when it was stirred by an angel.

Jesus approached him and asked, "Do you wish to get well?" That sounds like a yes-or-no question to me. But the man's response was, "Sir, I have no man to put me into the pool when the water is stirred up, but while I am coming, another steps down before me." I have encountered people who, like this man, actually identify with their medical condition. Their ill health has become their identity. Here it seems like the man had no hope of being healed, yet he sat there day after day. The people there were his acquaintances and associates. He was one with them and of them. To be healed would mean to lose his present identity, so it would be safer to remain there with his familiar friends, in his familiar environment, and in his familiar condition. Being healed would require venturing into new and uncharted waters.

Jesus did not even acknowledge the man's response, for He had already seen His Father healing the man. Jesus said to him, "Get up, pick up your pallet and walk." We know the result. The man was healed and caused quite a ruckus among the religious order for carrying his pallet on the Sabbath. When the religious leaders found that Jesus was responsible, they confronted Him. But He answered them, "My Father is working until now, and I Myself am working" (John 5:17).

Signs, wonders, miracles, and spiritual gifts from our Heavenly Father are normal, everyday occurrences in the kingdom of Heaven. They take place, not for our glory but for the glory of the Father and His kingdom. We are merely channels, or lightning rods, for heaven to touch the earth.

One night I met a young man as I walked along. We talked, and I could see he was open and receptive to the message I was sharing. When I asked him if he would like to receive Christ as his Savior and Lord, though, he politely declined my offer. That is when the Holy Spirit spoke to my heart, "He doesn't feel it would be sincere to make this decision right now because he is high on drugs."

I asked him, "You don't feel it is appropriate to make this decision because you are high, right?" He nodded yes.

Next, the Holy Spirit directed me to put my hand on his shoulder. When I did, the Holy Spirit said to me, "Ask him if he feels high now."

I asked, and he sort of shook his head back and forth a few times, looked at me in amazement, and replied, "Why, no, I don't feel high at all." I again asked him if he would like to invite Christ to be his Savior and Lord now, and he said yes, he would. This young man encountered the power of God, and it resulted in his salvation.

In our ministry in Mexico and El Salvador, we regularly provide beans and rice for the people. Most of the areas we work in are extremely poor, and dispensing food is a practical service we can provide and again is part of that presence element of evangelism. A kilo of beans and a kilo of rice can equal a day's average wage in many parts of those nations.

A couple of years ago, I led a youth mission team from my home church to El Salvador. The team was from my home church in northern Colorado. The team leaders were my dear friends Pastor Bob and his wife, Tammie. We were at our final ministry site of the week in a remote village called El Milagro, or "the miracle." We knew exactly how many bags of beans and rice we had with us, something like 94 bags of rice and 87 bags of beans.

Over three hundred people, nearly everyone in the village, had gathered under a massive tree to witness the presentation. At the conclusion of the ministry, about 250 adults and children responded to the Gospel invitation. After distributing New Testaments and praying for the sick, we asked the adults to line up for the food distribution, and I counted 120 adults in the line. Our entire team knew we did not have enough food in our bags for everyone. One of the adult leaders asked if we should just give either a kilo of beans or a kilo of rice rather than a kilo of both. The Holy Spirit rose up in my spirit, and I announced, "No, give each person a bag of each. The Father loves these people more than we ever could, and He wants to feed each and every one of them." The only requirement was to take only one kilo bag out of the larger bags at a time.

The line moved steadily, with each person receiving both a bag of beans and a bag of rice. I had counted to the 100th person in line, but still bags of beans and rice were being lifted out of the larger bags. Each time a team member reached in, a bag came out. After 110 people had come through the line, food still remained, and finally the last person came through the line and received a blessing. When we were finished, the entire team realized we had participated in a miracle. One bag of beans and one bag of rice were left, which emphasized the miracle, because we didn't start with an equal number of beans and rice.

As we all stood there, astonished at what had just taken place, a woman approached us. She had just returned to her home in the village and heard we were distributing food. Did we have a gift for her as well? Yes, we did. God knew. But then another young mother approached; sadly, we had to inform her we had no food left. She responded, "Oh no, I didn't come to ask you for food. I have already received your gift and taken it to my home. I came back to ask you some questions." She wanted to know more about her newfound faith in Christ. This was not the first or last time our team witnessed miracles of multiplication, but it may have been the most dramatic. This miracle was for the benefit of new believers. It increased our faith to see the Father's loving compassion for the poor and needy.

On another occasion, I was working in the city of Matamoros in Mexico, across the border from Brownsville, Texas. The third and final week of our summer "Invasion" conferences, three days of evangelism training were followed by three days of putting the training into practice. Our staff and students live in and work with the churches during those three days of outreach. On Saturday afternoon, the churches return for a night of celebration, testimonies, and statistics. We have seen more than 10,000 salvation professions of faith in a single city during the three days of outreach.

The church I was working with went out into a neighborhood one evening in an area where they had a cell group. It was a good ministry site, with 90 to 100 people attending. After praying for people for salvation, and then for individual healing, we dismissed the people to their homes. On the way home, some of them told neighbors sitting on porches about people in the park being healed by prayer. A group of five ladies responded by hustling on over. It was getting late, and the sun was setting when they arrived. The spokeswoman of the group had some sort of palsy, and her left side was paralyzed. The other ladies in the group, one being the spokeswoman's sister, also had various infirmities. The spokeswoman went on and on about her condition in a voice slurred by palsy.

As she continued her exhaustive dissertation, I was asking, "Father, what do you want to do here?" He showed me the woman's condition was due to her bitterness from a broken relationship. After persuading the woman to calm down, I asked her, "Is there someone you need to forgive?"

Immediately, she responded, "No, I cannot forgive my daughter!" She was emphatic about this. We convinced her that it was imperative for her healing to not hold any bitterness. She finally agreed to pray to forgive her daughter. After we led her in this prayer, without praying a specific prayer of healing, she reached up with what was previously a frozen left hand and began to touch the left side of her face. She could now feel it. Of course, this set her off like a fire in a fireworks factory, and it took an additional amount of time to calm her down again.

She then directed us to her sister, who had some sort of undiagnosed sickness that caused extreme bloating of her body. She wore a typical Mexican house dress that was literally bursting at its seams. I asked one of our students to ask Jesus what He was doing here with this woman. The student heard from the Lord and followed the course He was setting for her. As she ministered to and prayed for the lady, we watched as the swelling throughout her body diminished. The skin-tight house dress now hung loosely on her body. I directed our other students to pray for the remainder of the group, and each woman left whole and healed.

In a parking lot on Main Street in Longmont one night, I was witnessing with Steve, a good friend of mine and a co-worker in the harvest fields. As we shared with a group of young people, a car drove past us with the tailpipe dragging on the pavement. Steve and I made our way over to the group of four young men and women who exited that car. The driver and owner of the car became somewhat agitated when our conversation turned to eternal things. He wore dark glasses though it was dark and became very resistant to our message.

I told Steve to continue to share with the other three, who seemed open to the Good News message, while I invited the driver to help fix his tailpipe. We climbed under the back of the car with some steel bailing wire to assess the problem. As we lay on the pavement under the car, I asked him why he was wearing the dark glasses. He told me he had a welding accident that week which had severely burned and damaged his eyes. I asked him if I could pray for his eyes, and while we lay under the car, I prayed for healing and restoration of his eyes. We completed our task under the car, tied up the tailpipe, and emerged to meet with the rest of the group. Steve had led the other three to Christ during our absence and was following up by distributing New Testaments and "Next Step" booklets. We said our goodbyes and parted ways.

The following week, I was once again witnessing in the parking lot to a group of people, when I heard a call from behind me, "Hey, Bob. Hey, Bob." I turned and saw a young man, who asked, "Do you remember me?"

"Uh, no," I responded. He introduced himself as the young man I had prayed for the previous week. I did not recognize him, because the dark glasses were absent from his face. When I asked what had happened to his eyes, he said they were healed. After I had prayed and left, he removed the glasses and realized that his sight was restored. A doctor he visited confirmed the healing, and the young man attributed his healing to the prayer spoken on the pavement under the car. Now, he was totally open to the Gospel. I shared the message with him, and he received Jesus as his Savior and Lord. It took a miracle for this resistant skeptic to open his heart to Jesus and the message of salvation.

I have had numerous and diverse divine healings in my own body. For more than seven years, I suffered with plantar fasciitis in my feet. When your calling is to walk and talk with people about eternity, an infirmity like this can cause you to wonder, "What's going on here?"

At the time I was diagnosed with this problem, I was spending eight hours on the streets in Denver almost every Friday night, arriving home around 3:00 a.m. Getting up on Saturday morning meant facing incredible pain in my feet. The first six to ten steps would produce a ripping sensation in the arches my feet. A couple of courses of cortisone injections did not alleviate the problem. I was determined to continue to seek and save the lost regardless of this obstacle, but the condition continued into the first four to five years after I began mission work in Mexico.

For a number of years, our ministry teamed up with the YWAM base in Mazatlán, Mexico, to partner in their Carnival Outreach in the week before Ash Wednesday and the beginning of the Lenten season. A team of our staff worked to equip the YWAM group for this evangelism outreach. Each night, we brought our team into the gates of the wild celebration. Dozens of stages were set up along the two-mile waterfront road for bands. More than 100,000 people attended each night, especially during the weekends. Our ministry took place from about eight each night until two in the morning.

During the week, our small team would see upwards of 2,000 salvation professions of faith. I felt like a kid in a candy shop. During two separate years during the Sunday night outreach, I and my ministry partner witnessed 63 people come to Christ.

The first two years we participated, I struggled with this plantar fasciitis. Each night at midnight, we gathered in a big open plaza with a huge flagpole to see if all the ministry team members were okay. On this particular night, as I approached the flagpole, the pain in my feet was excruciating. I prayed silently, "Lord, I don't know how much longer I can keep this up tonight, but by your grace I will continue."

I did not tell anyone about the pain. My niece Harmony was the team leader of the YWAM intercessory prayer group. As we prepared to go back out, she asked if her team could pray for us. I got down on my knees on the pavement and bowed my head to the ground as a young man named Chris took hold of my hands.

While he prayed in front of me, I could feel someone behind me with a hand on each of my Achilles tendons. I tried to turn around nonchalantly to see who it was, without being noticed. Finally, I determined to just turn around and look. When I did, no one was there, but I could still feel the hands on my heels. When I got up afterwards, the pain was gone. To this day, that infirmity has not returned.

Signs, wonders, miracles, gifts of the Spirit. The Holy Spirit provides these wonders to us to perform the tasks Jesus has given us. We do not seek these wonders; we seek the presence of Jesus. But when Jesus is present, His power and glory are also present with Him.

Angels

> *Do not neglect to show hospitality to strangers, for by this some have entertained angels without knowing it. —Hebrews 13:2*

I would like to share some stories in which I am convinced that angelic beings were present. Many people are uncomfortable discussing the presence of angels in ministry, and you can determine for yourself the validity of my assertions. But I am sure I have had a number of encounters with angels during ministry on the streets and in other public places. And somehow, I believe I have entertained angels numerous other times without knowing it. Throughout Scripture, angels have been sent on assignment as messengers of the Lord to guard our ways.

> *For He will give His angels charge concerning you, To guard you in all your ways. —Psalm 91:11*

Just as we do not seek signs, wonders, and miracles, we do not seek angels. But I believe they seek us as they fulfill their instructions to guard and bring messages to us.

I made my way to my van at about 2:00 a.m. after a long night of street ministry in downtown Denver. A short fireplug of a man with olive skin, a shaved head, and a thin mustache approached me and asked if I was Jewish. What a strange question for two in the morning, I thought. I told him I did not know whether my heritage included a line to Israel.

Some in my family have speculated that my grandfather, Jacob Gabelman, may have had Jewish ancestry. Grandpa fought in Germany in World War I, suiting up for the Canadians. After the war, he moved to Akron, Ohio, and worked in the B.F. Goodrich tire factory until he retired. At that time, be bought a 70-acre farm where half the field was potatoes and the other half corn, with raspberry bushes running down the middle. His family had farmed potatoes on their farm in Canada. Grandpa had 35 grandchildren, which was helpful at the harvest. One year he planted the entire 70 acres with alfalfa, and I asked him why. Being a man of few words, he simply responded, "Because it's the seventh year." In Jewish culture the seventh year is the Sabbath year, and fields were to rest from planting and harvest. This was the source of the speculation regarding Grandpa's possible Jewish lineage.

The man on the street again asked me, "But are you Jewish?"

Again, I told him I did not know. I was not raised Jewish, but I did say, "I am a Christian Zionist." Not a Christian Scientist, a Christian Zionist, which means I support the development and protection of Israel as a sovereign state. Our strange discussion somehow came around to the study of theology, and he stated he was a student of theology. My response to him was, "We can take all of your books on theology and all of my books on theology and stack them here in a pile. Then we can take all the books of theology in the world and stack them on top of ours. And do you know what? The pile would not be tall enough to reach God. He can only be reached through His Son, Jesus Christ."

With that, the man placed his left hand around the back of my neck, gripping my neck tightly. With his right hand he began to lightly thump me on my chest saying, "You know, you can get hurt out here."

I then told him, "I am sorry, but you just don't see the two giant angels standing behind me guarding over me. No harm can be done to me out here except what my heavenly Father permits."

At that point, the strangest thing began to ensue, and everything went into slow motion. I mean everything, like I had been transported into another dimension. In this slow-motion sequence, I could see the man reach into his pants pocket with his right hand, while his left hand continued to firmly grip the back of my neck. Then I saw the knife handle, followed by the blade, coming out of his pocket. I began to move in the direction of his arm holding my neck. Of course, I had a big old backpack on when I initiated this move.

Then something supernatural occurred. I was transported about 20 feet down the sidewalk. Facing the man now from a distance, I could see him standing there with the knife in his hand and a stunned look on his face. At that moment, a police cruiser drove by, and the man turned tail and made a hasty retreat. The police, knowing I was the street preacher, pulled up next to me and asked if everything was okay. I said it was.

As I continued my trek to my van, I considered, "That was somewhat dangerous!" I had a firm grasp of the obvious. I then considered, "Boy, if Kathleen finds out about this, she'll never let me come out here again." My greatest fear at that moment was not being able to continue going out to seek and save the lost. I then determined not to tell anyone about this, and I did not until the following Wednesday.

On my way to church on Wednesday night, the Holy Spirit nudged me, "You have got to tell Kathleen." He was right, of course. (Did I just need to include that?)

When I got home that night, I sat Kathleen down and told her the entire story. She said, "I'm glad you told me. I know it can be dangerous out there, and I pray for you each night as you go. But now I know

God is protecting you. He will give His angels charge concerning you, to guard you in all your ways."

Another encounter involving protective angels took place a few years ago in the Mexican city of Torreon. We were holding an "Invasion" conference and were driving to the venue in an old, heavy, 15-passenger Dodge van. We must have had 20 young men in the van as we made our way across town. Behind me was a van with our women's staff and students. It had rained through the night, so the roads were wet and slippery, and I was taking precautions on the wet road. As we approached a traffic light, a man on a motorcycle was in front of us. The light changed, and I applied the brakes, but they locked up. We were sliding uncontrollably toward the now-stopped motorcycle. There was no way we would stop in time to avoid plastering this man.

Everyone in the van could see that a collision was imminent, and we braced for impact. From within my spirit, I cried out, "Jesus, save us!" Immediately, it felt like we hit a concrete wall. The van stopped immediately after I cried out, and those in the van behind us thought we had hit a concrete light pole. The front bumper merely brushed the rear fender of the motorcycle, not even moving the bike from its place. The driver turned and looked but did not seem concerned. What took place there was something supernatural. Every one of us knew there had been divine intervention.

At another time, I was hosting a youth mission team in El Salvador. Our long-standing mission trip assistant and ministry liaison to El Salvador, Marlana, had accompanied me. Marlana knew our system so well that she could do most things better than I could. We had scheduled a visit to a large high school in San Salvador and were expecting thousands of students in each of the morning and afternoon sessions. We arrived at the school a half hour before our scheduled presentation, but no one in the administrative office had been informed of our coming, despite it being scheduled and then later confirmed with the school director. We brought our team to the large gymnasium, which was locked up. More than 45 minutes later, someone finally opened it.

Over an hour after the scheduled presentation, the first students began to arrive, but only about one-third of the expected students showed up. No teachers or faculty were present, so the students were disorderly. After the presentation, we invited the students to make a decision to receive Jesus as Savior and Lord. Thankfully, in the midst of so much disorder, about 100 students made salvation decisions.

Afterward, Marlana and I headed towards the administrative building to thank the administrators for letting us present this program. Neither of us were in a very thankful mood. I told Marlana that I did not want to return for the afternoon session. As mission trip director, I felt the quality of this ministry site was lacking, and Marlana agreed.

As we reached the door of the administrative building, a woman met us and told us how important our work was to the students. It makes such a difference in their lives, she said, and she was thankful for people who were willing to come. We asked her if she was present at the event. "No," she said, "but I have heard." We wondered how she could have heard because we had just left the presentation ourselves. Was she a teacher here? "No," she replied.

"Are you an administrator here?"

Again, "No." She told us she worked in the area and was aware of the activities of the young people.

As she spoke, Marlana and I both sensed that something divine was taking place. An indescribable sense of presence, power, and mostly peace came over us. My heart's stinky attitude was being arrested by this woman's presence, and I began to cry. I turned to Marlana, and she was also crying. Then I asked the woman, "Are you an angel?" She politely smiled without answering and excused herself. Her few words had changed our hearts, and we proceeded to the administrator's office, thanked them, and promised to return for the afternoon presentation. That meeting was supernatural, with hundreds of students responding. Angels are sent as messengers, and I believe we entertained an angel that day.

I will share one last story, although I have more. Again, we were in El Salvador for a summer mission trip, working with a government agency which aided communities of displaced people. That year, we worked in eight different communities over two days. In these areas, the poorest of the poor eked out a meager existence. Many had lost their homes to fire, flood, hurricanes, or financial failure, and they lived in dirt floor hovels fabricated from wooden pallets and sheet metal. Hundreds of people crammed into a small space.

At this particular outreach, it was difficult to find enough space to give our presentation. A hundred or more people, mostly women and children, gathered in the cramped space. We played games with the children and then shared the Gospel. Several in our ministry team had noticed two ladies standing on the side of the ministry site. These women seemed different and out of place among the rest of the people, exhibiting a calm, peaceful, and joyful presence. Almost identical in appearance, they carried themselves with grace and beauty. There was truly something angelic about their presence. At the conclusion of the ministry, after we prayed with the people for salvation and healing, we invited the people to form a line to receive beans and rice. Instead of jostling for position in the line that was forming, these two ladies positioned themselves behind our distribution table and assisted us in dispensing the food. Afterward, I was not sure if they even received food for themselves, but they somehow departed without any of us noticing. A number of our staff and team had the same sense about the presence of these two angels.

Signs, wonders, spiritual gifts, and miracles are all part of the tools we have at our disposal to accomplish the task God has given believers of spreading the Gospel to all the world.

> *Our sufficiency is of God. Difficulties melt in His presence. In Him are those mighty, overcoming energies, which accomplish the possible and the impossible with equal readiness... The real resources are with Him for the evangelizing and*

the redeeming of the world. But He has not been able to do 'many mighty works' in the non-Christian lands, because of our unbelief as a Church. We have not possessed our possessions. God has been waiting to be honored by the faith of a generation that would call upon Him for really large outpourings of His power.[40] *—J. Lovell Murray (SVM)*

The secret of the success of the Apostles lay not in what they did and said, but in the presence of Christ in them and with them. They saw with the eyes of Christ, felt with His heart, and worked with His energies. They were nothing; Christ was everything. Christ was living, breathing, and triumphing in their personal lives. Their entire nature being replete with His life, their spirits bathed in His light, and their souls kindled with the fires of His love, they moved in the midst of men as embodiments of supernatural power... Brethren, this is what we must be, if this mighty Empire (China) is to be moved through us. But to be this, the throne of grace must be our refuge, the secret place of the Most High must be our daily and hourly habitation.[41] *—John Griffith*

13

OUR JOB DESCRIPTION—YOU ARE ANOINTED TO PREACH THE GOSPEL

*"21 Now **He who establishes us with you in Christ and anointed us is God,** 22 who also sealed us and gave us the Spirit in our hearts as a pledge." —2 Corinthians 1:21, 22*

*"20 But **you have an anointing** from the Holy One, and you all know." —1 John 2:20*

*"27 And as for you, **the anointing which you received from Him abides in you,** and you have no need for anyone to teach you; but as His anointing teaches you about all things, and is true and is not a lie, and just as it has taught you, you abide in Him." —1 John 2:27*

THE ANOINTING IS God's power and influence upon the person He has chosen for His service.

"Spirit filled souls are ablaze for God. They love with a love that glows. They serve with a faith that kindles. They serve with a devotion that consumes. They hate sin with fierceness that burns. They rejoice with a joy that radiates. Love is perfected in the fire of God."[42] —Samuel Chadwick

173

In this chapter we will look at: What is the Gospel, what is salvation, and the anointing we have to preach the Gospel of Salvation.

I have heard it said that the anointing is tangible and transferable. And I agree with this to a point. I believe that the anointing on our lives is constant. We have an anointing, and that anointing abides with us, is fixed upon us. The manifestation of the anointing in us seems greater at some times than others, but the anointing is always with us. We are anointed.

It is like being married. There are certainly times when I feel very married. The conscious fact of my marriage to Kathleen is very present. At other times, I am not consciously aware of being married. I may be preoccupied with other things, but it does not change the fact that I am married. The anointing is the same, always present regardless of our level of awareness of it. What makes the difference is the power and presence of the Holy Spirit upon us when we are functioning in the anointing. I will explain this in further detail as we continue in this chapter.

I wrote earlier of the night in downtown Denver when I sensed a powerful presence of the Holy Spirit upon me with an irresistible anointing to win souls. Everyone I spoke with responded positively to the Gospel message and invitation. I love those nights. I treasure them, and always hope and pray for such nights. Many times, I have walked in that kind of powerful anointing. Most of the time, though, while the anointing to win souls is present, the glorious power and presence of the Holy Spirit is not as strong, or at least not discernible. Souls are saved on those nights, but there is definitely a difference.

One of the most powerfully anointed nights I have ever experienced was on Main Street in Longmont several years ago. Two friends and I had entered a parking lot on Main Street where hundreds of young people would gather on Friday nights. This night, we came upon a group of about 20 young people milling about and visiting with one another. My friends and I began to share with small groups of them, but we sensed we were encountering some disruptive spiritual warfare.

Four or five times, as we engaged in significant Gospel conversations, a distraction interrupted the conversation.

After several such incidents, our group of evangelists gathered together. Recognizing the spiritual battle at hand, we paused to pray. As we finished praying, three young ladies we had spoken to earlier approached us. I began to speak with them, picking up from the previous conversation. A few other young people joined us, then a few more, until finally 20 people were listening, and I had to raise my voice to be heard. This was truly street preaching at its finest.

As I spoke, the Holy Spirit power came upon me. The anointed presence and power became overwhelming. The tangible powerful presence of God, thick like a cloud, and with an electric atmosphere, settled upon us. My flesh became so weak that I felt like I was going to fall to the ground. That parking lot had become a holy place by the manifest presence of our Holy God. My spirit was alive and animated, and my soul was focused on what God was doing at that moment. Body, soul, and spirit were united together for the task at hand, to proclaim the Gospel and set captives free. As I wrapped up the Gospel presentation, I went through the crowd one by one, asking each individual present, "Do you want to surrender your life to Christ right here and right now?"

Each person responded, "Yes!" I went through the crowd again, asking each individual if they wanted to pray with me to invite Jesus to be their Savior and Lord. Each person responded, "Yes!" Together we prayed a salvation prayer. Even as we prayed, my body quaked in the glorious presence of Jesus. It took all the strength I could muster to keep standing as we prayed. Afterward, we distributed New Testaments, follow-up booklets, and local church information. I love the anointing and the power of God that joins itself to our anointing to accomplish the work Jesus sends us to do.

After eight hours on the street, I sometimes return home at three in the morning to climb into bed. My body is aching and exhausted, but my spirit is alive and fresh. One night, I climbed into bed next to Kathleen. As I lay there with waves of glory rolling over me, Kathleen elbowed me and said, "Bob, will you turn out the light? I can't sleep with it on so bright." Umm, the light was not on, but she said that light was filling the room.

Another night, in a deep sleep after again returning during the wee hours of the morning, she elbowed me and told me she could not sleep next to me because of the glorious presence still upon me. I had to go sleep on the couch for a few hours until the glory faded. Moses spent 40 days in God's glorious presence and had to wear a covering over his face until that glory faded.

I have often said that if you want to catch fish, you must go where the fish are. Likewise, if you want to be a fisher of men, you must go where they are. Have you ever gone barhopping to proclaim the Good News of salvation? I was on Main Street in Longmont one very pleasant evening when I noticed several bars with doors open to the street.

Walking by one particular neighborhood bar, I noticed a man sitting alone at a table facing the street. The first time I walked by the man captured my attention, but I continued on my way. After speaking to several people on the streets, I walked by the bar a second time, again noticing the lone man. Again, he captured my attention. I walked into the bar and introduced myself, asking if I might sit with him and share a message. He invited me to have a seat. We talked a bit about this, that, and another thing, when I turned the conversation to eternal issues. Our conversation was tremendous, and the man was open and interested in what I had to say. I could see he was lonely and appreciated someone taking an interest in him.

After sharing the Good News message, I invited him to respond to Jesus's call, "Come to me, all you who are weary and heavy-laden, and I will give you rest" (Matthew 11:28). He decided to trust Jesus as his personal Savior and Lord. I took his hand, and we prayed together to invite Christ into his heart, whereupon his countenance transformed into great joy. His born-again experience was evident in his eyes. I provided a Bible and a "Next Step" booklet, along with information about local churches he could attend. We shook hands and parted ways. Jesus will meet a person anywhere, even in the most unlikely places.

One of my soul-winning heroes has been Arthur Blessitt, the guy who has carried the cross in every country and island group throughout the world. He began a street ministry on Sunset Strip in Hollywood, California, in 1968 and was one of the influential early Jesus Movement personalities. I had a chance to meet this dear brother while speaking at a church in the Denver area a few years ago. Arthur opened a Christian coffeehouse on the Sunset Strip called "His Place" in 1968 next door to a topless go-go club. He tells a story about how he requested and received permission from the owner of the club to hold Bible studies in the dancers' dressing room. Now that will probably ruffle some religious feathers, but if you want to catch fish, you have to go where the fish are.[43]

Arthur held these studies over a period of time, and after a while, he received a letter from a Baptist pastor in the heartland of America. It seems that one of those go-go dancers who joined in the Bible studies was the pastor's daughter. Because of Arthur's ministry to these lost souls, his daughter left Los Angeles, returned to her home, and renewed her faith in Christ. I imagine that Baptist pastor was more than happy that a street preacher would venture into the darkest places to seek and save the lost.

Once I was sent into a similarly unlikely place where God showed up to extend His great mercy. While living in Key West, Florida, I oversaw a men's discipleship home near Duval Street, the main party street. Key West was a final destination for many people who were on the move, for whatever reason. It was the end of the rainbow, the final island on the overseas highway. US Highway 1 was the end, or the beginning, depending on your perspective, and many people referred to it as "the last resort."

The elements were never so severe that people could not live on the streets. In our continual ministry on the streets, we would invite those being drawn to Jesus into our home. There, they received a consistent helping of discipleship. A number of the men struggled with alcohol and drug addiction.

Over time, I became aware of a continuing cycle these men struggled with. When they first came to us, having made a fresh start by their profession of Christ, they were all-in to advance their relationship with Christ and attain victory over addictive lifestyles. In those first few weeks, they would be very humble and contrite. After a while, I noticed those attitudes fading. They would begin to talk about their buddies on the street that were returning to their "vomit," as Proverbs 26:11 states, "Like a dog that returns to its vomit Is a fool who repeats his folly."

At this point, pride was hoisted up the yard arm, and I could see that a fall was imminent. This cycle repeated itself over and over in a number of these men. They would begin to sneak out for a drink. More than once I tracked them down, finding them in different bars, especially fishermen's bars, and with much persuasion brought them back home. I was fulfilling the Biblical example of leaving the 99 to bring back the one lost sheep.

One day, I came home at midday and noticed that no one was around. I had been observing the end of the aforementioned cycle in a couple of the guys and had a suspicion that they were at the bars. Going in search of my lost sheep, I visited all the usual places, but they were nowhere to be found. As I walked along the bars on Duval Street, I walked by a nudie bar and felt the moving of the Holy Spirit in my heart. After passing the bar, the feeling inside me diminished. I turned around and walked by again, and I felt that same stirring in my spirit. Oh no! I could not, I would not, I should not. Should I? I walked by that bar two or three more times, each time feeling that stirring in my heart.

"But what if someone sees me enter or exit the nudie bar?" was my great concern. I was known throughout the city. I met regularly with the local Pastors' Alliance, where I was addressed as Reverend Bob. Now I could damage or altogether lose my reputation. I knew in my heart I was supposed to enter that place, but reputation stood in the way.

I made one last approach to the door and quickly made my move to open and enter that dark place. In the back of the bar was a semi-clad dancer doing the hoochie-coochie all over the stage. As I entered, my great fears were realized. The guys I was looking for were not there, but worse, I was approached by a young woman, a dancer who had attended our church services a couple of times. Even worse, she recognized me. Stuttering and stammering, I struggled to get out a greeting. Quickly, I informed her of my mission. She told me the guys I was looking for had been there recently, and they told her I would never look for them there.

The young lady invited me to sit down at a table with her, and we talked for a bit. She was happier to see me than I was to see her. I maintained eye contact, making sure my eyes did not wander. "Be careful little eyes what you see." Then we began to talk about the things of God. Yeah, believe it or not, we talked about spiritual things in that place, which seemed like witnessing right outside the gates of hell. Somehow, I was able to share the Good News message with her, telling her God had another plan for her life. I took her hand, and we prayed together, in front of everyone present.

It was a divine appointment. The young lady began to regularly attend our Sunday services and even my Tuesday night discipleship classes. Kathleen and I have known her now for about 40 years. She has struggled off and on throughout her life with homelessness and other behavioral issues, but she continues to maintain her testimony in the saving power of Jesus Christ. Over the years, she has supported us financially from time to time in our mission work. It is always a great pleasure to receive her letters or calls. You never know where the Holy Spirit may lead you, and I learned a lesson that day about reputation. Our Father is more interested in souls than in our reputations among men.

So, let us talk about salvation. Salvation is more than just escaping hell. It is about escaping hell, but there is much more. Salvation is more than going to Heaven in some distant future. It is about entering Heaven in some distant future, but still it is more. Salvation is about entering the kingdom of Heaven that is present here and now. Look at Jesus's Gospel invitation:

The time is fulfilled, and the kingdom of God is at hand; repent and believe in the gospel. —Mark 1:15

In essence, Jesus's message was, "The time has come; the time is now. The kingdom of God is at hand, it is present, just an arm's length away. Repent, that is, change the way you are thinking about the kingdom of God, it is here and now within reach. And believe this Good News."

The Greek word used throughout the New Testament for salvation is *sozo*. It means more than going to Heaven in some distant future. It literally means wholeness in body, soul, and spirit. We will see that Jesus announced the purpose of His coming, which was to restore every area of humankind that was broken by sin. Let us look at a few verses from a couple of translations to highlight this point:

28: For she said—"If even his garments I may touch, I shall be saved." —Mark 5:28 YLT

28: For she said, "If I touch but his garments, I shall be made whole." —Mark 5:28 ASV

These words were spoken by the woman who had an issue of blood for 12 years. She came to Jesus to have that great need met. The Youngs Literal Translation uses the word *saved* and the American Standard Version uses the words *made whole*. Other translations use the word *healed*. The woman was desperate to be healed after 12 years of suffering.

In our Gospel concept of the word *saved*, did the saving mean she would go to Heaven? Or be healed? Or be made whole? She needed healing in her body, the "*sozo*" type of healing that brings wholeness.

Here is another example:

While he is yet speaking, there doth come a certain one from the chief of the synagogue's house, saying to him—"Thy daughter hath died, harass not the Teacher"; and Jesus having heard, answered him, saying, "Be not afraid, only believe, and she shall be saved." —Luke 8:49, 50 YLT

While he yet spake, there cometh one from the ruler of the synagogue's house, saying, Thy daughter is dead, trouble not the Teacher. But Jesus hearing it, answered him, "Fear not: only believe, and she shall be made whole." —Luke 8:49,50 ASV

We have the same thing, with one translation using the word *saved* and the other using the words *made whole*. And other translations use the word *healed*. The child had died. Did she need to be saved in our Christian concept of the word *saved*? Or did she need to be healed or made whole? She needed to be made whole, in this case resurrected to new life.

But, here again we see the Greek word *sozo* being translated as saved, or healed, or made whole in body, soul, and spirit. Therefore, we can conclude that salvation includes the saving and healing of the soul (mind, will, and emotions), the spirit, and the body. This is the salvation Jesus came to bring to humankind. We need to incorporate the full notion of this salvation in the Gospel we proclaim. Jesus did.

We will look at that further, but first let us look at the anointing. We are anointed. We are anointed to preach the Gospel. You are anointed to preach the Gospel. But what does that mean? Let us look again at the scriptures we opened this chapter with:

*21 Now **He who establishes us with you in Christ and anointed us is God,** 22 who also sealed us and gave us the Spirit in our hearts as a pledge. —2 Corinthians 1:21, 22*

20 But __you have an anointing__ from the Holy One, and you all know. —1 John 2:20

27 And as for you, __the anointing which you received from Him abides in you__, and you have no need for anyone to teach you; but as His anointing teaches you about all things, and is true and is not a lie, and just as it has taught you, you abide in Him. —1 John 2:27

Let us establish this fact from the Word of God: You are anointed! You have an anointing from the Holy One! God has anointed you!

Why has God anointed you? The anointing is God's power and influence upon the person He has chosen for His service.

The Father has a purpose for you and for me, and He has placed His power and influence upon us to accomplish that purpose. What is the anointing? The Greek word for anointed is *chrio*. We derive "Christ" from *chrio*. Jesus is the Christ, the anointed one. The literal meaning of *chrio* is to smear or rub with oil.

The symbolic meaning is to consecrate, to set apart for service. Throughout the Old Testament, prophets, priests, and kings were set apart for service by the pouring of oil upon their heads. Today we have the habit of dabbing a little oil on a person's forehead to anoint them. But in Old Testament scripture it was not "a little dab will do ya." It was a ram's horn filled with oil poured over the head of the person being set apart. Look at the setting apart of Aaron to the priesthood over Israel:

It is like the precious oil upon the head, coming down upon the beard, Even Aaron's beard, Coming down upon the edge of his robes. —Psalm 133:2

That is a lot of oil, running down his head, down his beard, and down to the very edges of his robe. Customarily, oil would be poured out to reach every limb of the person being anointed. This oil ran down to the very edge of Aaron's robes. That is the image of the anointing we have been given. We are soaked in the anointing.

In the past, I have taught this lesson on graduation nights at our "Invasion" conferences before the churches Invade their cities with the Gospel. I have illustrated this idea by pouring an entire liter (34 oz.) of oil onto the head of one of our institute students. Of course, I have him stand in a plastic trash bag when I do, because the oil runs down his head, onto his clothes, down his arms and legs, and into the trash bag. It is symbolic of how unreserved the anointing is upon us.

The world needs Jesus! Our purpose in ministry is for the world to have a head-on collision with Jesus. We are anointed, smeared, and soaked with oil, set apart for this service. We are anointed to carry the glory of God on the earth. When God's glory, power, and presence are present, things happen!

Oil is combustible, of course. Have you ever accidentally spilled oil on a hot stove? What happens? Fire! It is always good to keep a fire extinguisher at hand in the kitchen for moments like this. You and I are soaked in the oil of anointing. And then the fire of the Holy Spirit comes near us and: Fire! We do not need or even desire a fire extinguisher in these moments. John Wesley used to say, "I set myself on fire and people come to watch me burn."[44] We are soaked in oil, and then the Holy Spirit ignites the flame with power. Therefore, we must keep a tight connection with the Holy Spirit. We may not always feel anointed, but we are. It is in the moment the Holy Spirit arises within us that flame is ignited.

> *But you shall receive power when the Holy Spirit has come upon you; and you shall be My witnesses both in Jerusalem, and in all Judea and Samaria, and even to the remotest part of the earth. —Acts 1:8*

Why has the Holy Spirit come upon us? To animate within us the power to be witnesses. The gift of tongues is a bonus. But the purpose of the Holy Spirit within the Church is to enliven us with power from above to ignite the oil of the anointing that rests upon our lives. The anointing equips us to carry the Glory of God on the earth. Remember, the glory and the presence of God were intended to be carried by the anointed priests. Today, we are those anointed priests who are destined to carry the glory of God's presence throughout the earth.

> *9 But you are a chosen generation, a royal priesthood, a holy nation, a people for God's own possession, so that you might speak of the praises of Him who has called you out of darkness into His marvelous light. —1 Peter2:9*

We are anointed priests to "speak the praises of Him." Now, let us turn the corner and look at the job description of Jesus, which is our job description as well. After being baptized by John, Jesus came out of the water and went into the wilderness, "full of the Holy Spirit" (Luke 4:1). John had witnessed the Holy Spirit come upon Jesus in the form of a dove. In Hebrew tradition, a dove is symbolic of purity. After 40 days in fellowship with the Father in the wilderness, Jesus came out of the desert in the "power of the Holy Spirit" (Luke 4:14). He went in full of the Holy Spirit, and He came out in the power of the Holy Spirit.

When Jesus came out of the wilderness, He returned to His home village and synagogue. On the first Sabbath following His return, He was at His synagogue and was handed the scroll of Isaiah. Scripture says it was customary for Him to read from the scrolls when He was in attendance. He found the place in the scroll that we know today as Isaiah 61:1, 2 and a portion of Isaiah 42:7. Here Jesus announced what His ministry would look like:

> *18 The Spirit of the Lord is upon me, because he hath anointed me to preach the gospel to the poor; he hath sent me to heal the brokenhearted, to preach deliverance to the captives, and <u>recovering of sight to the blind</u> (Isa 42:7), to*

set at liberty them that are bruised, 19 To preach the accept-
able year of the Lord. —Luke 4:18, 19

The Spirit of the Lord is upon me. Why? Because He has anointed me. Jesus was the Christ, the anointed one, and that is why the Holy Spirit of the Lord was upon Him. We have established the fact that you and I are anointed, and that is why the Holy Spirit is upon us. Jesus was soaked with the oil of anointing, and that anointing was ignited by the power of the Holy Spirit. He came out of the wilderness in the power of the Holy Spirit. For what purpose? To preach the Good News.

His message was Good News, and our message must be Good News. Jesus was anointed to preach Good News to the poor, the poor in spirit. He saw the people as helpless and harassed, as sheep without a shepherd. It is the poor in spirit who are most ready to receive the message of hope we bring.

Healing the brokenhearted refers to restoration of the soul, the mind, will, and emotions. A whole lot of people around us are broken. This world tends to break the hearts, the souls, and the emotions of people. Jesus came to heal and restore them.

Jesus came to proclaim liberty to captives and prisoners. Whether a person is taken prisoner by his own doing or by no fault of his own, Jesus came to set them free.

Restoration of sight to the blind refers to physical healing. Can you see that, from the very beginning of His ministry, Jesus announced salvation, *sozo*, which means wholeness of body, soul, and spirit? Jesus's ministry was about restoring man in every area of his brokenness, the brokenness that resulted when sin entered the world.

So the Father sent the Son to: (1) Preach good news to the poor, (2) heal broken hearts (the soul and emotions), (3) proclaim freedom to captives (bound by sin, addictions, etc.), (4) recovery of sight to the blind (physical healing, to restore the body), (5) set at liberty those who are crushed (broken people), and (6) proclaim the year of God's favor with man. Now let us look at how the Son sends us:

*21 Jesus therefore said to them again, Peace be unto you: as
the Father hath sent me, even so send I you. —John 20:21*

As the Father sent me, I am sending you. Again, Luke 4 describes
how the Father sent the Son: to preach the Gospel to the poor, to heal
the brokenhearted, to preach deliverance to the captives and recov-
ering of sight to the blind, to set at liberty them that are bruised, and
to preach the acceptable year of the Lord. Jesus sends us in the same
manner that He has been sent by His Father. Now someone, somewhere, may say, "Yeah, well, Jesus was talking to the apostles in John
20:21, not to us." That may be a good point except for what Jesus says
in John 17:19–20, in the portion of scripture titled "The High Priestly
Prayer." This takes place at the Last Supper, where He is praying to the
Father for His followers. Look what He prays:

*18 As thou didst send me into the world, even so sent I them
into the world. 19 And for their sakes I sanctify myself, that
they themselves also may be sanctified in truth. 20 Neither
for these only do I pray, but for them also that believe on me
through their word. —John 17:18–20*

In John 20:21, Jesus states, "As You, Father, sent me into the world,
I am sending them into the world." Then here in John 17:20, He clearly
states that He is not just praying for the disciples present with Him but
for those who will believe in Him through their word. Do you see it?
Jesus is praying for you and me at the Last Supper. Try inserting your
name in verse 20. Like this: "Neither for these only do I pray, but for
<u>Bob</u> (or Joe or Mary, whatever your name is) also that will believe on
me through their word."

Do you see? We have been sent in the same way Jesus was sent to
preach good news to the poor, heal broken hearts, proclaim freedom
to captives, recovery of sight to the blind, liberty to those crushed, and

to proclaim the year of God's favor with man. Look how Jesus sent His disciples:

> *1 And he called the twelve together, and gave them power and authority over all demons, and to cure diseases. 2 And he sent them forth to preach the kingdom of God, and to heal the sick. 6 And they departed, and went throughout the villages, preaching the gospel, and healing everywhere.*
> *—Luke 9:1, 2, 6*

He gave them power and authority over *all* demons and to cure diseases. He sent them to proclaim the kingdom of God and to heal the sick. And they did it. We will see these common threads in Jesus's ministry, and the ministry of the twelve, and the ministry of the 70. Teaching, preaching, and healing. These are the elements of the Gospel. Look at Jesus's ministry:

> *23 And Jesus went about in all Galilee, teaching in their synagogues, and preaching the gospel of the kingdom, and healing all manner of disease and all manner of sickness among the people. 24 And the report of him went forth into all Syria: and they brought unto him all that were sick, holden with divers diseases and torments, possessed with demons, and epileptic, and palsied; and he healed them. — Matthew 4:23, 24*

> *35 And Jesus went about all the cities and the villages, teaching in their synagogues, and preaching the gospel of the kingdom, and healing all manner of disease and all manner of sickness. 36 But when he saw the multitudes, he was moved with compassion for them, because they were distressed and scattered, as sheep not having a shepherd. — Matthew 9:35, 36*

The Apostles followed the same pattern in ministry:

5 These twelve Jesus sent forth, and charged them, saying, Go not into any way of the Gentiles, and enter not into any city of the Samaritans: 6 but go rather to the lost sheep of the house of Israel. 7 And as ye go, preach, saying, The kingdom of heaven is at hand. 8 Heal the sick, raise the dead, cleanse the lepers, cast out demons: freely ye received, freely give. — Matthew 10:5–8

They went, teaching and preaching that the kingdom of Heaven was at hand. They healed the sick, raised the dead, cleansed the lepers, and cast out demons. These are all elements of the Gospel we are sent to proclaim. But wait, there is more. Jesus sent out another group, the Seventy:

1 Now after these things the Lord appointed seventy others and sent them two and two before his face into every city and place, whither he himself was about to come. 2 And he said unto them, The harvest indeed is plenteous, but the laborers are few: pray ye therefore the Lord of the harvest, that he send forth laborers into his harvest. 3 Go your ways; behold, I send you forth as lambs in the midst of wolves. 9 and heal the sick that are therein, and say unto them, The kingdom of God is come nigh unto you. 17 And the seventy returned with joy, saying, Lord, even the demons are subject unto us in thy name. —Luke 9:1–3, 9, 17

Jesus did it, the Apostles did it, the Seventy did it. Now it is our turn! Let us look at the Great Commission verses found in the 16th chapter of the Gospel of Mark:

*15 And He said to them, "Go into all the world and preach the gospel to all creation. 16 "**He who has believed** and* *has been baptized shall be saved (SOZO); but he who has disbelieved shall be condemned. 17 "These signs will accompany **those who have believed**: in My name they will cast out demons, they will speak with new tongues; 18 they will pick up serpents, and if they drink any deadly poison, it will not hurt them; they will lay hands on the sick, and they will recover. —Mark 16:15–17*

"Those who have believed," in verse 17 is the same as "He who has believed," in verse 16. The same deposit of faith (that is what believe means) resulting in salvation is accompanied by the signs, wonders, and miracles that will follow us into the harvest fields. In addition to being saved, believers will cast out demons, speak with new tongues, pick up serpents, and drink deadly poisons and not be affected. They will lay hands on the sick, *and they will recover.* These are the normal activities of the kingdom of Heaven! This is the normal Christian life! What we call supernatural from our perspective here on earth, *is natural and normal* in the kingdom of Heaven.

Chinese underground church worship.

Clandestine Peach Orchard meeting with Chinese underground leaders.

Brother Happy showing Chinese evangelist the Evangecube.

Brother Happy teaching Chinese evangelist how to use the Evangecube.

Teaching in underground Chinese Bible school.

Chinese underground church celebrating the Day of Pentecost.

Chinese underground church worship.

Chinese baptism on the Day of Pentecost.

China underground church three-day seminar.

Pastors and Leaders Conference, Camaguey, Cuba.

Pastors and Leaders Conference, Camaguey, Cuba.

Pastors and Leaders Conference, Camaguey, Cuba

Pastors and Leaders Conference, Camaguey, Cuba.

Now it is our turn to do it. You are sent—therefore, you are anointed, with power and authority! Over devils, over diseases! Anointed to teach. Anointed to preach. Anointed to heal the sick. Here is your commissioning, and it is the same as our Lord's commissioning.

> *18 The Spirit of the Lord is upon <u>me</u>, because he hath anointed <u>me</u> to preach the gospel to the poor; he hath sent <u>me</u> to heal the brokenhearted, to preach deliverance to the captives, and recovering of sight to the blind, to set at liberty them that are bruised, 19 To preach the acceptable year of the Lord. —Luke 4:18, 19*

Now, read it one more time, only this time proclaim it over yourself. Maybe even read it out loud so you can hear yourself speak the words. The Spirit of the Lord is upon *you*. He has anointed *you*. He has sent *you*! Do you believe it?

Before we close this chapter, I would like to share one more story. At the beginning of the chapter, I shared a story about 20 people in a parking lot who heard the Good News and made Jesus their Savior and Lord. Here I would like to share a story about the one. The Father has a passionate interest in the multitudes, but He is also just as passionately interested in the one. Even in a multitude, the Father sees each individual as unique and precious.

A number of years ago, I was in my office in Longmont, on a Friday about midday when it began to snow. When I arrived home late that afternoon, the snow was accumulating and continuing. I considered that the streets may be empty that night, but I went to my room to pray anyway. After a time of prayer and resting in the Lord's presence, I sensed Jesus would have me on the streets this night. I headed out onto Main Street in the cold and snow, confirming what I had suspected, that no one would be out on the streets. Even the normal Friday night traffic was absent in the inclement weather. For the next two and a half hours, I walked up one side of the street and down the other interceding for my city. The wind out of the north was stiff and frigid, making it disagreeable to walk north.

Finally, after more than two hours, I saw a lone figure standing at a bus stop. I thought to myself, "Surely this is the one I am out here for tonight." I reached into my pocket for one of my I.O.U. LOVE ministry cards.

As I made my approach toward the man, I heard the Holy Spirit say, "No, this isn't the one."

I thought, "What? Wait! Really?"

The word came back the same, "No, this isn't the one."

"Well," I thought, "at least there is one somewhere out here." I made my journey north along the street again, fighting the discomfort from the north wind. Making my way to my turnaround point, I crossed the street and began to walk south. Walking south at least provided me refuge from the hostile wind.

When I reached a row of storefronts running perpendicular between Main Street and the next street over, I heard the Holy Spirit say, "Turn in here," and I did so. I walked in the dark along the row of storefronts, and as I reached the midpoint, there was an opening between the storefronts that was occupied by the trash dumpster. Then I noticed the shadow of a figure sitting against a building. "Could this be the one?" I thought to myself.

"Yes, it is," came the response from that still small voice. I approached the shadowy lone figure and noticed it was a girl. Being a shadowy lone figure myself and approaching a young girl on a dark night in a lonely place, I was well aware that I needed to approach with caution. I asked the young lady if she was all right and if I might sit down to talk with her. I told her God had sent me out tonight, because He wanted me to speak to someone. I hoped that would calm her if she was feeling anxious. I sat down on the ground in the snow across from her with my back to the dumpster. She sat with her back to the side of the building. We talked for a bit, and I learned that her name was Rachel, and she was 17 years old.

As we chatted for a bit, I steered the conversation to the eternal, observing that each of her responses was penetrating. When I asked if she felt she would spend eternity in Heaven someday, she responded, "I really hope so." Her response sounded almost desperate. I shared the Good News of salvation, and she was eager to respond to my invitation to invite Jesus to be her Savior and Lord. We prayed together, and her prayer was as earnest and sincere as anyone I had ever prayed with.

I gave her a New Testament, and as I was about to leave she said to me, "You know, it is amazing that you are out here tonight." That was the opening I had been hoping for. I could tell she was in the midst of something intense, but I was being cautious in our conversation. I sat down again and asked her what was going on and why she was out here on such a dreadful night.

Then she told me her story. Earlier that day, she had received a letter from her doctor informing her that she had cancerous cells on her cervix. Our discussion took a whole new turn. I reassured her of God's love for her and His plan for her. I told her that God knew she would be out here tonight and sent me to reassure her that He knew what she was going through. We prayed together for her healing. We chatted and laughed for a long while, and I watched as her demeanor really changed.

Finally, she was ready to go home, so I helped her up out of the snow, and we parted ways. As I walked along, I considered that the Father knew Rachel would be out there that night, contemplating life-and-death issues. The Father cared for her enough to bring someone to find her and represent Himself to a scared young girl. I was glad I could be that someone.

We have talked about the anointing from God that abides in us to preach the Good News. We talked of how Salvation brings wholeness of body, soul, and spirit. We have seen what the ministry of Jesus, the twelve Apostles, the Seventy others, and ourselves as well includes: to preach good news to the poor, to heal broken hearts (the soul, the emotions), to proclaim freedom to captives (bound by sin, addictions, etc.) and recovery of sight to the blind (physical healing, to restore the body), liberty to those crushed (broken people), and to proclaim the year of God's favor with man. These are all the normal activities of the kingdom of Heaven. In the next chapter, we will talk about another anointing we have: The anointing to carry the glory and the presence of God on the earth.

Ordinary men with extraordinary power
Common men with uncommon results
Usual men with unusual anointing
Unschooled mortal men with immortal vision
Weak men with mighty deeds.[45] *—Ikechukwu Joseph*

"If God is going to use us for His honor and glory, if His power is going to rest upon us, if He is going to bless our soul-winning ministry, then our lives must be placed abso-lutely at His disposal.[46] *—Oswald Smith*

14

The Glory of God—Anointed to Carry the Glory of God on the Earth

"For the earth will be filled with the knowledge of the glory of the Lord, As the waters cover the sea." —Habakkuk 2:14

"What is the glory of God? It is who God is. It is the essence of His nature; the weight of His importance; the radiance of His splendor; the demonstration of His power; the atmosphere of His presence."[47] —Rick Warren

"You have the anointing of God flowing through you when God's heart touches another person's heart through your heart. The anointing of God is the Holy Spirit. He flows as a river of love, from the throne of grace, through the hearts of believers, bringing life to all that receive His touch."[48] — The Anointing of the Holy Spirit, God.net

"The anointing of the Holy Spirit is given through people to demonstrate God's love and power. Christ means the 'Anointed One.' Because Christ is in us the same anointing

that He had on earth we also have.[49] —*The Anointing of the Holy Spirit, God.net*

"For the anxious longing of the creation waits eagerly for the revealing of the sons of God." —Romans 8:19

THROUGHOUT OUR CHRISTIAN experience, we have those moments, many I hope, when we have powerful, life-changing encounters with God. It may be during our quiet times in His presence or it may be a powerful time in praise and worship where it seems like He peels back the veil of Heaven. We see and experience Him differently than ever before, and it changes us permanently. A time when a part of His character is revealed in a new way, with a fresh revelation of His nature. This is His glory.

These moments affect us in such a way that we walk differently from that day forward. Jacob walked differently after he encountered God at Penuel. These encounters with the glory of God enable us to carry this aspect of His glory on the earth in a new way. In this chapter I will talk about the glory of God. What is the glory? Perhaps you have been in one of those Holy Spirit–charged atmospheres that you can only explain as the glory of God. To the uninitiated who ask us to explain the glory of God, it is difficult to convey the meaning. We know when God's presence and glory are present. But what is His glory? I hope that by the end of this chapter, we will understand and be able to express it.

Also, in this chapter we will confirm the anointing we have to carry that glory on the earth. Our encounters with the very essence of God make us carriers of His glory. When will the knowledge of the glory of God fill the earth like waters cover the sea? Once the people of God recognize their anointing as priests of God to carry His presence and glory. All of creation is waiting eagerly for the revealing of the sons of God.

In the previous chapter, I opened with a story of God's glorious presence settling on a group of people in a parking lot. Another time, during a mission trip to Mexico City, the glorious presence of the Father stepped onto the playing field and took total control of the ministry. It was the final day of the trip, scheduled as a free day, where we would do the tourist thing and visit the Artist Market in the city's center. To start the day, we went to Mexico City's Alameda Park for a devotional time. Alameda Park is the large park in the center of the city, similar to New York's Central Park, and is filled with ornate, resplendent fountains, each circled with concrete banks of benches. It is also well shaded by Royal Poinciana and Jacaranda trees, two beautiful flowering trees.

That morning, I had shown the pastor of the group his team's statistic folder, which we maintain to document each ministry site. The folder has 22–24 individual lines that we fill in throughout the week, and all but one line of this folder had been filled, representing different ministry activities. The pastor told me that in all the years he had brought his students to work with us, he had never completely filled the lines in the folder, and he asked if perhaps we could do one more ministry site later that day. "Perhaps," I told him, not really expecting it to happen.

We started our devotional time with a few praise and worship songs in this vast public park. Our team took up one of the four concrete seating banks surrounding a fountain. Since it was still early on a weekday, about 8:00 a.m., not many other people were around. After a time of worship, I shared a short devotional called "Defining Moments in Our Lives." This devotional was intended to tie the week of ministry to their future walks with Jesus back home. I spoke out of Isaiah 6, the prophet's tremendous vision in the throne room of God. He is taken up into the glorious, holy presence of God, where he sees throne angels surrounding the Father. They are thundering back and forth, "Holy! Holy! Holy!" Isaiah is overwhelmed in this holy presence and becomes aware of his own human weakness. I can only imagine the powerful presence of God in this scene.

It was what happened next, though, that would define Isaiah's future. Verse 8 says, "And I heard the voice of the Lord, saying, 'Whom shall I send, and who will go for us?' Then I said, 'Here am I; send me.'" Isaiah's defining moment in this wonderful encounter was the moment when he said, "Yes, here I am, send me." Isaiah had already been a prophet for some time, but his response to this encounter in the Father's throne room resulted in a lifelong ministry. The remaining 60 chapters of the prophet's writings include many of the clearest prophetic descriptions of the life and ministry of Jesus to be found in the Bible. I challenged the young men and women present that morning to say yes to Jesus's call on their lives. I challenged them to respond as Isaiah had, "Yes, Lord. Here I am. Send me."

As we wrapped up our devotion time, our worship leaders played another worship song to give the students an opportunity to respond to the challenge set before them. Then it happened. God stepped onto the field and took control. His presence fell on us all like a ton of bricks. The ground became holy by His holy presence. Each team member went down on his knees in the holy presence of our Holy God. Then many were on their faces, weeping and crying out to God. Not a single person in that group of about 25 people was unaffected by the presence. This went on for the next three hours.

Several times, our worship leaders started to fall to the ground under the mighty presence of God. Fortunately, we had two worship leaders, and as one would go down, I would grab the guitar from him and hand it to the other leader. After a while as that worship leader was going down to the ground, I would do the same and bring the first leader back into the mix. As I walked through the group, I noticed that the students' faces were being impressed, from their tears, onto the concrete pavement surrounding the fountain. One young man caught up in the glory repeated for more than 30 minutes, "You are so real! You are so real! You are so real." In the middle of all this, I got a call on my cell phone from the senior pastor of their church back in Texas, wondering how the team was doing. I walked around the group with my phone to let the pastor hear for himself.

After the first two and a half hours, I felt that maybe it was time to wrap up. We had a schedule to keep, you know. I walked over to our speaker and took up the microphone, intending to stop the meeting. But there was a problem. I could not lift the microphone up from my side to my mouth. I tried, but my arm was frozen. All I could do was let out a laugh, acknowledging the Father's supremacy in what was taking place. After another hour, I tried to do the same thing, with the same results. I abandoned the idea of keeping the team schedule for that day.

As His manifest glory continued, people began to come from all over the park to sit on the other three concrete seating benches surrounding the fountain. The presence of God drew and kept them there for the next several hours. At one point, a young man approached me trembling, telling me how he had been drawn to our location. He had come into the city to bring his sister for a job interview. Since he had some time to spare, he decided to go to the nearby central library, which required him to cross the park. As he entered the park, he felt a holy, powerful presence of God. He followed that presence, and the closer he came to us, the more powerful the presence became. When he entered the fountain area, he saw two huge angels standing over us.

This glory had now continued for three hours plus the hour of the original intended devotion. The entire area was now filled with people, all the seating was occupied, and still many more people stood nearby to immerse themselves in this holy presence. I sent a couple of our staff back to the hotel, only three blocks away, to get some cases of New Testaments. When they returned, we turned our speaker to the crowd, and one of our Mexican national staff delivered a Gospel invitation. About 100 people responded to the Gospel invitation by flooding the area. Afterward, I allowed the team pastor to fill in the final line of the statistics folder.

God's glory is irresistible, and we are anointed to carry it. In the previous chapter, we established the clear fact that we are anointed. The word anointed comes from the Greek word *chrio* from which we derive the word "Christ," which means the anointed one. It literally means to smear or rub with oil. It symbolically represents to consecrate, to set apart, the person called to service. The anointing is God's power and influence upon the person He has chosen for service. What is our purpose in ministry? Our purpose is for the world to have a head-on collision with Jesus! The world needs Jesus, and we are anointed to proclaim Him to the world. Let this key statement permeate your soul: You are anointed to bring the Glory of God down to this earth and the people in it. When God's Glory is present, things happen, as illustrated by this story of the transfiguration:

> *2 And He was transfigured before them; and His face shone like the sun, and His garments became as white as light. 3 And behold, Moses and Elijah appeared to them, talking with Him. 4 Peter said to Jesus, "Lord, it is good for us to be here; if You wish, I will make three tabernacles here, one for You, and one for Moses, and one for Elijah." 5 While he was still speaking, a bright cloud overshadowed them, and behold, a voice out of the cloud said, "This is My beloved Son, with whom I am well-pleased; listen to Him!" 6 When the disciples heard this, they fell face down to the ground and were terrified. —Matthew 17:2–6*

Now imagine Peter, James, and John coming back down the mountain after this glorious encounter, leaning over to each other and asking, "I'm not really sure. Did something happen up there?" I think not. I imagine them coming down the mountain ready to burst, saying, "Whoa! Did you see that?" They encountered the glory of God, and it overwhelmed their flesh. We too may end up falling face down to the ground in the glorious presence of God. God's presence and glory is awesome and terrible to us. The world is not waiting for religion, but for the powerful presence of a powerful God to reveal His glory.

The anointing is the Father's power and influence upon us to carry His glory on the earth. The glory and presence of God is intended to be carried by anointed people. It has always been that way. The Ark of the Covenant, which represented God's glory and presence on the earth, could only be carried by anointed priests. A story in the Old Testament relates its capture by the Philistines during the reign of King Saul. Eventually, after the presence of the Ark had caused many disturbances amongst the Philistines, they put it on an oxcart and sent it back to Israel. By divine direction, the oxcart made its way to the home of Abinadab, a Levite (priest). It stayed there for more than a generation until David was King over Judah and desired to bring the Ark into Jerusalem.

David gathered the people to go out and retrieve the Ark. He set it on a new oxcart and started the journey to Jerusalem. It did not go far before God put a halt to that parade. Uzzah, the son of Abinadab, who grew up with the Ark on his front porch, drove the oxcart along. At some point, the oxen stumbled, and Uzzah reached out his hand to steady the Ark. God struck Uzzah dead, so King David abandoned the mission and returned to Jerusalem. He wanted dearly to bring the Ark, the place of God's presence and glory on the earth at that time, to Jerusalem. His motive was good and noble, but his methods were unacceptable to God. The Ark remained where the parade had stopped, at Obed-Edom's home, for three months. God blessed the house of Obed-Edom and everything he had. Where the Lord's presence is, there lies His blessing. King David heard of the Lord's blessing on the house of Obed-Edom and inquired further into what was needed to bring the Ark into Jerusalem. Look at what he discovered:

> *2 Then David said, "No one is to carry the ark of God but the Levites; for the LORD chose them to carry the ark of God and to minister to Him forever."*

11 Then David called for Zadok and Abiathar the priests, and for the Levites, for Uriel, Asaiah, Joel, Shemaiah, Eliel and Amminadab, 12 and said to them, "You are the heads of the fathers' households of the Levites; consecrate yourselves both you and your relatives, that you may bring up the ark of the LORD God of Israel to the place that I have prepared for it. 13 "Because you did not carry it at the first, the LORD our God made an outburst on us, for we did not seek Him according to the ordinance." 14 So the priests and the Levites consecrated themselves to bring up the ark of the LORD God of Israel. 15 The sons of the Levites carried the ark of God on their shoulders with the poles thereon, as Moses had commanded according to the word of the LORD.
—*1 Chronicles 15: 2, 11–15*

Do you see? The presence and Glory of God has always been intended to be carried by anointed people. The Philistines sent the Ark back on an oxcart because they did not know any better. King David and the people of God, who should have known what God required, tried to put it on a new oxcart. I believe the Philistine's oxcart represents the ways of this world. Too often we try to use the same methods as the world, except maybe to clean them up a bit, to promote the things of the kingdom of God. It does not work, and there is no anointing on it. The anointing lies on the people of God, the contemporary anointed priests of the kingdom.

9 But you are A CHOSEN RACE, A royal PRIESTHOOD, A HOLY NATION, A PEOPLE FOR God's OWN POSSESSION, (WHY?) so that you may proclaim the excellencies of Him who has called you out of darkness into His marvelous light. —*1 Peter 2:9*

6 and He has made us to be a kingdom, priests to His God and Father—to Him be the glory and the dominion forever and ever. Amen. —Revelation 1:6

10 You have made them to be a kingdom and priests to our God; and they will reign upon the earth. —Revelation 5:10

Today, God's people are the anointed priests called to proclaim His excellencies and glory on the earth. We are anointed to carry His glory, just as the priests of old carried His glorious presence on their shoulders.

But what is God's glory? How do we define the Glory of god? We know when His glory is present, but what is it? That is a good question. Let us look to the Word of God to define the glory of God:

18 Then Moses said, "I pray You, show me Your glory!" 19 And He said, "I Myself will make all My goodness pass before you, and will proclaim the name of the LORD before you; and I will be gracious to whom I will be gracious, and will show compassion on whom I will show compassion." —Exodus 33:18, 19

22 "and it will come about, while My glory is passing by, that I will put you in the cleft of the rock and cover you with My hand until I have passed by." —Exodus 33:22

Moses asks the Lord, "Show me Your glory!"

The Lord responds, "I will." In the Old Testament, whenever you see the word "Lord," it is translated from the personal name of God, Jehovah, or Yahweh, which means "I Am." Immediately, Yahweh suggested that His glory is His character, His goodness, graciousness, and compassion. God's character includes His glory, and another aspect of His glory is His name, "The Lord." In the Old Testament especially, names were given to define the character of the person. Often, names would be a prophetic description of what a parent proclaimed over a child. This day-to-day proclamation would mold the character of the child, with the desired end result being a child who would grow into that character trait.

When God revealed Himself to Moses at the burning bush, He revealed Himself as "I Am." I Am what? It sounds open ended: I Am. Throughout the Lord's dealings with Israel, He would fill in that blank. "I Am your provider." "I Am your healer." "I Am your victory." There are many more, and we will look at this shortly.

The Lord didn't give Israel a laundry list of "I Am's." During times of great need, though, He would reveal Himself. "Oh, by the way, I Am the One who fights this battle." "Oh yeah, I am the one who will provide your needs." Therefore, Moses requested, "Show me Your glory!" and the Lord obliged His request with a foretaste of what was to come the next day. The Lord tells Him, "I will make my glory pass by you." He tells Moses, "Prepare yourself and come up the mountain in the morning." I love Moses's response. He prepared himself and came up *early* in the morning. Now let us have a look at what God's glory is.

> 5 The LORD descended in the cloud and stood there with him as he called upon the name of the LORD. 6 Then the LORD passed by in front of him and proclaimed, "The LORD, the LORD God, compassionate and gracious, slow to anger, and abounding in lovingkindness and truth; 7 who keeps lovingkindness for thousands, who forgives iniquity, transgression and sin; yet He will by no means leave the guilty unpunished, visiting the iniquity of fathers on the children and on the grandchildren to the third and fourth generations." 8 Moses made haste to bow low toward the earth and worship. —Exodus 34:5–9

What is God's Glory? It is the revelation of His character, His nature, and His essence.

What is the glory of God? It is who God is. It is the essence of His nature; the weight of His importance; the radiance of His splendor; the demonstration of His power; the atmosphere of His presence.[50] —*Rick Warren*

His Glory begins with His name, "The Lord!" "The Lord God." "Yahweh." "Yahweh, God." Or in Hebrew, "Yahweh El." "I Am!" "I Am God." Yahweh is the personal name of God. "El" was the common name of God. Every nation had an "El" or a multitude of them, but Yahweh was the El of Israel. Then Yahweh announced specific aspects of His glory. He is compassionate; He is gracious; He is slow to anger; He abounds in lovingkindness; He abounds in truth; He keeps His lovingkindness for multitudes; He is forgiving; He forgives iniquity, transgression, and sin. But He is holy, and He will punish the guilty. This is the God of the Old Testament, the God who is the same yesterday, today, and forever.

We may encounter these glorious characteristics at different stages of our Christian walk. I am talking about the deep revelation of God's compassion, or His lovingkindness that is burned into our spirits. Often, when we encounter these qualities of God, we are undone, like Moses, making haste to bow low to the earth and worship. Moses got the full dose of God's glorious essence in one shot. No wonder he had to cover his face when he came down the mountain. His face was shining, and that is what we look like when we have these glorious encounters with God.

A single revelation of His character can change our lives radically. People can walk in the glory and power of a single revelation for years. Lifelong ministries are birthed out of a single revelation of a single feature of God. When we have these encounters with the Glory of God, we are then capable of carrying these glorious attributes with us in this world. When we have encountered the Lord as compassionate, we become fit to carry that trait and impart it to others. When we have encountered the Lord as gracious, we are then capable of carrying His graciousness to the lost living around us. When we have met the Lord in His lovingkindness, we are able to extend His lovingkindness to the broken people of this world. It is the same with every glorious attribute of our Heavenly Father. Do you know what His lovingkindness is? It means He loves to do acts of kindness for us and for the multitudes, and He abounds in it. He overflows in lovingkindness and truth.

And then there is His name! I Am! Yahweh! As I wrote earlier, The Lord revealed Himself to Israel in the time of their present need. Today, scripture gives us a record of how He revealed Himself. Let us not stop here, but let us press on, press in, to know Him in our experience as the I Am in all of these.

Yahweh, Jehovah, I Am, literally means to exist, to be self-existent. Jehovah is the combination of three Hebrew words that mean, "Who was, who is, who is to come." Before God revealed Himself to Moses as Yahweh, He revealed Himself to Abraham, Isaac, and Jacob as El Shaddai, El Elyon, and El Olam. The God of Abraham, Isaac, and Jacob was not like the gods of the nations. He was El Shaddai, God Almighty, El Elyon, God Most High, and El Olam, the Everlasting God. He distinguished Himself from the "El's" of other nations as Almighty, Most High, and Everlasting.

When the Lord revealed His personal name to Moses as Yahweh, the I Am, He planned to introduce the nation of Israel to His personal character and attributes, usually in the time of their need. He still desires to reveal Himself today to each of His sons and daughters. When you find yourself in the place of sickness, seek His presence, wait upon Him, and let Him come near and say to you, "Son, daughter, I Am here, I Am your healer." When you are in great need and not sure where your provision will come from, seek His presence, wait upon Him, let Him come near, and announce, "Son, daughter, I Am here. I Am your provider." When your peace is disrupted, and you have no rest, seek His presence, wait upon Him, until He appears and declares to you, "Son, daughter, I Am here, I Am your peace." As we encounter our Heavenly

Father in these ways and gain the sweet revelation of who He is, we can then carry that revelation to the waiting world.

Who is the I Am? He is Yahweh Jireh, The Lord will provide (Genesis 22:14). He is Yahweh Nissi, The Lord is my banner, our means of victory, He fights for His people (Exodus 17:13–16). He is Yahweh Shalom, The Lord is our Peace, our rest (Judges 6:22–24). He is Yahweh Sabbaoth, The Lord of Hosts, Captain of the Armies of Heaven, (1 Samuel 17:45–47). He is Yahweh Maccaddeshem, The Lord our Sanctifier, He makes us holy, He sets us apart for His purpose, (Exodus 31:13). He is Yahweh Ro'I, or Rohi, Ra'ah, or Ro'eh, The Lord, my Shepherd, (Psalm 23). He is Yahweh Tsidkenu, the Lord, our Righteousness, He is the means of our righteousness, Jesus! (Jeremiah 23:2–6). Yahweh Rapha, the Lord who Heals you, He is the source of our healing and wholeness, (Exodus 15:26). And Yahweh Shammah, the Lord is there, His presence is with His people, the Lord's personal presence in His millennial kingdom, (Ezekiel 48:35).

Yahweh Shammah is one of the Lord's attributes that really excites me. I Am there! This expression of who the Lord is can be found in Ezekiel, where the prophet describes the New Jerusalem, a Heavenly place. Even at this point in Ezekiel's life, long ago, the Lord announced Himself as I Am there. I am already there. It suggests to me that He is already in the future. He occupies the past, present, and future, meaning He is in my past, present, and future. He has written my story, and from what I already know of His glorious attributes, He knows the end of my story. Since He does all things well, I know that this story will end well. And so will yours.

Do you see it? His Name is His glory. I am God Almighty. I am the Most High God. I am the everlasting God. I am your provider. I am the one who fights your battles. I am your victory. I am your peace. I am the captain of armies. I am the one who sets you apart. I am the one who makes you holy. I am your shepherd. I am your righteousness. I am the one who heals you. I am there wherever you go, and wherever you are, I am there. When we are challenged by difficult situations, it is time to seek and wait upon Him until He reveals to us who He is in that moment. When Paul was imprisoned in Rome, when his future was unsure, he cried out, "I want to know you in the situation I am in this very moment."

> *That I may know Him and the power of His resurrection and the fellowship of His sufferings, being conformed to His death. —Philippians 3:10*

Look at King David's understanding of the glory and the character of the Lord Most High. It seems to me that David had revelation of the many attributes of Yahweh that God had previously revealed to Moses:

> *1 A Psalm of David. Bless the LORD, O my soul, And all that is within me, bless His holy name. 2 Bless the LORD, O my soul, And forget none of His benefits; 3 Who pardons all your iniquities, Who heals all your diseases; 4 Who redeems your life from the pit, Who crowns you with lovingkindness and compassion; 5 Who satisfies your years with good things, So that your youth is renewed like the eagle. 6 The LORD performs righteous deeds And judgments for all who are oppressed. 7 He made known His ways to Moses, His acts to the sons of Israel. 8 The LORD is compassionate and gracious, Slow to anger and abounding in lovingkindness. 9 He will not always strive with us, nor will He keep His anger forever. 10 He has not dealt with us according to our sins, nor rewarded us according to our iniquities. 11 For as high as the heavens are above the earth, so great is His lovingkindness toward those who fear Him. 12 As far as the east is from the west, So far has He removed our transgressions from us. 13 Just as a father has compassion on his children, So the LORD has compassion on those who fear Him. 14 For He Himself knows our frame; He is mindful that we are but*

dust. 15 As for man, his days are like grass; As a flower of the field, so he flourishes. 16 When the wind has passed over it, it is no more, And its place acknowledges it no longer. 17 But the lovingkindness of the LORD is from everlasting to everlasting on those who fear Him, And His righteousness to children's children, 18 To those who keep His covenant and remember His precepts to do them. —Psalm 103:1–18

God's glory is His character, and we encounter His glory in those moments when He pulls back the veil of heaven and reveals Himself. God's glory is the revelation of His character. We must pursue His presence to position ourselves for these fresh outpourings of His glory, which change us. In His glorious presence often, we become like Moses or Peter, James, and John on the mount of transfiguration, we make haste to fall with our faces to the ground and worship Him. When we stand again, we are changed by His glorious presence. We walk differently from that point on. Many people can continue in a single revelation of His Glory for years. Lifelong ministries are birthed out of a single revelation of a single aspect of God. We must seek Him, pursue Him, and like Moses cry out, "Show me your glory!" Encountering His glory throughout our lives we become carriers of His glory to impart to others. As a result of God's dealings with us, people can encounter God and His glory through us.

> *For the earth will be filled with the knowledge of the glory of the LORD, As the waters cover the sea. —Habakkuk 2:14*

As we, the contemporary anointed priests, carry the glorious attributes of our Lord throughout the earth, the earth will be filled with the knowledge of the glory of the Lord. *We are called to carry His glory throughout the earth.*

On Tuesday, April 20, 1999, I was in my office in Longmont around midday, when we began to receive reports about a tragedy unfolding in Littleton, Colorado. Two armed students entered Columbine High School and massacred 12 students and a teacher. The gunmen would later take their own lives. Twenty-four additional students were injured, 21 by gunfire. The gunmen entered the school at 11:19 a.m. The first 911 call came in at 11:21 a.m. Between 11:29 a.m. and 11:36 a.m., the gunmen shot and killed 10 students in the school library and wounded 12 additional students.

In the weeks following the tragedy a group of well-known professional athletes visited the Columbine students after they resumed classes at nearby Chatham High School. Among those was Reverend Reggie White, perennial All-Pro defensive end who played 15 years with the Philadelphia Eagles and Green Bay Packers. Pastor/Author Rick Joyner was also invited by the group to join them. After the school assemblies a rally was held at nearby Orchard Road Christian Center and was well attended by the area students.

During the rally the founder of the group, Keith Johnson, remarked that the first 911 call on that terrible day came in at 11:21 a.m. John 11:21, says, "Martha then said to Jesus, 'Lord, if You had been here, my brother would not have died.'" He challenged those students that night to take a moment each day at 11:21 a.m. to pray for their schools. Do you find that coincidental? Then look at John 11:32, the moments during the slaughter in the school library, "Therefore, when Mary came where Jesus was, she saw Him, and fell at His feet, saying to Him, 'Lord, if You had been here, my brother would not have died.'" We can shake our heads and wring our hands and ask why. But I would remind you of Martha's words to Jesus after her brother Lazarus died. "Lord, if You had been here, my brother would not have died" (John 11:21). The truth is, we have removed Jesus from our public institutions and wonder why they have experienced such death and decay.

Revelation 3:20 reveals that the Lord will not enter where He is not invited. As Psalm 115:16 states, "The heavens are the heavens of the LORD; but the earth He has given to the sons of men." The Lord delegated authority over the earth to man, and "the gifts and calling of

God are without repentance" (Romans 11:29, KJV), which means that he will not take them back. That is why the Lord will not do things on earth until we ask Him, even though He knows what we need before we ask Him. This is why Jesus had to become a man to redeem the earth, and why He always referred to Himself as the "Son of Man" when He walked the earth.[51]

In the days following the tragedy, there was a tremendous outpouring from local and national communities to comfort the young Columbine students whose lives and sense of security had been shattered. Christian groups also raced to Littleton to console the traumatized Columbine community. In prayer, I sought the Lord as to whether I should participate in this outpouring of comfort, and the Holy Spirit confirmed that I should go. I did not want to go as another onlooker; I wanted to bring healing to the brokenhearted.

Over the next few days, I made several trips to Clement Park, which is adjacent to Columbine High. Students, families, onlookers, local and national news teams, and others like me descended upon the park to somehow make sense of this heartbreak. The scene was indescribable. Multitudes of young people walked about in a state of disorientation and bewilderment. Makeshift memorials were loaded with stuffed animals, flowers, and notes from the survivors.

As I said, the local Christian community was doing its part to comfort the brokenhearted. Ongoing prayer and worship were taking place at a tent set up by a local ministry, and I was glad for that. The tent was full the entire time I was there, and they were reaching the churched students with care and comfort.

There was also some weird religious stuff taking place also. One group of about 10 people huddled together, backs to the crowds, spewing out hellfire, judgment, and damnation through their 20-dollar speaker system. That saddened me. They were not reaching anyone, and they were an annoyance to all.

A number of young people stood on the fringes, lost, dazed, marginalized, and unchurched. No one was reaching out to them. Who would reach out to them? I guess my ministry has always been to the people outside the walls of the church.

I met one young man standing vigil over his best friend's pickup truck, which had become one of the makeshift memorials in the park. His friend was one of the 21 wounded students. At that time, his prognosis was uncertain. Eventually, his friend would survive but with crippled legs. He became a spokesman for Columbine at other school assemblies. At this point, though, his future was unsure.

I asked the young watchman if I could pray with him regarding his friend. He invited me to pray. Taking his hand, I began to pray for the wounded friend's survival and healing. The young man grabbed hold of me tightly, sobbing and sobbing. It took some time for him to regain his composure. A crowd of people stopped and witnessed this outpouring of brokenness. Afterward, the young man was deeply appreciative and had renewed hope in his friend's restoration. An older fellow who had been watching approached us with tears in his eyes. He was a teacher at nearby Dakota Ridge High School and said, "That was beautiful; we need more people like you here, loving on these students."

I continued through the masses and came upon a group of about 10 young students sitting in the mud. Because it had snowed that day, the hundreds of stuffed toys were soaked and the ground was muddy. I joined these ninth and tenth grade students to console them. They were very alternative, with dyed hair and multiple piercings, my kind of people. We talked for a long time. I spoke healing words to them, and they were open and receptive to the Word I shared. One young lady with magenta hair looked up at me from her place in the mud and said, "You know, if I had heard you speak a couple years ago, I might still be in youth group today." I do not feel this is an indictment on any church youth group. There are just some people out there who do not fit into the context of our typical youth ministries, and they must be reached under a different framework.

On the Saturday after the shootings, I made my last trip to Clement Park. While talking to a group of people, I noticed a young man slipping through the bevy of local and national news trailers that had set up shop on the edge of the park. He caught my attention because he was a skinhead, with a swastika-adorned T-shirt, shin-high black jackboots, and the look of a real Nazi. I tried to catch up with him but lost him in the crowd of people. I prayed that the Lord would lead me to him later, and I continued to talk to huddled groups of broken young people. After a while, I caught sight of the young Nazi, again sneaking through the news trailers, and made a beeline to intercept him.

I caught up with him and gave him one of my I.O.U. LOVE ministry cards. As we talked, he offered, "Man, I've been raised on hate my whole life, but I had to come see this." Josh was raised in Chicago and had moved to the Denver area recently. The entire story surrounding the Columbine massacre had cut him to the core; it had made him tender and open to another point of view. I shared with him the peace that can be had in Jesus, and the Good News of Jesus's salvation. Then I invited him to respond to Jesus's invitation to, "Come to me, all who are weary and heavy-laden, and I will give you rest." Josh declined my invitation, and we parted ways.

But the story did not end there. Almost exactly a year later, I received a phone call on a Saturday afternoon. It was Josh. He told me his life was in the dumper, and he did not know where to turn. He remembered that little I.O.U. LOVE card that had been in his wallet for the past year. We had a great conversation, and he was open to the Good News message. When I invited him to respond to Jesus's invitation, he said yes. We prayed together over the phone, and Josh was born again.

My I.O.U. LOVE ministry card has our names, Bob & Kathleen Gabelman, on the front, along with our phone number. When you unfold it, you see scripture verses leading to salvation. Over the years, many people, especially pastors, told me it was unwise to put our home phone number on the card. I prayerfully listened to their concerns but had never received that instruction from the Holy Spirit. Over the 10 years I handed them out in Colorado, yes, we got many crank calls at two in the morning. But we received many more calls from people desperate for help, yes, also at two in the morning. But it is worth it to throw a lifeline when someone is in an hour of desperate need.

Let me share one more story to conclude this chapter. On a Friday night in Longmont, I was witnessing in the parking lots on Main Street. It was already a good evening, and I had prayed for salvation with seven people. Then I heard the Holy Spirit say, "You need to go home! You need to go home now!"

I said in my heart, "What? But it's early, and people are getting saved."

Immediately, I heard again, "You need to go home! You need to go home now!"

I made my way to my parked VW van a couple of blocks away and started the ten-minute drive home. When I entered, my entire family was seated in the living room. They greeted me with, "Dad, what are you doing home?" It was still early, and my family knew I did not come home until the wee hours of the morning after a night on the streets. I told them, "The Holy Spirit told me to go home now. So here I am." I didn't tell them that He had told me twice.

Kathleen told me that, less than an hour before, she had received a collect call, and it was from Satan. She could not understand the person at first, so she asked the operator to verify who the call was from. The operator came back and said the call was from Satan. My dear Kathleen is a frugal, Proverbs 32 woman. Yes, Proverbs 32, because she far exceeds the standards of Proverbs 31. Because she is thrifty, she would not pay the charges for a collect call from hell. She received a second call just moments before I walked in the house. Needless to say, my family was alarmed. When they told me, my first response, perhaps not the best, was to laugh.

When I sat down with them and assured them that God knew about the calls and sent me home to protect them, they all had a sense of relief. The next thing I did was to get my Bible and place it on the counter next to the phone. I opened it to Revelation chapter 20 so I could read it to Satan if he called again. Chapter 20 tells of the defeat and final judgment of Satan. Then we gathered together as a family to pray for the perpetrators of this ruse, that they would be convicted and eventually saved. Then I laughed again when I considered, "The economy of hell must be in the dumper when Satan has to terrorize God's people with collect calls."

> *Give me the love that leads the way, The faith that nothing can dismay, The hope no disappointments tire, The passion that will burn like fire, Let me not sink to be a clod: Make me Thy fuel, Flame of God.*[52] *—Amy Carmichael*

> *Talking to men for God is a great thing but talking to God for men is greater still.*[53] *—E. M. Bounds*

15

The Great Commission—Go into All the World

"People who do not know the Lord ask why in the world we waste our lives as missionaries. They forget that they too are expending their lives... and when the bubble has burst, they will have nothing of eternal significance to show for the years they have wasted."[54] —Nate Saint, missionary martyr[1]

"He is no fool who gives up what he cannot keep to gain that which he cannot lose."[55] —Jim Elliot

"If missions languish, it is because the whole life of godliness is feeble. The command to go everywhere and preach to everybody is not obeyed until the will is lost by self-surrender in the will of God. Living, praying, giving, and going will always be found together."[56] —Arthur T. Pierson

---

[1] Martyr who lost his life in the late 1950s trying to reach the Auca Indians of Ecuador.

"This gospel of the kingdom shall be preached in the whole world as a testimony to all the nations, and then the end will come." —Matthew 24:14

19 "Go therefore and make disciples of all the nations, baptizing them in the name of the Father and the Son and the Holy Spirit, 20 teaching them to observe all that I commanded you; and lo, I am with you always, even to the end of the age." —Matthew 28:19, 20

I WANT TO caution you. After reading the stories in this book, you may begin to think that every encounter we have in reaching lost souls will be dramatic. Yes, I have shared many dramatic stories, I will share more in this chapter, and many more are yet unrecorded. But most encounters are not as dramatic as the ones I have written herein. Oh, every soul reached for the kingdom of God is wonderful and powerful, and the destiny of that person is changed. It is a great thrill every time a person says, "Yes, I want to receive Jesus as my Savior and Lord." But the reality of the matter is this: I have found that soul-winning is more like pulling the plow the length of each furrow through the harvest fields. I want you to get that image, you or me pulling the plow. Not a beast of burden, or a mechanized tractor, but you and me. It is always rewarding, but it is tedious, arduous, work. Yet I would not exchange my life working in the harvest fields for anything.

Throughout my Christian life, I have heard people say, "Even so, Lord, come quickly!" While it is a good thing to live in constant expectancy and desire for the Lord's return, we need to understand that if Jesus were to return today, 2.5 billion souls who have never heard the name of Jesus or the Good News message of salvation would be doomed to an eternity separated from Christ. Another 2.5 billion people may have heard the way of salvation and live within reach of the established church in their cultures but have either rejected the message or never really heard it clearly. I have lost track of the numbers of times I have shared the Gospel message and people have responded, "I have never heard that before." That response is in a culture where there is a church on nearly every corner. We play an integral part in the Lord's return; Jesus has chosen to partner with His people in the work of world evangelization.

> *11 Since all these things are to be destroyed in this way, what sort of people ought you to be in holy conduct and godliness, 12 looking for and hastening the coming of the day of God, because of which the heavens will be destroyed by burning, and the elements will melt with intense heat! 13 But according to His promise we are looking for new heavens and a new earth, in which righteousness dwells.*
> *—2 Peter 3:11–13*

We are to be those who look for and hasten the day of God. Peter tells us this should be our holy conduct. How do we hasten the day of the Lord? We proclaim the Good News message in the whole world to all nations.

> *This Gospel of the kingdom shall be preached in the whole world as a testimony to all the nations, and then the end will come. —Matthew 24:14*

To *all* nations. Not just geopolitical nations, but Biblical nations as well. What is a Biblical nation? The Greek word for nations is *ethnos*, so it is saying that every ethnic group shall hear the Good News before the end will come. Within geopolitical nations, defined by geographic boundaries and politics, there can be hundreds of Biblical nations. God's covenant promise to Abraham in Genesis 12:3 was, "Through you, every family of the earth will be blessed." *Every* family. Paul restates this in Galatians 3:8. "The Scripture, foreseeing that God would justify the Gentiles by faith, preached the gospel beforehand to Abraham, saying, 'ALL THE NATIONS WILL BE BLESSED IN YOU.'" Here again, that word "nations" is the Greek word *ethnos*. Who are these "families" the scriptures are referring to? The list of the Seventy Gentile nations, or families, can be found in Genesis chapter 10, and they were the families descended from Noah and his sons who were present at the Tower of Babel.

Genesis chapter 11 records the incident at Babel when God confused men's languages, and the people scattered across the earth. Even after the scattering, new families, or ethnic groups, continued to multiply. Abraham was the father of two additional nations. Lot, Abraham's nephew, fathered two nations.

Today, over 17,000 distinct ethnic groups fill the earth. Over 7,000 remain unreached with the Gospel. This means that no missionary has gone to them, and the Church of Jesus Christ has not been planted among them. Having not received the Bible in the language of their culture, the language of their hearts, they are still waiting to hear the Good News.

When will the end come? When the Gospel has been preached in the whole world to each ethnic group. This concept is made even clearer when we look at the diversity of the people of the earth who will gather before the throne of the Father in His coming kingdom.

> *And they sang a new song, saying, "Worthy are You to take the book and to break its seals; for You were slain, and purchased for God with Your blood men from every tribe and tongue and people and nation." —Revelation 5:9*

Every tribe, every tongue, every people, every nation—if we are to hasten the Day of the Lord, we must make haste to proclaim the Gospel of the kingdom to the remaining 7,000 people groups on the earth who have never heard the Good News message. Today's modern mission strategies do just that. What is lacking are the resources to accomplish world evangelization. What resources are lacking? People, finances, and prayer. The Church today lacks none of these resources, but we have not allocated the resources available to the primary purpose of the Church, world evangelization. Missionaries are still needed to go to the unreached people groups. Finances are needed to send them. And most of all, prayer is needed to prepare the way to the uttermost parts of the earth.

Since the Acts of the Apostles, the Gospel message has always come from outside the target culture as evangelists crossed cultural boundaries. At the beginning of the Gospel expansion, it was people from the Jewish culture who entered new cultures to bring the Gospel, first to the Samaritans, then to the Gentiles, and then to the ends of the earth. The ends of the earth are still waiting.

Over 2,000 years have passed since the commission to "Go into all the world" was given to the church, and still one-third of the world is waiting. Coca Cola has the same world vision as we do, in their case to put a Coke in the hands of every person on earth. Coke was introduced in 1886, only 135 years ago. They have done a better job in accomplishing their vision than we have. There is hardly a place in the world where you can go and not find Coca Cola. "Even so, come, Lord Jesus!"

Since 2004, Kathleen and I have served as missionaries. Our journey into the harvest fields of Mexico, El Salvador, and Cuba began in faithfulness. We were first faithful to serve our local church and communities. If you are looking for the key to step into future ministry, this is it: be faithful where you find yourself now.

> *You will never make a missionary of the person who does no*
> *good at home. He that will not serve the Lord in the Sunday*
> *school at home, will not win children to Christ in China.*[57]
> —*Charles Spurgeon*

For 25 years prior to launching out into the harvest fields, we faithfully served in many capacities in our home churches. We were actively engaged in soul-winning in our local communities. One day in 1998,

Kathleen told me she felt Jesus was going to send us out as missionaries. When she spoke, it rang true and felt like a Holy Ghost dart to my heart.

In the months that followed, I began to look for mission opportunities on the beloved worldwide web and found there were many opportunities out there. One evening, as I searched the Internet, I heard the Holy Spirit say, "Bob, it's not going to happen this way." That word arrested my efforts to make something happen on my own.

Over time, the notion that we would become foreign missionaries began to fade. Years went by until we virtually forgot it, but we continued to be faithful in serving in our home church and soul-winning in the communities of northern Colorado. We also went on four mission trips to Mexico with the junior high youth from our home church, Resurrection Fellowship, and our good friends Pastors Bob and Tammie Groeneman.

One evening in 2002, I was driving my old VW van into the heart of Denver for a night of ministry outreach. I prayed as I exited Interstate 25 onto Colfax Avenue leading into downtown, and the Holy Spirit spoke, "Bob, I am going to promote you." That is all He said, "I'm going to promote you." When you get a word from the Holy Spirit, do you try to put it into the context of your will and not His? Do you add to the word, or edit it in a way that fits into your expectations? Well, I began to consider that my home church would hire me, maybe as the evangelism pastor. I imagined getting an office at the church and being on the payroll. Life would be beautiful, right? Wrong!

In a short time, the plan began to unfold, and not as I expected. In January of 2003, Pastor Bob approached me on a Sunday night, as we were setting up for the youth service, and told me of a dream he recently had. In the dream, he saw Kathleen and I working in Mexico with David and Donna Blanchard and their ministry, Victorious Christian Harvesters. Then Pastor Bob said, "I was so sure about it that I called to tell them too." Talk about being sent out.

So the promotion was to world missions, and I would get to raise my own financial support. I remembered what the Holy Spirit had spoken months earlier when I crossed over the Colfax Viaduct. "I'm going to promote you." This was a promotion. He had called it a promotion. I would now get to live by faith for my finances. That seemed a little scary. Actually, it was very scary. I also remembered the sense Kathleen and I had five years earlier that Jesus was going to send us to the mission fields. I remember when He arrested my efforts to find mission opportunities on the worldwide web by saying it would not happen this way.

I could clearly see that going to work with David and Donna was a God thing. We already had a relationship with them from our four mission trips over the previous four years, and we regularly supported their work financially. God, the master planner, had been working His plan into our lives over the past five years. Throughout the remainder of 2003, we prepared to move to the border of Mexico.

In January of 2004, Kathleen and I moved our family from Longmont to Laredo, Texas. Since that time, we have worked with our dear friends David and Donna Blanchard, founders and leaders (servants) of Victorious Christian Harvesters (VCH). David and Donna are true examples of laying your life down for the sake of the Gospel. They work tirelessly to expand the kingdom of Heaven here on the earth. They continually pour into the lives of the VCH staff, as well as the staff and students at the International Harvesters Institute (IHI) in Nuevo Laredo, Mexico. It has been an honor and privilege to serve them and the vision God has given them.

Here is the description of the vision David received during a prayer meeting:

David Blanchard, president and founder of VCH, received a vision from the Lord while in a prayer meeting in 1990. He saw the country of Mexico covered with ocean waves. When the waves receded, they left big black Bibles with gold crosses on them. In this vision, God spoke to David telling him to get His Word out, "for it will not return to Me empty or void without accomplishing what I've sent it forth to do." "How many Bibles do you want me to get out, Lord?" David asked. "How many souls do you want to see saved?" was God's reply. David answered, "The whole nation of Mexico!" "Me too," said God, "but how many souls do you want to be responsible for?" "I'm not Dr. Billy Graham nor Dr. T.L. Osborn," David said, "I'm just me. But I want to see a million souls come to know You." "Then," God commissioned David, "get one million Bibles for one million souls." Thus, the vision for Victorious Christian Harvesters was born— One Million Bibles/One Million Souls. With this vision VCH began ministering 28 years ago and continues to do so today with more passion than ever. Since we began to train and make disciples through the International Harvesters Institute, we have sent more harvesters into the field to help fulfill the vision. God is causing our efforts to be successful, and we are grateful to be a part of His master plan. We are trusting God to use VCH as a unique instrument to fulfill the great commission of Jesus Christ by planting His Word in lost souls and harvesting lives for an eternity. For the glory of God and with the vital support of its partners, VCH has seen this vision completed in August 2016. More than one million souls have come to know Jesus Christ through the evangelism of VCH, and more than one million Bibles, New Testaments, and Gospel booklets have been given to these new believers and to the national church evangelism teams who are regularly sharing the Gospel! We continue to share the gospel, equip the national people, and train new harvesters so that the kingdom of Heaven may be established here on earth.

Thus, the vision of this ministry was birthed in 1992, "One million Bibles for one million souls." Kathleen and I came alongside David and Donna to serve them in this vision in January of 2004. Before joining full time, we participated in the previously mentioned four short-term mission trips to Mexico, often accompanied by our church junior high team. In addition, during the fall of 2003, Kathleen and I also participated in a medical mission trip to remote indigenous villages near Poza Rica, Veracruz, Mexico.

After fulfilling the vision of "One million Bibles for one million souls" during the first days of August 2016, David was given a ring from his staff, inscribed with one of his favorite verses which he quotes often. Proverbs 11:30: "The fruit of the righteous is a tree of life, And he who is wise wins souls." Shortly after receiving the gift, he and Donna were in a worship service. As he lifted his hands in worship, he saw the ring, and he had a vision of ten rings on his fingers, one on each finger. From that vision, the current ministry vision was birthed. "Ten million Bibles for ten million souls."

Does that sound improbable, unlikely, impossible? We never really embrace faith until we believe the impossible. Faith comes by hearing the current, spoken word of God. When we hear the voice of Jesus, even though it seems implausible, and when we believe against all odds what Jesus has spoken, and when we take hold of that word with assurance and conviction, then we step into the realm of faith.

> *We never test the resources of God until we attempt the IMPOSSIBLE.*[58] *—F. B. Meyer*

> *What are Christians put into the world for except to do the impossible in the strength of God.*[59] *—General S. C. Armstrong*

Shortly after David received the vision of "One million Bibles for one million souls" before launching VCH, he shared the vision with

Doctor Lester Sumrall, who was visiting in Laredo. After hearing the vision, Dr. Sumrall responded, "David, that's a vision from God. Now go out there and do it!" Throughout my Christian life, I have always considered three men as being the missionary statesmen for my generation: Lester Sumrall, T.L. Osborn, and Wayne Meyers. I find it interesting that all three of these men have had personal connections with VCH. When I first heard David quote Dr. Sumrall's response to the vision on my first mission trip to Mexico in 1998, I thought to myself, "If there is ever anything I want to expend my life and my strength on, it is a vision from God."

As a result, we have been planted since 2004, working alongside many dedicated laborers in the harvest fields. My responsibilities are primarily as the mission trip director. I have planned, coordinated, and carried out hundreds of mission trips to Mexico and El Salvador. I have also had the privilege of working with VCH in China and Cuba. I estimate I have been on over 3,000 ministry sites since 2004.

It is also an honor and privilege to teach the young future leaders of the churches of Mexico at the International Harvesters Institute in Nuevo Laredo. I teach a four-semester class called World Mission, teaching the four perspectives of God's mission to reveal Himself to the peoples of the earth. Since 2010, VCH has been training the national churches in Mexico, El Salvador, and Cuba to win their cities for Jesus Christ and the kingdom of God.

We do this through the outreach ministry we call "Invasions." An "Invasion" seminar is a week-long event in a city, which begins with three days of training, followed by three days of soul-winning outreaches, and concludes with a night of celebration for the harvest of souls. The Saturday night celebrations are electric, with God's people, many who have never shared their faith or won a soul to Jesus before, return full of the Spirit. They have been used by God, in the flow of the Holy Spirit, and when they return it is explosive. To date, we have hosted more than 100 city-wide "Invasions" throughout Mexico. In a single week during the three days of outreach, more than 10,000 new salvations have been recorded by the churches. And the churches are following up with the people that come to Christ. Churches have out-grown their places of worship in the weeks and months following an "Invasion." This is a recurring story among the churches that incorporate soul-winning into their church culture.

In the city of Tulancingo, in the state of Hidalgo, Mexico, I was working with some churches during the "Invasion" week. The seminar begins Monday night, but often we arrive on the Saturday before to send out our staff on Sunday to minister in the participating churches. I was invited to preach in a church of 250 people on Sunday morning, and my message was about being disciples. At the urging of the pastor, I concluded the service by inviting people to surrender to Christ's call to follow Him as a disciple. There was a great response to that invitation.

While ministry was taking place for the first group of respondents, I gave an invitation for salvation. One young man in his early twenties responded. He seemed to be an artsy sort of fellow, and it was a genuine first-time salvation. On Monday night, this young man attended the "Invasion." I opened the conference by teaching a good portion of the contents of this book, condensed to an hour-and-a-half window. The first night's presentation includes "The Heartbeat of God" and "The Heart of the Evangelist."

The second night of Invasion is titled "The Power of Evangelism." During the ministry time on the second night, we pray for the bap-tism of the Holy Spirit, who *is* the power of evangelism. Over the years, multiple thousands of believers have received the baptism of the Holy Spirit during the Tuesday night ministry times. Again, the young man who surrendered to Christ on Sunday participated in the conference all day Tuesday and came forward for the baptism that evening. Because I felt a personal interest in him, I had been watching him all day. I saw him being powerfully touched by the Holy Spirit during the ministry time. He was baptized in the Holy Spirit and was speaking in tongues.

Following each morning of workshops, we use the afternoon ses-sions to teach the dramas they would perform as they evangelized on the streets, and in parks, plazas, markets, and so on. It turned out this artsy young man was cast into all the lead parts of the dramas by his new church family.

The third night of the conference is the graduation night, where we impart the "Anointing to Preach the Gospel." Graduate credentials are distributed to all in attendance, and Gospel literature is provided for distribution during the outreaches.

On Thursday, Friday, and Saturday, the teams hit the streets. Most of our staff goes to live with the churches during these days to assist the church outreach teams to be effective in their ministry. I traveled around to different teams during these days to video their outreaches and provide support. Throughout these three days, I continually saw the young man who surrendered his life to Christ on Sunday. Everywhere I saw him, he was engaged in soul-winning. On Saturday night, as we were about to begin the celebration, I chatted with him. He had personally won 15 people to Jesus Christ. In addition, his church team had seen over 400 salvations take place through the drama presentations. I asked him to share his testimony of what had taken place in the past week. On Sunday he was born again, and on Tuesday he was baptized in the Holy Spirit. By Saturday, he had personally led 15 people into a relationship with Jesus Christ. Pretty awesome for his first week in Christ. I love serving Jesus!

I would like to share some stories of my trips to Cuba and China. It is such a blessing to serve the King in His kingdom. He is always faithful to His children and so desires to show His faithfulness to all people groups.

In May of 2012, I went with a team of four VCH staff to Cuba. These young men and women were Mexican nationals and graduates of the IHI Bible Institute. I was the lone old American guy on the trip. Our purpose was to train the leaders of our Cuban churches in the "Invasion" format, so they could then train the people in their churches. 2 Timothy 2:2 says, "The things which you have heard from me in the presence of many witnesses, entrust these to faithful men who will be able to teach others also."

Cuba is such an austere place, both economically and spiritually. Since the fall of the Communist-bloc nations in Europe in 1989, the Cuban economy has suffered greatly. Before the fall, Russia pumped 5–8 billion dollars each year into Cuba, in addition to oil subsidies, which bolstered the transportation industry. With those benefits withdrawn, the already ailing economy fell further into chaos. The average wage in Cuba is $10 to $20 each month. Throughout Havana, the infrastructure is crumbling. Majestic old buildings have deteriorated, many having fallen to rubble where they once stood. In many ways, it is also a spiritual desert, as the darkness of Communism and witchcraft have drawn a veil of darkness over the people. One shining report is the strength of the illegal underground church. The church in Cuba is strong and active in advancing the Gospel. Believers there are not nominal believers but true disciples of Jesus Christ. They understand the cost of following and serving Him.

Our plan was to go from Havana to the city of Camaguey at the center of the island and then work our way west back to Havana, visiting all our churches and church leaders. We spent our first couple of days at the Havana Riviera Hotel, a once-impressive and majestic high-rise structure on the waterfront, which has now fallen into severe disrepair. The time there provided an opportunity to meet with our church leaders in the area to plan our mission. Then we headed to Camaguey by bus, arriving in late afternoon, and met with local church leaders to chart our course for the next few days. Afterward, we checked into a tourist hotel in the city's historic center.

The following morning, we headed to our first meeting with 120 pastors and leaders, but on the way, we had to lose the Communist government agent who was following us. The authorities keep a sharp watch over foreigners, especially Americans. The churches we work with are illegal, which means they will not comply with the strict demands of the atheistic Communist leadership. After being dropped off about two blocks away, we cut through an overgrown field and entered the meeting through an opening in a 12-foot block wall. Those 120 dear brothers and sisters were anxiously awaiting our arrival. The meeting was held in a walled-in open area in the back of a small concrete block home. A tapestry of old tarps strung overhead protected us from the sun.

I spoke to the group first, sharing with the congregation for nearly two hours in the humid morning heat. The assembly of church leaders hung on my every word. At times, when you teach or preach, it seems like the word is going out like a hammer, breaking hard, stony hearts. Then there are those wonderful times when it seems the people are drawing the word out of you, and it just flows effortlessly. God's people were hungry that day for the Word, and I did not want to disappoint. Later, I heard the comment, "We need more of this kind of teaching." I can get quite animated when I minister God's Word, and in the morning heat and humidity, it was not long before I was being baptized in my own sweat.

I taught our church leaders what I teach during the opening night of an "Invasion": "The Heartbeat of God" and "The Seven Essentials of Evangelism," which are also the main body of this book. Then we took a break and went into the small house to plan the next sessions. Half an hour later, the pastor of the church where we were meeting came to tell us that an officer from the Ministry of Interior was there and wanted to talk to the American preacher. That would be me.

I stepped outside to meet a young man in uniform with mirrored sunglasses. He wanted my credentials, that is, passport and visa. After inspecting my papers, he handed them back to me and ordered me to appear at the Ministry of Interior at 1400 hours, or 2:00 p.m. That is all he said. He did not tell me what, or if, I had done wrong, just to appear. It was not yet 11:00 a.m. when I re-entered the house church. My young team, shaken by the transpiring events, were too upset to continue with any further teaching. Therefore, I said to the assembled group, "Well, he didn't tell me why I was to report to the office. He did not tell me I could not teach further. Why don't I go out again and teach the next section of the 'Invasion' manual?"

The main leader we work with felt that was a great idea, responding, "Yes, we can make Bob a sacrificial lamb." Most of these church leaders have had their own run-ins with the Communist authorities, and some have spent years in prison for their work. For them, this is just the cost of following Jesus, the cross they pick up every day.

I went before the assembly of leaders a second time. With two and a half hours left before my appointment with the Ministry of Interior, I taught for another two hours. My teaching was the contents of chapter 13, "You Are Anointed to Preach the Gospel." After this second session, our missionary team had calmed down, and as I left for my engagement with the authorities, they continued teaching.

I arrived promptly at 2:00 p.m. and was ushered into a room with an elevated platform where three officers of the Ministry of Interior were seated at a long table. The senior officer was a two-star territorial colonel named Martin. My mirrored-glasses friend, named Mejia, was present and still sporting the mirrored glasses. And a third, lower-ranking officer named Freddy rounded out the roster. You may ask how I remember their names after all these years? Because I still pray for their salvation regularly, and I continue to maintain prayer campaigns for them. I was directed to turn over my passport, visa, and my old 3G smart phone, which was promptly removed for further inspection.

I was instructed to take a seat in a little chair on the floor in front of the platform. It was like sitting in a child's "Little Tykes" chair. I immediately understood the psychological objective of this arrangement. I had been trained in interrogation techniques during my military training, and it quickly became evident that an interrogation was about to take place. Of course, I neglected to tell my adversaries about my training in interrogation techniques or my military experience.

As they inspected my passport with a number of visas from previous mission trips to El Salvador, they began to ask me questions about who

I was, where was I from, what was I doing there in Cuba, and so forth. At one point I told them my passport was from the United States, but I was a citizen of another country. That grabbed their interest. I told them I was a citizen of the kingdom of Heaven. To borrow a phrase from the Chinese pastor and evangelist Brother Yun, I am a "Heavenly man." His story of ministry and extreme persecution under the Communist, atheistic government of China is detailed in a book called *The Heavenly Man*, a tremendous book that I have now read five times. I told these Cuban officials that I was a "Heavenly man." In fact, I told them, I was an ambassador of that kingdom, and I represented Jesus Christ, the King of that kingdom.

They began to fire questions at me faster than I could answer. Often, I acted like I did not fully understand what they were saying. I told them my Spanish was poor. Some of it was true, and some was just an act. They told me of five Cuban men known as the Cuban Five or the Miami Five, who were convicted of espionage in Miami and sentenced to federal prison. At the time of my interrogation, four were still imprisoned in the United States. In Cuba, these guys were heroes, with their pictures displayed on huge banners and billboards throughout the country.

My interrogators apprised me that these Cubans were in prison for breaking the laws of the United States, and likewise I had broken the laws of Cuba and deserved the same punishment. The law I had broken was preaching in an illegal church. I asked, "Aren't all churches illegal in Cuba?"

They responded, "We ask the questions here!" I was glad they did not arrest me due to the poor quality of my preaching, which would have been hard to bear. You will be glad to know that I have been arrested for teaching the contents of this book. As the examination continued, they persisted that my crime deserved punishment. Now, I am a pretty smart feller, and I began to consider, "This might not end well."

As threats continued, I embraced the presence of the Holy Spirit. The course of the interrogation began to change to what I could do for them to compensate for my transgressions. While they pressed me for names and information, I drew near to the presence of Jesus. In His presence, I made the most profound surrender I have ever made. Realizing that this may not end well, I prayed in my spirit, "Jesus, I trust you now with my life. I trust you with everything I am and everything I have. Regardless of how bad this gets, whether that means prison and separation from Kathleen, I trust you. I trust you to bring me through the worst moments I may face. I trust you to watch over my wife and family, to provide for them, to comfort them, to communicate with them." In those moments I was fully aware of just how bad this could possibly get.

Throughout our lives, we are often faced with moments of surrender. This moment was the deepest surrender I have ever made. But in doing so, something happened. Something wonderful, something powerful, something intense. That surrender gave me a sense of freedom I have never experienced. What could they do to me? I had just laid my entire life down before my Lord. They could not take away what I had already surrendered. This is what is known as grace in the moment of need.

After this incredible feeling of freedom overwhelmed me, something else happened. First, I experienced compassion for these men's souls and for their families' souls. I began to feel a burden for their lostness, understanding their eternal destiny without Christ. Then a fiery boldness came over me. I wondered who, if anyone, would ever have the opportunity to speak to these men about their eternal destinies.

I stood up from my little chair and proclaimed, "Right now, I am not as concerned about my future as I am about your future. What is your eternal destiny? Where will you and your wives and children spend eternity when this life is through? There are only two destinies existing, Heaven or hell! We are all on the road to hell. God has provided the way for us to escape that destiny and gain His desired destiny of Heaven for each of us. God made Heaven available to us through the life, death, and resurrection of His Son, Jesus Christ. Receive Jesus, turn to Him, and you will be saved."

What followed was a stunned silence, a long silence. My antagonists decided to call a recess. They left me in the room, in my little chair, locking the door as they exited. They left me alone with my thoughts, but honestly, I felt such a great peace. I felt free. After about 15 minutes, they returned with my papers and phone and told me I could leave. They obtained my hotel information and sent me on my way.

As I exited the Ministry of Interior, I noticed that it was 4:45 p.m. I had spent over two and a half hours as a guest of the Communist authorities. Returning to our hotel, I waited for more than an hour for my team to return. They had completed the day of training in my absence. Upon seeing them, I signaled them to meet me in another location in the center of the tourist section of the city. I was being followed, and we needed to talk. We met in a plaza several blocks away where several historic monuments were displayed. The others went before me, and I followed. As they walked around the plaza acting like tourists, I approached, acting like it was a first-time acquaintance. While we discussed our situation, the son of one of our pastor contacts approached and invited us to come to their home for dinner. We all separated and made our way to the pastor's home one by one. In the home that night, we discussed what we should do next. I heard the voice of the Holy Spirit say, "This isn't finished." We returned to our hotel, and I told my team what I heard the Spirit say.

I was awake early in the morning, spending quiet moments in prayer and the Word. At 7:00 a.m., we were roused by loud, authoritative knocking on our doors. We had two rooms side by side, one for the ladies and one for the gentlemen. I opened the door, and there standing in front of me was my new friend Freddy. The four of us were ordered to return to the Ministry of the Interior at 10:00 a.m. Being accommodating folk, we appeared at the time requested.

The officers took my three partners in crime before me, but only for 20 minutes each. After the first of my cohorts returned, she told me the only questions they asked were about me. Huh, what? Yes, they wanted to know if I was crazy. Each subsequent accomplice returned with the same report.

Then it was my turn. Now, instead of three interrogators, there was a fourth, a woman, there to translate anything I did not understand. While my three previous antagonists fired questions at me over the next two hours, she threw in some of her own. They had determined that I was unstable mentally, probably because I did not respond to them in fear. They resumed their previous line of questioning from the day before, but with a new angle.

They wanted to know who I called after leaving them the day before. They insisted that I called someone, and they demanded to know who it was. They even bolstered their demand with this, "Right now we are in contact with the American phone provider who is cooperating with us. You know they have the best communication systems in the world, and it is only a matter of moments until they return our call and confirm who it was you spoke with." They were giving me a small window of time to cooperate with them before the communication company responded. If I did not, they would not show any leniency toward me.

Jesus is eternal, and He dwells outside of time, past, present, and future. While our team was in the airport in Mexico City, ready to board our flight to Havana, I had received a call from David Blanchard. We chatted for a bit, going over our schedule and Cuban contacts. After the call, I erased all my recent calls. As I did so, the Holy Spirit spoke to me, "While you are in Cuba, do not call anyone, anyone!" So I determined I would not call anyone while I was in Cuba. And I did not.

Now, with these new accusations from my gracious hosts, I realized, "These guys don't know anything, except for what I tell them." That was a game changer for me. At that point, I quit cooperating with them in any way. They were lying, threatening, and playing head games, all in the hope that I would freely offer them any information I had.

The interrogation quickly deteriorated, and after two hours they let us go. We were told we must leave Camaguey and return to Havana immediately and then report to the main offices of the Ministry of the Interior. I had never been kicked out of town before. I do not think I even know anyone who has. I thought that only happened on old TV Westerns.

Leaving the Ministry of Interior building, we decided to walk back to our hotel, about two miles away. It turned out to be a God decision, because we came across the pastor of the house church from the day before. We passed him a note letting him know we had to leave. He in turn began to contact our associates in Cuba and the United States, so word about our situation began to travel fast. And prayer began to be offered by many people.

We did not know what would happen when we returned to Havana. After returning to our hotel room, my Bible was still lying open on my bed. It was opened to Genesis 46:3, "He said, 'I am God, the God of your father; do not be afraid to go down to Egypt, for I will make you a great nation there.'" It is funny, because I was not reading in Genesis that morning, but I took this as a present Word of the Lord.

The next day, we were at the bus station waiting to leave. Freddy, one of the interrogators, was there to ensure we were indeed leaving. It gave us further opportunity to share Jesus's message of salvation with him. While waiting in the bus station, I watched a government-sponsored children's television program. It was in every way like Sesame Street, with the same kind of Muppets, but they had Communist characteristics. The lessons being propagated by these puppets were Communist ideologies. At first, I was aghast that someone would use such a medium to promote their system of belief to children. Then I had a profound thought. American Christians use vegetables to promote Christian ideals to our children. I know it is a weird thought, but true. It did help me to extend some grace to the Communists.

We returned to Havana that day, after another daylong trip. I am sure government agents were following us. During rest stops when we left the bus, men sat all around me, never taking their eyes off me. That is really the way it is in Cuba. The Cuban government also strictly separates foreign tourists from Cuban national citizens. We were required to ride buses which only allowed foreign tourists, but I could tell there were several Cuban nationals with us that day. There are even two forms of currency in Cuba, currency for the foreign tourist and currency for the Cuban citizen.

Well, we returned to Havana that day, and the next day we reported to the main offices of the Ministry of Interior. When we arrived, we were met by a three-star colonel named Robert. He had no prior knowledge of our coming. We had to wait for some time until he communicated with Colonel Martin in Camaguey. Afterward, Colonel Robert ordered us to leave the country as soon as possible.

It would take four days to arrange an early departure. In the meantime, we were ordered into house arrest at our hotel, which would be periodically supervised. I made a request of the Colonel, "Could we perhaps, with your permission, tour the old city while we await deportation?" He thought for a moment and gave us permission, but we could not change hotels or have contact with any of the pastors we had been working with. We gave him our word that we would comply.

I have already told you about our remaining days in Cuba, winning souls on the streets, and praying for healing and for the nation. It was a great blessing to work among the saints in Cuba, to win the untold lost to Christ, and to see His healing power manifest.

Next, I will tell you about our ministry trip to China in 2008. In these two stories from Cuba and China, please note that I am being intentionally vague with names of the people we worked with and some locations so as not to expose those people to unwanted attention from the Communist anti-Christian authorities.

In May of 2008, we made a VCH staff mission trip to China. I believe that our team consisted of eight staff members, four men and four women. We had arranged to spend seven days with an American missionary and his family in several southwestern provinces. He worked with a network of illegal underground churches. In preparation for the trip, we had all packed various bits of Gospel literature, including solar-powered radios with the entire Bible recorded in Mandarin, the primary dialect of China. We also brought tracts, literature, and Evangecubes, which are 3"by 3" Rubik's-cube contraptions that fold out into the Gospel message. I have used Evangecubes for many years, and I find them to be valuable tools in sharing the Gospel message one-on-one with people. They provide a visual context for each point of the Gospel message.

We packed our bags with our Gospel contraband and wondered how it would all work out. In prayer, we felt positive that we were to do this. In the pants and shirt pockets in my bag, I packed 200 Mandarin "The Answer" tracts. I was familiar with the tract, having used the English and Spanish versions on the streets in the United States, Mexico, El Salvador, and Cuba. It is about the size of the palm of your hand, and as you proceed through the tract, it unfolds into the form of the cross. It is another powerful evangelism tool. Some of these evangelism tools were pretty obvious within my baggage.

We flew from San Antonio to San Francisco and were scheduled to have a couple of hours layover before our flight to Beijing and then to western China. In San Francisco, we kept seeing that our connecting flight to Beijing was delayed, first two hours, then four, and then six. We decided to take the train to Chinatown in San Francisco. After our excursion into the city, we returned to the airport to find that our connecting flight had been delayed even further. As the day slipped into evening, we were finally given a definite departure time. But our new arrival time in Beijing would mean we would not make our connecting flight to western China. With the bad news, bad attitudes began to surface.

Finally, we boarded our 12-hour flight to Beijing, arriving at two in the morning. The airlines planned to take us to a hotel where we would get about two hours of sleep before returning to the airport early in the morning to make our connecting flight. We made our way through immigration at about two-thirty in the morning. From there, we collected our bags and headed to customs. Knowing our bags were laden with smuggled goods, we all wondered how it would work. After picking up our bags, we arrived at the customs desk at around 3:00 a.m., but no one was there. The agents had all gone home. We walked through the doors with our bags and were suddenly out on the streets. Our bags did not even get checked. In that moment, we all could see God's divine providence in delaying our flight from San Francisco.

We arrived at the hotel around 4:00 a.m. and needed to leave by 6:00 a.m. to return to make our connecting flight. In the morning, we returned to the Beijing airport, which was in chaos, but we managed to get through it all. Finally, we were on our way to Kunming in the western Yunnan province. We met our host missionary and spent two days in Kunming in a hostel. These two days gave us a chance to recuperate from our travel and meet our host team, a group of American missionaries and a couple of Chinese national Christians.

Our translator for the trip was a young Chinese Christian who had worked with the underground church network associated with Brother Yun, the "Heavenly man." She had been with him in a meeting with a group of underground church leaders but left just moments before the PSB, Public Security Bureau, stormed the meeting. Brother Yun jumped out of a window, broke his legs, and was captured and sent to prison. His book, *The Heavenly Man*, details his miraculous Acts chapter 12 escape from that prison.

Another team member was a Chinese evangelist we named "Happy" because he was continually filled with great joy. I gave "Happy" one of the Evangecubes I had brought, and he received the gift with tears and great joy. He had seen one once before and understood how it worked. To him, it was as valuable as gold. Subsequently, when we gave other Chinese workers the Evangecubes, Happy was able to show them how they worked. As we traveled, we left our Gospel materials with the national workers.

After two days' rest, we were off by train to the regions north and west, near the Tibetan border. We traveled by train to a city called Dajitan where we would begin our work with the Chinese underground church. The day after we arrived, David and I were asked to meet with a group of underground church leaders in a remote location. We climbed on the back of motorcycles along with Happy and our translator and sped off over the hills. Riding through the hills at high speeds, on the edge of rocky trails, I watched the rocks breaking away under the tires and rolling down the steep hills. Also, my Chinese escort was much shorter than me and did not take my height into consideration as he continually maneuvered us under low-hanging tree branches. More than once, I had my hair parted by the trees. We came down the mountain into a valley loaded with peach trees as far as you could see. We arrived at a small mud hut structure in the middle of the orchard.

Upon entering, we were met by seven underground church leaders. One leader may have been approaching his forties, but these and most underground church leaders are noticeably young, some in their late teens and early twenties. Church leaders do not last long in leadership before they are arrested and imprisoned. Here in the west, church leaders offer their credentials based on the Bible institutes or seminaries they graduated from. In China, a leader's credentials are more likely where they were imprisoned.

David and I were asked to address and encourage these young faithful leaders. I felt totally inadequate for this, these young men and women were an encouragement to me. Nevertheless, we shared, prayed with them, and fellowshipped for several hours. We said our goodbyes and loaded up on our motorcycles for the harrowing return trip to Dajitan.

That night, our entire team visited a large house church gathering with well over 100 believers in attendance. The Holy Spirit's presence was powerful. The believers were filled with great joy and enthusiasm. Each of us shared a short message with our Chinese brethren. What a blessing it was to be with our brothers and sisters in Dajitan.

The following day, we left Dajitan in several small taxi-vans for a small village high in the hills. The taxis could only take us so far to our destination before the paved road ended. Then it was back on a caravan of motorcycles for the final couple of miles on rocky trails, straight up into the hills, surrounded by mountains. A three-day conference had been arranged for us to address the believers living and working in the mountain villages. The believers in this area were all farmers, farming of course for the Communist government. They owned no land, and each family was responsible for certain plots of land and certain crops. The government assigns the land and crops to be grown on the land. At the time of our visit, the hills were filled with pomegranate trees in bloom with bright red-orange flowers. Up and down every hillside, as far as you could see, were red-orange flowers.

Our team was welcomed into different walled-in farm compounds where families lived. The structures were very rustic, constructed of mud and unfinished tree limbs and branches. There were no bathrooms per se, except in the hog quarters. The hogs were kept in a walled-in area of the compound with a dividing wall separating the hogs from the person entering in need of relief. A wooden lattice was on the dirt floor in front of the wall, so those who came in stood or squatted on the lattice to do their business. The person's offering could then float under the wall for the hog's consumption.

I am not kidding. Because of the travel and time difference, my regular constitution was at two each morning. Each of the three nights we were guests in the farming compound, I made my way to the hog room in the darkness of night. Every time I opened the door to the hog pen, a joyful ruckus arose among the hogs. I could tell they were excited to see me. They knew they were about to be fed.

Each morning, our host family squatted around a little bowl of water to bathe. Chinese are squatters, and everywhere you go in China, people are squatting close to the ground. In the rural farming areas, the Communist government permits parents to have two children instead of the one child allowed in urban areas. When the family finished washing, they brought the bowl into our room to allow us to wash as well. This was the time in my missionary career that I learned to take hand sanitizer baths.

For three days, we met with these Chinese believers from about 7:00 a.m. until 8:00, 9:00, or 10:00 p.m. There was a break at midday for a communal meal. Each meal we ate, regardless of the time of day, consisted of white rice, noodles, and pork. In the larger cities, there would also be vegetables. But I noticed there was little variation in the diet of the Chinese.

This is when I came to realize how much of our Western mealtimes are more for recreation than for subsistence. The Chinese eat for sustenance and survival, and they can eat the same diet day in and day out. Westerners eat more with the mindset of entertainment. Each day, in an open area in the compound, 100 or more Chinese believers squatted down in small groups to eat their rice, noodles, and pork.

The all-day meetings were tremendous. The Chinese Christians have an insatiable hunger for the Word of God. They love to hear the Word read; they love to hear the Word taught. They sat there all day long, hanging on every word. No chairs or seats were in the meeting hall, so the people squatted. Some brought little cushions, but even the cushions were no higher than a person could squat. Throughout the day, this person or that person would nod off in their squatting position, but after a while they would wake up and join back in the proceedings.

Praise and worship was held in the morning and after mealtime. There was no worship team, and no instruments, just this little guy with a tambourine who could jump up and down about four feet into the air, like a Jack Russell terrier. The worship was powerful and intense, a blessing to us and I am sure more so to the Father whom they worshipped.

As I said, the meetings started at 7:00 a.m., but the meeting hall was filled by 6:00 a.m. with the saints interceding. At about six the first morning, I was out walking around the hills and praying, feeling rather good about my devotional discipline. Then I began hearing the sounds of prayer and praise coming from the meeting hall. Many of these believers had walked a long way through the surrounding hills each morning to get there, so they surely left their farms long before 6:00 a.m.

On Saturday, the day of Pentecost was being observed. After morning sessions and the midday pork and rice offering, the entire congregation climbed down a steep hillside to a muddy pond at the bottom. Pentecost is a traditional day for water baptisms in China, and a large group of believers had lined up to be baptized in water. We spent most of the afternoon at that little pond, baptizing about 20 believers.

Late in the afternoon, we all climbed back up the rocky hill for the final session we would have with our new friends and family. A special anointing was upon the service that night, and the entire congregation knelt throughout the praise and worship ministry. The atmosphere was charged with the presence of the Holy Spirit. After a long time of worship, our American missionary team washed the feet of the Chinese believers. The entire hall was filled with weeping and tears.

Our host had told me the Chinese believers hold the foreign missionary in high esteem because they recognize that foreign missionaries first brought the Gospel to China. Throughout the history of the Chinese church, foreign missionaries have remained faithful to them, even during seasons of persecution. The meeting went well into the night, till after ten. It was the culmination of a wonderful three days of fellowship.

One afternoon, I stood with our host outside the meeting hall. He pointed up to a range of mountains straight in front of us. Ten years earlier, he told me, some pastors from the mountain villages had made their way down to larger urban cities to ask for some help. It seemed that a great number of believers in the villages were suddenly speaking in unknown languages. The pastors asked if some missionaries could come up to their villages to explain what was happening. During the following five-year time span, about 20,000 believers in those areas were baptized in the Holy Spirit and spoke in new tongues.

Then my host turned to the east and pointed out another mountainous area. He told me that, after working with the local churches to the south, our group of missionaries went up to work in that region. After years of hard labor among the believers, though, there was little in terms of results. When we discussed the difference in the results between the two regions, we concluded that it was God who began the work in the first region, while it was man who began the work in the second region. God will be sure to bless His work. While man's efforts without God's blessing may not meet with the same results.

My host also told me about a government meeting just held in the larger city below while we were holding our meetings. The Communist authorities had called a meeting with the area party leaders to discuss the partitioning of land for specific crops to plant the following season. These authorities intended to come up to the villages where we were ministering that afternoon to partition off the land. The area representative, though, was a member of the house church network, so he told the authorities, "No, comrade brothers, why trouble yourself? It will be my pleasure to go back up and meet with the other villagers to assign your plan. Then I will return and report to you." The Communist leaders were more than thankful and appreciative for this cooperation. This man surely protected us. As foreigners, we were definitely in what was considered a forbidden zone, an area off-limits to foreigners. The appearance of the authorities would have meant great trouble for us and for the house church believers.

After leaving the house church conference in the mountains, we returned to Dajitan to board a bus that would take us north and west to the Tibetan border and the city of Shangri-La. We spent five hours on a bus winding through the mountains and were traveling in the southern Sichuan province when an 8.0 magnitude earthquake hit in the northern Cheng-du region of the province. Seventy thousand people lost their lives in that disaster.

In Shangri-La, we spent an evening with some house church believers, including two young ladies sent out from an underground Bible training center. These two young believers, still in their late teens or early twenties, were working to reach an unreached people group in the area. Thus far, they had made contact by working with them side by side in the agricultural fields. Despite working for three months, they had not begun to share the Gospel message. This is part of the strategy in reaching unreached people groups. The young ladies, of course, were not paid for their labor but were supported by local house church members with food and shelter. When we met with them, they had just been invited by the village leader to join them in a meal, an inroad that encouraged them. Even though it was late when we arrived, the believers pressed us to share a message with them that night. After sharing, we prayed with the group and distributed Gospel evangelism materials and then departed into the night.

China has a population of 1.4 billion people. There are 544 Biblical nations, that is unique people groups, in China, and 443 of those ethnic groups are considered unreached. The underground church of China has a vision and a plan to reach the unreached groups in China as well as the rest of the word. The illegal, underground house churches are training missionary evangelists to reach their nation and the nations of the world.

During our final days in China, we were invited to speak at an underground Bible training center. For all practical purposes, this was a factory that produced a product used throughout the world. Each morning, the young "factory workers," all in their teens and early twenties, gathered in a room for training to take the Gospel to unreached people groups of China. In the afternoon and evening, they worked in the factory. It was from this training center that the young believers in Shangri-La had come. Our Chinese evangelist friend, Happy, had a fifteen-year-old daughter in this training center. I welled up with tears when I saw him greet his daughter the morning we arrived at the school. We entered through a back door via a wooded area behind the factory so that none of the villagers down below would notice a contingent of Americans. The curtains on the large windows were drawn shut tightly.

I had the privilege of addressing the students first, assisted by our translator, who was a teacher and organizer of the school. Again, I taught much of what I have written in this book, though in a much-abbreviated form. Several times, I was forced to pause as students wept at my words. When I shared my vision of hell, from Jesus's own words in Luke chapter 16, several students broke down in tears. They got it. Like our Father, their hearts were tender toward those on their way to hell.

The Church in China is a church of vision. They have a vision for the evangelization of their own nation and a vision for world evangelization as well. The house church networks in China, working together, have formed an undertaking called the Back to Jerusalem Movement. A number of Chinese missionaries are in the process of moving to Jerusalem. This is not some kind of pilgrimage from China to the Holy Land. The fact is most of the unreached people groups in the world live in the nations between China and Israel. This movement is for the purpose of bringing the Gospel to those 7,402 remaining unreached people groups on the earth today.

Western Christian leaders have suggested that the Chinese Christian is not trained or prepared for such an undertaking. And besides, the nations between China and Jerusalem are some of the most hostile nations on earth in their opposition to Christianity. "They will kill you or imprison you." The Chinese Christian responds, "Atheistic Communist opposition has prepared the Chinese Christian for just such an endeavor for the past 70 years. We are prepared to go." In Brother Yun's words, "What started as a small trickle of missionaries leaving China has now become a steady flow, and soon I believe a mighty torrent of workers will leave China's borders with the Gospel."

We must learn to live with a vision to reach this world for the Gospel of Jesus Christ. Remember, we can hasten the day of the Lord's return by completing the task of world evangelization.

11 Since all these things are to be destroyed in this way, what sort of people ought you to be in holy conduct and godliness, 12 looking for and hastening the coming of the day of God, because of which the heavens will be destroyed by burning, and the elements will melt with intense heat! 13 But according to His promise we are looking for new

heavens and a new earth, in which righteousness dwells.
—2 Peter 3:11–13

This Gospel of the kingdom shall be preached in the whole
world as a testimony to all the nations, and then the end
will come. —Matthew 24:14

Let us review. We started with the understanding that the first essential in effective evangelism is our personal relationship with Jesus. We must know him personally, not just know about him. Evangelism should be introducing someone to our dear friend Jesus Christ. Few people struggle with introducing their friends to their other friends. Passion for Christ is the greatest and most important essential in soul-winning.

The second essential comes from the first. Our passion for Jesus will lead to His compassion for the world of lost souls. As we lay our head on His chest day by day, we will hear His heartbeat of, "None lost! All saved!"

Third, we have seen the end of the lost soul in eternity. They are eternally lost in a hell created for the devil and not for man.

Fourth, we have seen the power in praying for the lost in our realm of influence. We have begun prayer campaigns and determined that we will pray for those we know who are without Christ until (1) they are saved, (2) they die, or (3) we die.

The fifth essential is knowing how to focus our spiritual warfare on behalf of the lost. (1) The devil has taken the lost captive, and (2) our adversary, the devil, has also blinded their minds to the truth of the Gospel, making lies appear as truth. This is our warfare focus in prayer, to bind the enemy, to bind his lies, to expose his lies, so that when the truth is made known, it will be recognized as truth, and truth will set the captives and prisoners free.

And the sixth essential is that we can expect to go with the Gospel message. After we have prayed, we must be ready to be the answer to our prayers. We can expect to hear the voice of the Lord of the harvest as He says to us, "Now go, for I am sending you."

Then, finally, we learned about the greatest tool we have been given to win the lost: the Gospel message. We saw what that message is and the power that accompanies our message when we faithfully share it. We looked at signs, wonders, miracles, the gifts of the Holy Spirit, and even the ministry of angels in evangelism ministry.

In chapters 13 and 14, we saw the two anointings that we carry. The first is to preach the Gospel, and the second is to carry the glory of our Father on the earth. In this final chapter, we saw that the Great Commission to go into all the world is still valid today, and if we desire to hasten the day of the Lord's return, we must complete the task of world evangelization.

All of God's people on the earth are commissioned to bring in the world harvest in one way or another. We all have a part to play. While some may be called to go across the seas to bring the Good News message, others are called to simply go across the street. All around us are lost souls waiting to hear this Good News of salvation that is available to them through the life, death, and resurrection of our Lord, Jesus Christ.

I have written this book in hopes that you, the reader, would be inspired, encouraged, and blessed by this journey I have been on for over 40 years. I started the book over 10 years ago and then put it down after creating the framework and writing the first chapter. Over the past 10 years, total strangers have approached me to say I have a book in my heart that needs to be written. After encouragement from Kathleen and my good friend Pastor Bob to pick it up again, I set my heart on writing these things down.

In the week before I began to write, I considered how I wanted the first chapter to look. After I found and opened my ten-year-old file and began to read the first chapter I had written so long ago, I was surprised to find that what I had written 10 years ago was everything I had been considering before beginning this project anew. This confirmed to me that I was on the right path.

> *I thank God the Father for His grace over these many years; I have only done what He has empowered me to do. I thank God the Holy Spirit for His continual guidance and comfort. I thank God the Son, Jesus, my Savior, my Lord, and my friend, for giving me the hope of eternal life. I never set out to witness to so many lost souls. I guess I have lived with the desire to share with just one more. And then, just one more. And after that, just one more ... God bless you and keep you! —Bob G.*

> *All the resources of the Godhead are at our disposal![60] — Jonathan Goforth, Missionary to China 1888–1935*

> *Untold millions are still untold.[61] —John Wesley*

> *We are called to proclaim His great Salvation and rescue the captives.... But we are busy spending 33 billion a year in diet products for ourselves or for our overweight cats. We are busy redecorating our temporal housing, we are spending every evening for our own pleasure, and every spare dollar for our own retirement. And somehow the unreached in their life and death eternal struggle slip our minds and concern... we never get around to being serious about Jesus and his command to take the good news to them.[62] —John Willis Zumwalt, Passion for the Heart of God*

Since January of 2004, Kathleen and I have committed our lives to the Great Commission, working in the harvest fields of Mexico, Cuba, and El Salvador. We live by faith in our Father's provision. In 18 years of missionary service with Victorious Christian Harvesters, the Father has always been faithful to us. We have always had enough, often as a result of unexpected supernatural provision. If you would like to support this work, we invite you to ask our Father what He would have you do. And then, do it. Any gift you send to the following address is tax deductible and it will be placed into an account out of which we are paid on a weekly basis. Thank you, you are a blessing!

Address for giving: Bob & Kathleen Gabelman
Victorious Christian Harvesters
P.O. Box 450108
Laredo, Texas 78045

Web Page: www.vcharvesters.org
e-mail: bob@vcharvesters.org

Home Address: Bob & Kathleen Gabelman
2004 Los Suenos Ct.
Laredo, Texas 78045

e-mail: ioulove@att.net

Endnotes

1   Melody Green and David Hazard, *No Compromise – The Life Story of Keith Green* (Eugene, Oregon: Harvest House Publishers, 1996), 334.

2   Ministry 127, "William Booth," accessed February 9, 2022, https://ministry127.com/resources/illustration/quotes-on-missions.

3   Send.org, "Carl F. H. Henry," accessed February 9, 2022, https://send.org/files/ResourcePDFs/resource-missions-quotes.pdf.

4   The Bible Portal, "John Wesley," accessed February 9, 2022, https://bibleportal.com/bible-quotes/topic/righteousness.

5   David Brainerd, *Oswald J. Smith Pastor People's Church of Toronto* (London: Marshall, Morgan & Scott, LTD., 1949), 55.

6   Claude Hickman, "The History of Mission, Count Zinzendorf, The Traveling Team," June 20, 2021, http://www.thetravelingteam.org/articles/count-zinzendorf.

7   Inspiring Quotes, "Leonard Ravenhill," accessed February 9, 2022, https://www.inspiringquotes.us/author/1322-leonard-ravenhill.

8   Grace Quotes, "Charles Spurgeon Quote #23," accessed February 9, 2022, https://gracequotes.org/topic/evangelism-passion/.

9   Christian Quotes, "Andrew Murray," accessed February 9, 2022, https://www.christianquotes.info/quotes-by-author/andrew-murray-quotes/.

10   Inspiring Quotes, "Alan Redpath," accessed February 9, 2022, https://www.inspiringquotes.us/author/5419-alan-redpath.

11   Inspiring Quotes, "Hudson Taylor," accessed February 9, 2022, https://www.inspiringquotes.us/author/3068-hudson-taylor/about-heart.

12   Inspiring Quotes, "John Wesley," accessed February 9, 2022, https://www.inspiringquotes.us/author/8540-john-wesley.

13   Christian Quotes, "Jack Wellman," accessed February 9, 2022, https://www.christianquotes.info/quotes-by-author/jack-wellman-quotes/.

14   Oswald Smith, *The Revival We Need Sixth Edition* (Toronto, Canada: Marshall, Morgan & Scott, LTD., 1933), 22.

15   Moody Adams, *The Titanic's Last Hero* (West Columbia, South Carolina: The Olive Press, 1997), 25.

16   Moody Adams, *The Titanic's Last Hero* (West Columbia, South Carolina: The Olive Press, 1997), 24.

17   Goodreads, "John Stott," accessed February 9, 2022, https://www.goodreads.com/quotes/464217-his-authority-on-earth-allows-us-to-dare-to-go.

18   Christian Quotes, "John R. Rice," accessed February 9, 2022, https://www.christianquotes.info/quotes-by-author/john-r-rice-quotes/.

19   Goodreads, "Charles Spurgeon," accessed February 9, 2022, https://www.goodreads.com/author/quotes/2876959.Charles_Haddon_Spurgeon.

20   Watchman Nee, *Let Us Pray* (New York: Christian Fellowship Publishers, Inc., 1977), 11.

21   Soulwinning.info, "Quotes on Prayer and Revival, A.T. Pierson," accessed February 11, 2022, https://www.soulwinning.info/prayer/quotes.htm.

22 Inspiring Quotes, "Hudson Taylor," accessed February 10, 2022, https://www.inspiringquotes.us/author/3068-hudson-taylor.

23 AZ Quotes, "William Booth," accessed February 9, 2022, https://www.azquotes.com/author/1671-William_Booth?p=2.

24 QuotIr.com, "John Mott," accessed February 9, 2022, https://quotlr.com/author/john-mott.

25 AZ Quotes, "Catherine Booth," accessed February 9, 2022, https://www.azquotes.com/author/30084-Catherine_Booth.

26 Goodreads, "Billy Graham," accessed February 10, 2022, https://www.goodreads.com/quotes/search?page=17&q=Billy+Graham.

27 Henry Drummond, *The Greatest Thing in the World and Other Addresses* (London: Hodder & Stoughton LTD., London, England, c1920), 4.

28 Christian Quotes, "Charles Spurgeon," accessed February 10, 2022, https://www.christianquotes.info/quotes-by-topic/quotes-about evangelism/.

29 Christian Quotes, "Vance Havner Quote #28," accessed February 10, 2022, https://gracequotes.org/author-quote/vance-havner/.

30 Christian Quotes, "Dwight L. Moody," accessed February 9, 2022, https://www.christianquotes.info/quotes-by-author/dwight-l-moody-quotes/.

31 Shelton Smith, *Do it Again Lord* (Murfreesboro, Tennessee: Sword of the Lord Publishers, 2002), 96.

32 Harvest Ministry, "C.T. Studd Quote #61," accessed February 9, 2022, https://harvestministry.org/category/missions-and-your-family/mottos.

33 Harvest Ministry, "T.L Osborn Quote #58," accessed February 9, 2022, https://harvestministry.org/category/missions-and-your-family/mottos.

34 Quote Fancy, "Lee Strobel Quotes," accessed February 9, 2022, https://quotefancy.com/lee-strobel-quotes.

35 Oswald J. Smith, *The Cry of the World Eleventh Edition* (Toronto, Canada: Marshall, Morgan & Scott, 1959), 36.

36 AZ Quotes, "John Wesley," accessed February 10, 2022, https://www.azquotes.com/quote/1312191.

37 John Wimber with Kevin Springer, *Power Evangelism* (Ventura, California: Regal from Gospel Light, 1986) 137.

38 Quotestates.com, "John Wimber," accessed February 10, 2022, https://quotestats.com/topic/wimber-quotes/.

39 AZ Quotes, "Theodore Epp," accessed February 10, 2022, https://www.christianquotes.info/quotes-by-author/theodore-epp-quotes/.

40 J. Lovell Murray, "Limitless Spiritual Resources," *Far East Division Outlook Newsletter* 13, no. 13 (October 1924) 3, https://documents.adventistarchives.org/Periodicals/FEDO/FEDO19241001-V13-13.pdf.

41 Soulwinning.info, "Quotes on Prayer and Revival, John Griffith," accessed February 11, 2022, https://www.soulwinning.info/prayer/quotes.htm.

42 Soulwinning.info, "Quotes on Prayer and Revival, Samuel Chadwick," accessed February 11, 2022, https://www.soulwinning.info/prayer/quotes.htm.

43 Arthur Blessitt, *Arthur Blessitt's Street University* (Ventura, California: Vision House, 1978), 73.

44 Goodreads, "John Wesley," accessed February 11, 2022, https://www.goodreads.com/quotes/375171-i-set-myself-on-fire-and-people-come-to-watch.

45 Quotestats.com, "Ikechukwu Joseph Quote #2," accessed February 11, 2022, https://quotestats.com/topic/quotes-about-unschooled/.

46   AZ Quotes, "Oswald Smith Page #2, accessed February 11, 2022, https://www.azquotes.com/author/26117-Oswald_J_Smith?p=2.

47   AZ Quotes, "Rick Warren," accessed February 11, 2022, https://www.azquotes.com/quote/1571942.

48   God.net, "The Anointing of the Holy Spirit Page #1," accessed February 11, 2022, https://god.net/god/articles/the-anointing-of-the-holy-spirit/.

49   God.net, "The Anointing of the Holy Spirit Page #1," accessed February 11, 2022, https://god.net/god/articles/the-anointing-of-the-holy-spirit/.

50   AZ Quotes, "Rick Warren," accessed February 11, 2022, https://www.azquotes.com/quote/1571942.

51   Rick Joyner, "Morning Star Ministries, Columbine and the End Time," *Prophetic Bulletins*, June 30, 1999, https://publications.morningstarministries.org/columbine-end-time.

52   AZ Quotes, "Amy Carmichael," accessed February 11, 2022, https://www.goodreads.com/quotes/59566-give-me-the-love-that-leads-the-way-the-faith.

53   Grace Quotes, "E. M. Bounds Quote #7," accessed February 11, 2022, https://gracequotes.org/author-quote/e-m-bounds/.

54   Send.org, "Nate Saint #30," accessed February 9, 2022, https://send.org/files/ResourcePDFs/resource-missions-quotes.pdf.

55   Send.org, "Jim Elliot #29," accessed February 9, 2022, https://send.org/files/ResourcePDFs/resource-missions-quotes.pdf.

56   Inspiring Quotes, "Arthur T. Pierson," accessed February 9, 2022, https://www.inspiringquotes.us/author/2259-arthur-tappan-pierson.

57   Send.org, "Charles Spurgeon #44," accessed February 9, 2022, https://send.org/files/ResourcePDFs/resource-missions-quotes.pdf.

58   Christian Quotes, "F.B. Meyer," accessed February 9, 2022, https://www.christianquotes.info/quotes-by-author/f-b-meyer-quotes/.

59   Daniel Johnson Fleming, *Marks of a World Christian* (New York: Association Press, 1919), 152.

60   Missionaries of the World, "Missionaries to China, Jonathan Goforth Missionary to China," September 13, 2012, https://www.missionariesoftheworld.org/2012/08/jonathan-goforth-mission-ary-to-china.html.

61   Harvest Ministry, "John Wesley Quote #87," accessed February 9, 2022, https://harvestministry.org/category/missions-and-your-family/mottos.

62   John Willis Zumwalt, *Passion for the Heart of God Sixth Printing* (Chocktaw, Oklahoma: HGM Publishing, 2007), https://www.aamboli.com/quotes/author/john-willis-zumwalt.

CPSIA information can be obtained
at www.ICGtesting.com
Printed in the USA
LVHW071802200123
737358LV00001B/1